MENTALLY ILL OFFENDERS AND THE CRIMINAL JUSTICE SYSTEM ✦✦✦ Issues in Forensic Services

PRAEGER PUBLISHERS
Praeger Special Studies

New York • London • Sydney • Toronto

104933

Library of Congress Cataloging in Publication Data

Main entry under title:

Mentally ill offenders and the criminal justice system.

   1. Insanity--Jurisprudence--United States--Addresses,
essays, lectures. 2. Insane, Criminal and dangerous--
United States--Addresses, essays, lectures. 3. Insane--
Commitment and detention--United States--Addresses,
essays, lectures. I. Beran, Nancy J. II. Toomey,
Beverly G.
KF9242.A5M46   345'.73'04   78-19782
ISBN 0-03-046426-9

PSYCHIATRY AND SOCIAL CONTROL: TWO CONTRA-
DICTORY SCENARIOS, by Seymour L. Halleck, is reprinted with
permission from THE HUMAN MIND REVISITED, by Sidney Smith,
Ed., Copyright 1978, International Universities Press, Inc.

PSYCHIATRIC DIVERSION IN THE CRIMINAL JUSTICE
SYSTEM, by Thomas S. Szasz, is reprinted with permission from
ASSESSING THE CRIMINAL, Copyright 1977, Ballinger Publishing
Company.

PRAEGER PUBLISHERS
PRAEGER SPECIAL STUDIES
383 Madison Avenue, New York, N.Y. 10017, U.S.A.

Published in the United States of America in 1979
by Praeger Publishers,
A Division of Holt, Rinehart and Winston, CBS, Inc.

9   038   987654321

MENTALLY ILL OFFENDERS AND THE CRIMINAL JUSTICE SYSTEM ✦ ✦ ✦

Edited by
Nancy J. Beran
Beverly G. Toomey

PREFACE

This book is the culmination of five years of work by many people on the area of overlap between the criminal justice and mental health systems that serve the mentally disordered offender. The purposes of the book are to report research findings describing and evaluating one such service delivery system in the state of Ohio and to explore critical issues that face professionals involved in the provision of diagnostic and treatment services for mentally ill offenders.

Since these services traditionally have been provided by physicians with a psychiatric specialty, the service delivery system for mentally disordered offenders has long been known as forensic psychiatry. Today, however, this appears to be a misnomer, since psychologists and social workers also currently bring their professional knowledge, perspectives, and skills to the service of clients in the criminal justice system. * While in portions of this book we have succumbed to the traditional designation of "forensic psychiatry," we caution against a narrow interpretation of the term. In other sections we deliberately use the phrases "forensic services" or "psychosocial forensic services" to most accurately designate the area under consideration.

The evaluation research project reported here was conducted from 1972 to 1975 by the Ohio State University Program for the Study of Crime and Delinquency. It produced eight monographs. In order of completion these are:

An Evaluation of the Toledo Court Diagnostic and Treatment Center: An Experiment in Community-Based Forensic Psychiatric Services (April 1974)
An Evaluation of the Dayton Center for Forensic Psychiatry: An Experiment in Community-Based Services (September 1974)
An Evaluation of the Akron Criminal Courts Psycho-Diagnostic Clinic: An Experiment in Community-Based Forensic Psychiatric Services (October 1975)

---

*Psychologists are now even being acknowledged in statutes as official expert witnesses for the court. See the Ohio Revised Code 2945.381.

An Evaluation of the Butler County Forensic Psychiatric Center: An
  Experiment in Community-Based Services (October 1975)
An Evaluation of Community-Based Forensic Psychiatric Services in
  the Cincinnati Area (October 1975)
An Evaluation of the Columbus Forensic Psychiatric Center: An Ex-
  periment in Community-Based Forensic Psychiatric Services (Octo-
  ber 1975)
The Forensic Psychiatric Centers of Ohio: An Integrative Report
  (October 1975)
An Analysis of the Forensic Psychiatric Services Delivery System in
  Ohio: A Final Report (March 1976)

The book, presented in two parts, is comprised of both edited
papers (Chapters 2, 3, 4, 6, 9, and 11) and papers authored by the
editors (Chapters 1, 5, 7, 8, and 10). It begins with a historical
overview of the management of the mentally disordered individual in
conflict with criminal law from colonial days to the present and traces
trends that have set the stage for current legal and medical concerns.
In Chapter 1 the historical perspective identifies perennial problems
in the definition of criminal responsibility and the disposition of the
mentally disordered offender. The chronicle of years of effort and
energy that have been spent on many of the issues inspires respect
for the size and scope of the problems we still face today.

Chapters 2, 3, and 4 present papers addressing major forensic
questions that were delivered at a 1977 conference entitled "Ohio's
Forensic Services: One State's Response to National Issues." Seymour L. Halleck, Nicholas N. Kittrie, and Thomas S. Szasz, nationally known experts on the interface between psychiatry and the law,
discuss the social-control function of psychiatry, the prediction of
dangerousness, and psychiatric diversion from the criminal justice
system. The interaction of these experts with each other and with other
professionals attending the conference are included in discussion sections following each chapter.

Chapter 5 analyzes similarities and differences in the three experts' perspectives. In an attempt to bring focus to the issues, it
draws together their opinions and the ideas of others and identifies
dominant themes and current trends. This chapter then suggests future paths that policy and practice might take in the medical-legal
area.

Chapter 6 introduces Part II of the book. Dee Roth, Chief of
the Office of Program Evaluation and Research of the Ohio Department
of Mental Health and Mental Retardation, notes the necessity for research such as the reported evaluation and discusses its utility and
impact in the formulation of mental health policy and program planning.

Chapter 7 outlines the design of the evaluation, defining details of methodology and the necessary framework for understanding findings that are presented in Chapters 8 and 9. In Chapter 8 the data are used to compare and contrast the services of Ohio's community-based forensic centers with each other and with similar services provided in a traditional institutional setting. Chapter 9 offers an analysis of the forensic service delivery system pictured as it interfaces with the civil mental health and criminal justice systems. Conclusions drawn from the research are discussed in Chapter 10.

Timothy Moritz, director of the Ohio Department of Mental Health and Mental Retardation, completes the picture in Chapter 11 with a discussion of the future of forensic services in Ohio. His chapter, presented at the conference referred to above, considers both institutional and community services as well as legislative reform. The chapter ties together the theoretical predictions evident from academic speculation and the policy recommendations that flow from the research.

Chapters 2, 4, 7, and 8 are based on materials previously published in other forms. We wish to gratefully acknowledge the following sources:

Universities International Press, Inc. for permission to print Seymour Halleck's paper, "Psychiatry and Social Control: Two Contradictory Scenarios," which is a version of an article by the same title that appears in their publication The Human Mind Revisited, 1978;

Ballinger Publishing Company for permission to reprint Thomas Szasz's paper, "Psychiatric Diversion in the Criminal Justice System," from Assessing the Criminal, copyright 1977;

The Legal-Medical Quarterly, which published an article reporting the findings of the evaluation project in June 1977.

Many people contributed to the success of this project. From the inception of the research design to the preparation of this manuscript we owe much to many. First, we wish to acknowledge the support and cooperation of the Ohio Department of Mental Health and Mental Retardation and the Division of Forensic Psychiatry, which funded the research and provided linkages to the various state and local agencies we included in the study. Specifically, we would like to recognize John H. Vermuelen, Charles A. Mahoney, Ronald J. Averbeck, and Guy Nicholson. We appreciate the contribution of Timothy Moritz to this book. Special thanks are extended to Dee Roth for her chapter as well as her continuous support of the research and its application in the field of mental health.

Throughout the mental health and criminal justice systems we found many cooperative people who facilitated our work. We thank all the judges, probation officers, parole officers, mental health professionals, lawyers, and administrators who completed our questionnaires and responded to our interviews. We are grateful to all who talked with us and helped us carry out the effort. Particularly we wish to acknowledge the following center staff for their help: Kenneth Atkins, Charlene Cassel, Larry Chase, Dorothy Mack, Daniel Reinholt, Howard Sokolov, Dorothy Turner, Sam Waxman, and John Wells. Also we thank June Frucey, who aided us in our data collection at Lima State Hospital.

The research was conducted under the auspices of the Ohio State University Program for the Study of Crime and Delinquency. We wish to acknowledge the assistance of Harry E. Allen, director of the program, for his part in the project. Too numerous to mention are the many people who worked on the collection and analysis of the data. We wish, nevertheless, to recognize those who contributed greatly to the success of this phase of the project: Josephine Ann Colli, Dwight Ely, and Franklin Marshall. We also thank Eric Carlson, who authored Chapter 9 and worked on the project for more than two years (one as project coordinator).

Finally, we would like to thank our families and friends for their understanding of our intense investment in the book, which distracted us from participation in our usual social activities with them.

CONTENTS

Page

PREFACE   v

LIST OF TABLES   xiii

PART I: CRITICAL ISSUES IN FORENSIC SERVICES:
         THE OPINIONS OF THE EXPERTS

Chapter

1   THE MENTALLY DISORDERED OFFENDER: A
    HISTORICAL PERSPECTIVE   5

    The Colonial Period   5
    The Rise of Institutional Confinement   7
    The Evolution of a Special Category   8
    Tests of Insanity   9
    Competency to Stand Trial   11
    "Psychopaths" and Special Treatment   12
    Hospitals for the "Criminally Insane"   16
    Court Clinics Established   18
    Current Directions   21
    Notes   22

2   PSYCHIATRY AND SOCIAL CONTROL: TWO
    CONTRADICTORY SCENARIOS
    Seymour L. Halleck   24

    Psychiatrists as a Clean-up Crew   25
    A "Belegaled" Profession   27
    Trends in Civil Commitment   28
    Informed Consent to Treatment   29
    Research Curtailed   30
    Increase of Psychiatric Practice in Criminal
        Justice Settings   32
    Psychotherapy and Drug Prescription as Social
        Control   35
    Value-Based Criteria of Mental Health   37

ix

Chapter   Page

       Conclusions   38
       Discussion   39

3   THE PREDICTION OF DANGEROUSNESS: THE
      EXPERTS, THE COURTS, AND THE CRIMINAL
      JUSTICE SYSTEM
      Nicholas N. Kittrie   43

       Identifying the Dangerous   43
       Defining and Predicting Dangerousness   45
       Experts, Judges, and Juries   47
       Discussion   49

4   PSYCHIATRIC DIVERSION IN THE CRIMINAL
      JUSTICE SYSTEM
      Thomas S. Szasz   54

       Cases of Psychiatric Diversion   55
       Suicide: A Historical Example   57
       The Young, the Old, and the Insane   61
       The Responsibility to Punish   63
       Discussion   65
       Notes   72

5   INTEGRATION AND FUTURE DEVELOPMENT   74

       Integration   74
        Incompetency to Stand Trial   76
        Criminal Responsibility   78
        Sexual Psychopathy   82
        Right to Treatment, Informed Consent, and
          Right to Refuse Treatment   83
       Future Developments   85
        Incompetency, Insanity, and Psychopathy   85
        Right to Treatment, Informed Consent, and
          Right to Refuse Treatment   87
        Mental Health–Criminal Justice Relations   89
        Two Models   90
        The Politics of Therapy and Criminal Justice   92
       Conclusions   94
       Notes   95

Chapter   Page

PART II: THE OHIO EVALUATION PROJECT

6   COMMUNITY-BASED MENTAL HEALTH SERVICES
     FOR THE CRIMINAL JUSTICE SYSTEM: THE OHIO
     EXPERIENCE
     Dee Roth   103

7   COMMUNITY VERSUS INSTITUTIONAL CARE:
     AN EVALUATION PROJECT   107

     Community Centers Established   110
     The Evaluation Project   111
     Data-Collection Procedures   113
     Sampling   113
     Some Terms   114
       Competence/Incompetency to Stand Trial   115
       Not Guilty by Reason of Insanity   115
       Psychopathic Offender   116
       Ascherman Act   117
     Notes   117

8   FINDINGS: THE COMMUNITY FORENSIC CENTERS   119

     Centers' Operation and Service   119
     Client Caseloads   122
     User Satisfaction   125
     Clients and Their Movement through the System   127
     Time Involved in Moving through the System   136
     Cost Analysis   137
     Summary   139
     Notes   140

9   FINDINGS: THE STATEWIDE SERVICE
     DELIVERY SYSTEM
     Eric W. Carlson   141

     Introduction and System Overview   141
     System Elements   142
       The Community Forensic Centers   142
       Lima State Hospital   145
       The Courts   145
       Local and State Correctional Facilities   146
       Civil Mental Health   147

Chapter   Page

        System Environments   148
          The Legal Environment   148
          The Administrative Environment   148
        Activities and Functions   149
          The Information-Generation Function—
              Forensic Examinations   151
          Treatment and Custody   156
          Decision Making in the FPSDS   159
        Findings   160
          Forensic Services—Issues of Supply and Demand   161
          Quality of Forensic Services   170
          Multiple Admissions to LSH   170
        Summary and Conclusions   171
        Notes   173

10   REMAINING ISSUES AND RECOMMENDATIONS   175

        Remaining Issues   175
        Recommendations   177
        Discussion   178

11   OHIO'S FORENSIC SYSTEM: FUTURE PLANS
        Timothy B. Moritz   181

        Administration of Forensic Services   182
        The Community Forensic Centers   183
        The State Inpatient Facility   184
        Legislative Reform   185
        Facilities and Services for the Future   186
        Discussion   188

ABOUT THE EDITORS AND CONTRIBUTORS   192

LIST OF TABLES

Table   Page

8.1   Client Frequencies and Rates per 100,000
       Population for the Six Forensic Centers, 1971-75   123

8.2   Admissions to Lima State Hospital by Commit-
       ment Type and Calendar Year for Center
       Counties, 1968-74   124

8.3   Admissions to Lima State Hospital by Commit-
       ment Type and Calendar Year for Noncenter
       Counties, 1968-74   125

8.4   Project Data Collection Periods and Client
       Numbers for All Six Centers and Corresponding
       LSH Samples   128

8.5   Percentages of Ascherman and Competency/
       Sanity Referrals for Six Centers and LSH Samples   130

8.6   Recommendations for the Six Centers and the LSH
       Samples   134

8.7   Categorized Recommendations for the Six Centers
       and LSH Samples   135

8.8   Processing Times for the Six Centers and the LSH
       Samples   137

8.9   Cost per Client Based on Budget and Caseload Size
       for All Six Centers   138

8.10   Costs for Ascherman and Competency/Sanity
       Evaluations at the Six Centers   138

9.1   Functions Performed by Elements of Forensic
       Psychiatric Service Delivery System   151

9.2   Examinations by Type, Lima State Hospital and
       Community Forensic Centers, 1968-74   153

9.3   Total Annual Commitments to LSH by Examination
       or Indefinite Commitment, 1968-74   157

Table   Page

9.4   Commitments to Civil Institutions by Type, Year,
          and Presence or Absence of Local Forensic Centers   163

9.5   Estimated Total Forensic Examinations, 1971–75   164

I

CRITICAL ISSUES IN FORENSIC SERVICES: THE OPINIONS OF THE EXPERTS

INTRODUCTION

To provide an overall perspective on forensic services, Part I opens with a historical review of the definition and management of mentally disordered offenders from colonial days through to the present time. Chapter 1 traces trends that have set the stage for the current legal and medical concerns discussed in Chapters 2 through 5.

Chapters 2, 3, and 4 present the opinions of three renowned experts on some of the most pressing problems in contemporary forensic services. The problem areas are identified in the research described in Part II of this book; and the experts were invited to address them at a conference and to discuss them with conference participants. Seymour Halleck argues that psychiatrists must accept the social-control functions of their activities and proceed with them as humanistically as possible. In contrast, Thomas Szasz contends that diversion of offenders into psychiatric statuses is undermining the criminal justice system. We have become, he concludes, unwilling to shoulder our responsibility to punish certain people. Nicholas Kittrie reviews the problems involved in the definition and prediction of dangerousness and draws very pessimistic conclusions. Each of three experts' presentations is followed by a dialogue with other conference participants.

The last chapter in Part I provides a comparative analysis of Halleck's, Szasz's, and Kittrie's presentations and attempts to integrate the issues they raise. With this as a backdrop, an effort is made to outline future developments in the field of forensic services.

1

THE MENTALLY
DISORDERED OFFENDER:
A HISTORICAL PERSPECTIVE

The label "mentally disordered offender" has been variously
used to describe a number of groups of persons who have been differ-
entially identified in both the mental health and criminal justice systems. These individuals share two common characteristics: All have
come before the courts accused of some violation of the criminal law
and all have had their mental health status questioned at some time
during the process. They differ in the type and severity of mental disability as well as in their status before the courts. The individual may
be mentally retarded, psychotic, or diagnosed as having a personality
disorder. He or she may be pretrial, at trial, a convicted offender-
presentence, or a convicted offender serving time.

Society has been interested in these individuals and in understanding the relationship between their mental disabilities and their
crimes for two major reasons: to establish criminal responsibility and
to classify offenders in order to make better dispositions of them. In
the last hundred years, particularly as the hope of rehabilitation or
cure increased, the latter became a more important issue. The case
law that defines various groups of mentally disabled offenders is well
documented in the forensic literature; however, little is written of the
disposition and treatment of these people. Therefore, this chapter
will focus on the provision of evaluation and treatment services. It
will review the history of the provision of care for this especially difficult group of people who are today the clients of what has been called
the forensic psychiatric services system.

THE COLONIAL PERIOD

The growth of population and the development of community living in colonial America brought with it the need for an increase in

social order and social control. The type of order and the methods of control prevalent in the colonies were linked with both the English law the colonists brought with them and the colonists' sense of good and evil derived from their intense religious convictions. Also, then as now, control procedures reflected society's need to deal pragmatically with the problematic individuals while satisfying the philosophical demands of justice. However, in the last analysis, pragmatic solutions to control problems were utilized whether they fulfilled philosophical demands of fairness or not.

Both pragmatic needs and philosophical justifications for social control in communities have changed throughout history and appropriate changes in methods of control have resulted. The earliest methods were quite harsh. As the colonies grew, humanitarian concerns brought less physical punishment, and other forms of punishment were developed.

The early colonists were basically concerned with controlling two groups of people, the criminal and the poor. The mentally disordered offender was sometimes classified and treated as a criminal and at other times as one of the poor, as were all other persons who were recognized as mentally ill. Frequently identified as a criminal without recognition of his mental disability, this offender received standard corporal punishment, banishment, or death. Based on English law, the criminal code for most of the colonial period identified all felonies except larceny as capital offenses. Other crimes merited such punishments as branding, whipping, the stocks, the pillory, or fines.[1] Because punishment was also seen as moral instruction and a factor in deterrence, the imposition of the punishment was a public ritual.

In relatively few cases, however, the offender would be recognized as a lunatic without criminal intentions, and disposition usually would be determined by the person's need for care and the perceived danger of the individual to the safety of the community. These people would be placed in the care of a family (either their own or one willing to take them in), cared for in the poorhouse, or, if violent, confined in a cage at the poorhouse or in a small outbuilding specifically constructed for the purpose of isolation and restraint. Most of the time these procedures were informally, possibly haphazardly, handled at the whim of the decision makers.[2] Deutsch relates an incident that illustrates the punitive attitudes, limited understanding of mental illness, and limited dispositional resources of the colonists. In 1674 in Flushing, New York, a court acquitted a man who was charged with "running amok, breaking down doors, setting fire to houses, beating women and children" as "not being in his right reason."[3] While the recognition of mental disability in this case is encouraging, the disposition is more revealing. The defendant was banished to Staten Island to the custody of the local magistrate where he was to work. The magistrate was empowered "to punish him according as he may deserve" if he behaved badly.[4] This reveals the court's lack of understanding of mental illness and implies a belief that although a man can be excused once for actions acknowledged to be the result of mental disability, he is expected to be deterred from acting out again by the threat of punishment.

For the most part, whenever a crime was committed the colonists were concerned with both community safety and punishment for evil. As noted, the punishments were public and severe. They were intended to eliminate or at least discourage a repeat performance by the offender and also deter others from behaving in a similar fashion. The severity of punishment was justified by the belief that the person had freely chosen to commit the evil deed. This implied that the individual understood the evil nature of the deed and also could control his actions. While little was understood about the linkage between free will and mental illness, occasionally, especially in capital offenses, the offender might be spared the prescribed penalty through a pardon when it was decided he was insane or a lunatic.[5] In 1794 Benjamin Rush is reported to have been appointed by President Washington to examine a person sentenced to death for treason to see if he might be pardoned.[6] Nevertheless, what to do with the dangerous individual after the pardon remained a problem.

THE RISE OF INSTITUTIONAL CONFINEMENT

Although the Pennsylvania Hospital, one of the first general hospitals in the colonies, cared for a few "lunaticks,"[7] it was not until late in the eighteenth century that places of confinement and care expressly for the mentally ill became a part of the social structure. The establishment of the first mental hospital in Williamsburg, Virginia, in 1773, was a rudimentary beginning. According to Russel, this facility housed about 30 patients and was a holding place without a medical organization or a resident physician.[8] A second mental hospital was not opened until 1824. The absence of facilities left the mentally ill, criminal and noncriminal alike, without care. The New York Board of Governors at this time noted that few facilities were available for the mentally ill, with only a small percentage hospitalized. Others, if dangerous, were confined in crowded jails, in almshouses, in lockups, and in private homes. Many were on the streets.[9] To ease the situation, the board approved the development of a special psychiatric department at the New York Hospital in 1808.[10]

Similarly, the criminal justice system offered little space for confinement. Jails and workhouses were intended to detain those awaiting trial, as well as petty offenders and debtors, for short periods.

Since long-term incarceration was <u>not</u> a punishment for serious crimes, no facilities for such confinement existed. It was not until Quaker reformers moved to substitute confinement with hard labor for capital punishment that the first "penitentiary-house" was established in 1790.[11] Opened as a section of the Walnut Street Jail, this first long-term corrections setting was an alternative that offered society protection from dangerous criminals (whether mentally ill or not) without putting them to death.

As so comprehensively described by David Rothman in his remarkable work, <u>The Discovery of the Asylum</u>, the nineteenth century was a time of vigorous development of institutional care for both the insane and the criminal.[12] During this period the mental health and correctional systems expanded by building numerous large institutions. The influence of philosophical humanitarianism, pragmatic needs for community security, and later a belief in the possible efficacy of confinement for rehabilitation and cure were powerful stimuli behind this massive building program. With the development of these extensive systems, confinement for the insane and the criminal became a more available option.

THE EVOLUTION OF A SPECIAL CATEGORY

Throughout the nineteenth century, as institutional care became the modal form of disposition for both convicted criminals and the insane, the law and courts struggled to more clearly define the situation of the mentally disordered offender. As a result of changing social values and a growth in knowledge and understanding of mental illness and defect, the mentally disordered offender slowly began to be differentiated from others violating the criminal law. Legal decisions began to reflect evolving societal attitudes, and in the ensuing decades the courts have identified a variety of mental conditions that provide a basis for mitigation of criminal process.

The criminal law today deals with three major categories of mentally disordered offenders: those who plead the insanity defense, those incompetent to stand trial, and those variously identified from state to state as some type of psychopathic offender. Each of these groups has a different legal history that affects current definitions and treatment.

The earliest concerns with the mental status of an accused offender derived from a court interest in determining insanity, which usually meant lack of criminal intent and criminal responsibility. The element of will, volition, or criminal intent has been recognized as a component of criminal responsibility for hundreds of years. Roman law recognized legal irresponsibility due to mental disease.[13] Bracton, a thirteenth-century English priest and legal analyst, defined insanity and provided basic concepts that influenced thinking for many generations.[14] As early as the reign of Edward I (1272-1307), insanity was "admitted as an excuse to crime."[15] From that time to this, the concept of insanity has been discussed, defined, and often derided but nevertheless used. While the term has been most broadly employed in criminal law to identify a state that "exempts a person from responsibility for crime, or limits such responsibility" and "affords ground for preventing or delaying trial, sentence or punishment of a person accused of a criminal act,"[16] Glueck contends that definitions of insanity in both law and medicine have been and continue to be vague and imprecise. He notes: "No two writers define the term in exactly the same manner; and a few, wiser than their colleagues, refuse to define it altogether."[17] That statement is applicable to early definitions of insanity as well as to the current state.

TESTS OF INSANITY

The concepts of insanity has a long history in English law. The specific definitions evolved in court decisions as perceptions and knowledge of mental illness, and also social values, changed. An English case that has had major impact on American legal interpretations of insanity was that of M'Naghten in 1843.[18] M'Naghten, while attempting to assassinate the prime minister, actually mortally wounded the leader's secretary. After it was established that he was suffering from paranoid delusions, M'Naghten was acquitted on the grounds of insanity. The decision caused such a public controversy that the House of Lords held an inquiry to clarify the criteria for insanity. Out of the debate came the following test, which has come to be known as the M'Naghten rule: "[T]hat to establish a defense on the grounds of insanity, it must be clearly proved that, at the time of committing the act, the party accused was labouring under such a defect of reason, from disease of the mind, as not to know the nature and quality of the act he was doing, or if he did know it that he did not know he was doing what was wrong."[19]

This test became the accepted basis for determining criminal responsibility both in England and the United States. In common usage in the United States, the M'Naghten test is most frequently interpreted to mean "whether the defendant had the capacity to know right from wrong in respect to the particular act charged."[20]

Although the M'Naghten rule has been criticized by both the medical and legal professionals who have used it in criminal trial work, this general definition of insanity has been the prevalent test in the United States in the past and continues to be applied as part of a widely employed formula for the determination of insanity. A major criticism of M'Naghten is that it presents a "minimalistic" position.[21] Experts contend that some mentally disabled individuals are not acquitted on a M'Naghten test when reason, not to mention psychiatric opinion, would indicate they should not be held criminally responsible.

The irresistible impulse test offers another perspective for the definition of insanity: It is applicable to the person who may well appear to know the difference between right and wrong and is aware of what is wrong but not able to resist committing the deed. As early as 1834, Ohio courts recognized such a mental condition as mitigating criminal responsibility;[22] however, many states have rejected this test. Critics contend that whether an impulse is resistible or not is impossible to determine; therefore, the test is not utilitarian. Some states, however, do apply this test in conjunction with M'Naghten, and the concept of irresistible impulse is a component of the American Law Institute Model Penal Code test that is becoming widely accepted throughout the states.

Another test that has not been widely accepted in the United States but has had significant impact on the definition of insanity is the Durham test. Drawing on early philosophical foundations in a New Hampshire Supreme Court opinion of 1871,[23] the Washington, D.C. Court of Appeals in 1954 in Durham v. United States[24] said, "An accused is not criminally responsible if his unlawful act was the product of mental disease or mental defect."[25]

The Durham decision expanded the definition of criminal responsibility substantially. It also had the effect of increasing input from mental health professionals, especially psychiatrists, into the judicial process since their testimony was necessary to make the determination of mental disease or defect. The Durham definition of what constituted "mental disease or defect" was vague and left to the jury or court to decide with the help of the expert medical testimony. Even though subsequent cases sought to make the Durham test easier to apply, in 1972 Durham was rejected in the Brawner case.[26] Brawner adopted the American Law Institute (ALI) Model Penal Code definition of insanity.

The ALI in its Model Penal Code combines many of the elements of the tests discussed here and provides an updated version of the thinking on what constitutes insanity as it affects criminal responsibility. The major provisions of the test set forth in the Model Penal Code are that "a person is not responsible for criminal conduct if at the time of such conduct as a result of mental disease or defect he lacks substantial capacity to appreciate the wrongfulness of his conduct or to conform his conduct to the requirements of the law."[27] Although this test specifically defines mental disease or defect to exclude "an abnormality manifested only by repeated criminal or otherwise antisocial conduct," it, like <u>Durham</u>, is criticized as vague about what really does constitute mental disease. Also the Model Penal Code test is the recipient of the same criticism as the irresistible impulse test. Nevertheless, the Model Penal Code test is currently applied in all federal circuit courts and it is gaining acceptance in the state courts.

COMPETENCY TO STAND TRIAL

The history of the use of the insanity defense and the various tests of insanity in this country illustrates the way in which growing knowledge about mental illness and mental defect changed the legal definitions of criminal responsibility. This same knowledge has had similar impact on definitions of competency to stand trial. In most jurisdictions, competency to stand trial is entangled with the issue of criminal responsibility in statutes using the term "insanity" for both. This results in a great deal of confusion about the competency question, even though it is quite distinct from that of criminal responsibility. While the concern in a case claiming the insanity defense is with the mental condition of the accused at the time of the offense, the competency question pertains to the mental condition of the accused at the time of trial. It is important to remember that competency does <u>not</u> involve the questions of guilt or innocence or criminal responsibility.

A long-standing tenet of common law is that no individual could be indicted, tried, sentenced, or executed if he was known to be insane. Blackstone's Commentaries (1765) state the position:

> If a man in his sound memory commits a capital offense, and before arraignment for it he becomes mad, he ought not to be arraigned for it, because he is not able to plead to it with that advice and caution that he ought. And if, after he has pleaded, the prisoner becomes mad, he shall not be tried; for how can he make his defense?[28]

The tests for competency to stand trial have followed Blackstone's reasoning and as defined in numerous cases have sought to determine if the accused was sufficiently able to appreciate the charges and the proceedings and assist in his own defense.

In the United States one of the earliest cases raising the issue of insanity at or before trial occurred in 1804.[29] Case law from that point to the present identifies an assortment of tests to determine the competency of an accused to be tried. Most of them reflect the same common-law thinking. Even though statutes vary from state to state and frequently utilize confusing language, the current tests of competency are relatively simple and well stated by the Supreme Court in Dusky v. United States. [30] The Dusky court said that the legal criteria for competency were: "Whether he has sufficient present ability to consult with a lawyer with a reasonable degree of rational understanding, and whether he has a rational as well as factual understanding of the proceedings against him. "[31]

Although these appear to be relatively straightforward criteria, problems that arise in the application of these criteria are not so simple. Stone criticizes the courts for vagueness about what is a "reasonable" degree of understanding. [32] In addition, many point out that these statutes provide for the confinement of those incompetent to stand trial until they are restored to reason and able to be tried. Since many found incompetent to stand trial are not treatable, until quite recently the result was an involuntary commitment, perhaps for a lifetime, for an individual who was not adjudicated guilty of any crime. Contemporary thinking, enlightened by a new appreciation of the nature of some types of mental disabilities and the inability of medicine to bring about cure, is reflected in recent litigation that decries the injustice inherent in the process. The Supreme Court opinion in Jackson v. Indiana, [33] contending that this type of prolonged confinement violated due process rights, directs that persons who are not likely to be restored to competency within a reasonable time be committed by "customary civil commitment proceedings"[34] or released. This decision has resulted in the revision of state statutes and procedures for the treatment of the incompetent accused.

"PSYCHOPATHS" AND SPECIAL TREATMENT

A third category of offenders who have been defined by law as suffering from some impairment of mental health are called psychopaths, sometimes more specifically sexual psychopaths. Both psychiatry and the law put them in a different compartment from the insane or the incompetent.

The concepts of criminal responsibility and competency to stand trial historically were defined as a deficiency or defect in the cognitive capacity of the individual. These definitions reflected the medical and philosophical position that viewed insanity as an intellectual impairment; however, some psychiatrists of the eighteenth century began to note mental illness where the intellect seemed intact. Pinel, Rush, Pritchard, and Ray defined a type of mental illness (insanity) that they described as a defect of the moral faculty. Philosophically, a distinction was being made between the intellectual, the cognitive parts of the mind, and the emotional, the feeling portions. The defect of the emotion was defined by Pritchard as "moral insanity."[35] By the middle of the nineteenth century the concept was established in psychiatry, but opinion within the field was divided. This expansion of the concept of mental illness was resisted in American courts. The doctrine of moral insanity was rejected as a defense in the famous case of Charles Guiteau, who killed President James A Garfield.[36]

Even though the law did not recognize moral insanity, the concept gained credence in the psychiatric literature. By the beginning of the twentieth century a social maladjustment component was added to the term. In his study of prisoners at Sing Sing, Bernard Glueck identified a category of prisoner that he called psychopaths. This group was described as predisposed to excessive use of alcohol, drugs, and gambling.[37]

Throughout the last 50 years the term psychopath has increased in usage but not in clarity. The definition has remained a catch-all category. Brakel and Rock indicate "the term 'psychopath' is not susceptible of precise definition."[38] A reading of the literature supports this contention. The vagueness is evident in the American Psychiatric Association (APA) Manual (1957 edition) description. According to this volume, the individual with a psychopathic personality is "a person whose behavior is predominantly amoral or characterized by impulsive, irresponsible actions satisfying only immediate and narcissistic interests without concern for obvious and implicit social consequences accompanied by minimal outward evidence or anxiety or guilt."[39] In its 1968 revision of the manual the APA replaced the term psychopath with antisocial personality; but the definition was still difficult to apply with precision.

Despite the lack of clarity in the medical definition, the psychopathic offender has been identified in the law. Responding to public concern about socially dangerous, habitual criminals and sex offenders, the legislatures of many states have defined for special treatment a category of criminals called the sexual psychopath, or, more broadly, the psychopath. The action in this direction constituted a major expansion of communal powers of social control utilizing the guise of mental defect to impose indefinite confinement on a special class of people.

Although psychopathy had been claimed as a defense in trials since the turn of the twentieth century, courts were reluctant to see it as insanity.[40] Nevertheless, there was a belief that psychopaths were not ordinary criminals;[41] they were viewed as exceptionally dangerous to society. Given the hesitancy of courts to interpret insanity statutes to cover the psychopath, legislatures moved toward new codes to cover the situation. Most often spurred by public outrage following a particularly heinous sex crime, state legislators authorized laws that provided for the psychiatric examination and the indeterminant sentencing of sex offenders and other especially dangerous habitual offenders. Ostensibly predicated on the belief that while traditional incarceration only prevents the person from committing additional crime while he remains confined, indefinite confinement for treatment in special institutions would provide "rehabilitation" or "cure" for these mentally defective criminals before their return to society. Then, theoretically, those released would not commit crimes again. In this legislation there was the implicit guarantee that these more dangerous offenders would remain in confinement until they were "safe." In effect, it provided for indefinite control and fulfilled requirements of a social philosophy that valued both prevention and humanitarian treatment.

Beginning with the Goodrich Act in Michigan in 1937, psychopath control legislation was enacted in state after state. By the early 1950s about half the states had some special provision to control psychopaths. Currently about 31 states have some form of psychopathic offender legislation. [42] In most states the legislation specified sexual psychopaths, but in some it was broadened to include psychopaths in general.

The general psychopath laws are similar to those covering only the sexual psychopath, except they cover greater numbers and types of offenders. Laws covering sexual psychopaths are applied to persons charged with or convicted of a range of sexual offenses, but the broader statutes could include almost any repeat offender. The Maryland Defective Delinquent statute is a prime example of the expanded psychopathy statute. It provides for special confinement for the defective delinquent defined as

> an individual, who, by demonstration of persistent aggravated antisocial or criminal behavior, evidences a propensity toward criminal activity, and who is found to have either such intellectual deficiency or emotional unbalance, or both, as to clearly demonstrate an actual danger to society so as to require confinement and treatment. [43]

While statutes differ on the time of examination and who is subject to examination, in general all of the statutes include vague definitions of the psychopath (as might be expected given the psychiatric controversy about the existence of the condition) and provisions for psychiatric evaluation, indeterminant hospitalization, and release dependent on "recovery" or sufficient improvement to no longer pose a threat to society.

From the beginning, the constitutionality of these statutes has been challenged, but largely the laws have stood as civil statutes providing for care and treatment of convicted mentally ill offenders. In this regard, courts have noted the necessity to provide treatment. [44]

Critics of the psychopathy statutes identify issues of self-incrimination and preventive detention as significant concerns. Citing the inability of psychiatry to even define, let alone treat, psychopathy, they challenge the practice of indefinite commitment until "recovered" as preventive detention. A similar question arises if the justification for confinement of the defined psychopath is the protection of society from a dangerous person. Psychiatry has not demonstrated a facility for predicting dangerousness, but courts continue to act as if this skill can be assumed.

According to the statutes, individuals are categorized as psychopathic offenders so that they may be placed in special institutions established to treat and control them. It is a well-accepted fact that until quite recently public mental hospitals were severely deficient in active treatment programs; in general, hospitals for the criminally insane have fewer programs. If staffing is difficult in public civil mental hospitals it is next to impossible in hospitals for this type of mental patient with greater stigma and less treatability. Citing a 1972 survey of mental health and correctional institutions for adult mentally disordered offenders, Stone suggests that "few American institutions have full or active treatment programs,"[45] and he notes that they are understaffed and primarily security conscious. Stone also states, "Where treatment was available, it was usually not with a psychiatrist because that profession has largely ignored these problems and avoided these institutions. And ironically, the panoply of new treatments for the quasicriminal, e.g. hormones, stereotoxic psychosurgery, behavior modification, etc., some of which may have considerable potential, all present grave constitutional questions."[46]

The problems of treating the psychopathic offender and particularly the sexual psychopath are monumental. Both the inadequate understanding of the diagnosis of psychopathy and the lack of knowledge of how to treat it are compounded by the insufficient resources in institutions to develop and implement treatment programs. Current litigation and forensic research are investigating this situation and bringing about revision in those statutes and conditions of confinement. Most significant is a more toward more community-based services for both evaluation and treatment of the psychopathic offender.

In addition to the insane, the psychopath, and the incompetent, some mentally disordered offenders who become clients of the forensic services system get there by administrative transfers rather than by court action. One group of these transfers is civilly committed mental patients who are regarded as dangerous. Another group is made up of convicted offenders who become mentally ill in prison. These individuals are lumped with the court-defined commitments in the institution for the criminally insane.

HOSPITALS FOR THE "CRIMINALLY INSANE"

Through the decades, court opinions and new legislation increased the involvement of mental health professionals, particularly psychiatrists, in the criminal justice system. As noted above, their input to the court expanded as they became expert evaluators to aid in determining mental health status that influenced the adjudication of the case. Also, mental health professionals became increasingly involved in the care and treatment of mentally ill offenders once the adjudication process was complete.

More specifically, the development of mental illness treatment facilities and the more careful definition of mental disability in criminal courts raised concern about the disposition of the mentally disabled individual within the criminal justice system. As was suggested in the beginning of this chapter, in the seventeenth and most of the eighteenth centuries American jurisprudence acknowledged few instances of mental disability in criminal cases, and even when it was recognized the mental condition made little difference in the disposition of the case. Following the Revolutionary War the criminal justice reform movement created the prison as a place of long-term incarceration. The few mentally ill or mentally deficient offenders acquitted for insanity were usually confined with the prisoners or in special security portions of almshouses. Some began to complain that this was not appropriate for the acquitted individuals; others complained that the insane person caused difficulty in the institutions for the more appropriate residents. During this same period public hospital facilities for the mentally ill were becoming more available and the policy of confining the mentally ill offender in the hospital rather than prison was established. The persons affected, those in the category of mentally ill offender, included the few accused identified as insane, either because of mental illness or extreme deficiency, and acquitted, and some who were recognized as mentally ill while serving sentences in prison.

The problem of finding the appropriate place to house the mentally ill offenders was an important one because during the better part of the nineteenth century the emphasis in prison was on punishment and repentance, while in the mental hospital it was on care and cure. Although psychiatric knowledge was not developed enough to make an accurate distinction between criminality and mental illness (and, in fact, as was more readily acknowledged later, both states can exist at once), the determination had grave implications for the kind of treatment the individual would receive. Therefore, the laws reflected the societal belief that if an individual could be found mentally ill, he should receive care rather than punishment. The problem was sorting out the mentally ill person while not excusing the criminal.

A New York State law passed in 1818 provided for the transfer of insane offenders from prison to the Lunatic Hospital at New York. [47] By the midnineteenth century several states had laws mandating that persons acquitted by reason of insanity should be committed to mental hospitals, not confined in prisons. [48] Although holding these mentally ill in prison was then specifically outlawed, Deutsch reports that the enforcement of these laws was often ignored and the mentally defective were still routinely held in prison settings.

On the other hand, applying the law—committing the mentally ill offender to the hospital—also caused difficulty. These "special" persons, whether acquitted by reason of insanity or transferred criminals who were found to be mentally ill while serving a sentence, were not welcomed in the mental hospital. Friends and relatives of the noncriminal mentally ill in hospitals complained that the special class of mental patient should be kept separate.

Responding to this issue, New York State was the first to open a special institution for these doubly stigmatized individuals, the mentally ill touched by criminal court contact. In 1859 the State Lunatic Asylum for Insane Convicts was opened adjacent to the state prison in Auburn. This institution was established to house convicted persons transferred from other prison settings. It is not surprising that there were many convicts in this category since it appears that the juries ignored all but the most flagrant indicators of mental defects and disorders in the trial process to avoid possible acquittal. [49] In addition, in 1869 this hospital began to take commitments of not convicted insane individuals directly from the criminal courts. These cases increased as case law more carefully defined insanity as a defense and at the time of trial.

In the first quarter of the twentieth century about a dozen states established separate facilities for the mentally ill offender. [50] In general these settings were meant to house the mentally ill tainted by contact with the criminal court, but their domain was extended as they became the dumping ground for noncriminally involved individuals perceived as particularly dangerous as well. Most of these institutions received commitments of the so-called dangerous insane who were civilly commitable and suspected of having "dangerous criminal tendencies."

Through the first half of this century, institutions for the criminally insane and the insane criminal proliferated. These institutions became warehouses for the most stigmatized of the society. Since the connotation of criminal was foremost, institutions placed more emphasis on control than cure. At the same time, science was affirming the entangled relationship between criminality and mental illness and new hope that treatment could cure began in the mental hygiene movement. More zeal for the possibility of cure than actual knowledge of how to affect it characterized this period. Nevertheless, the growth of psychological theories to explain social problems such as crime and delinquency by linking them to mental defect and mental disease fostered new emphasis on treatment and laid the foundation for later psychotherapies based on individual personality adjustment models. Ironically, as knowledge about mental disease and mental defect increased, it became harder rather than easier to determine which individuals were "insane."

COURT CLINICS ESTABLISHED

Concurrent with all these trends was the expansion of the role of psychiatry to include postconviction evaluations as aids in the disposition of offenders. This practice began in 1909 with a clinic attached to the Chicago Juvenile Court. The first adult court clinic was established in that same city in 1914. In 1921 Massachusetts passed the Briggs Law, which required psychiatric evaluation of all persons charged with capital offenses and those charged with felonies after one previous felony conviction. This promoted the growth of clinics in Massachusetts. Other states became interested in clinics as a possible aid to understanding the criminal. Halleck indicates that about 10 percent of the courts of the country had clinics by 1930.[51] It should be noted, however, that most of the clinics were in the states of California, Illinois, Massachusetts, Michigan, New York, Ohio, and Pennsylvania. While the purpose of these clinics was largely to aid in the disposition of convicted criminals, they also made evaluations of the mentally ill accused at the pretrial stage and assisted in the determination of insanity when it was the defense.

Although the earliest reason for psychiatric intervention in the criminal court was to help determine which persons violating the law should really be excused and treated and which ones deserved to be punished, more and more psychiatrists were now suggesting that all offenders needed mental health treatment. The distinction between the "sick" and the "bad" was becoming even less clear and the role of psychiatry in the criminal justice system was expanding.

During these early decades of the twentieth century, the American Medical Association, the American Psychiatric Association, and the American Bar Association all agreed that the alliance of psychiatry and law would benefit society and clients of the criminal justice system and all supported programs to increase psychiatric input to courts. This cooperation was not destined to continue, however, and disenchantment with the mental health approach to criminal behavior began about the same time as World War II.

Reasons for the loss of interest can be identified. First it should be emphasized that to this point most of the activity of psychiatrists revolved around the classification and placement of the criminal, not treatment. Halleck contends that the major contribution of the psychiatrist during this period was to deviance management (to classification and control), not to individual treatment.[52] Concurrently, the growing impact of psychoanalytic theory moved mental health professionals away from classification with its major interest in causality and prevention to practice that focused on treatment and cure. Since the psychoanalytic therapeutic method is most effective with highly motivated individuals, resistant, difficult, nonvoluntary clients were not appealing to the mental health professionals who embraced the new method of treatment. The institutionalized individuals, whether in a prison or hospital, received less of this emphasis than those seen in private practice, which became the major interest of psychiatrists.

In ironic contrast to this movement away from forensic practice, the passage of the sexual psychopath laws during this period created new linkages between psychiatry and the law and a larger client population in the forensic domain. The passage of the first sexual psychopath laws in the late 1930s was the foundation for the return of the medical model to the courtroom. Passed in state after state during the 1940s, these laws reflected the growing impact of social and psychological theory on the values of the times and the law. The courts and legislatures believed that certain criminals could be identified as psychopathic offenders and that this justified indefinite commitment to institutions of a special type to protect society. As legal scholars argued the constitutionality of these laws, the psychiatric community debated the reality of the psychopathic personality as a diagnostic category. To legislatures and juries the term psychopathic offender meant "dangerous, habitual offender," and inherent in the definition of this type of offender was a demand for special treatment.

Laws mandating special treatment for so-called psychopathic offenders, habitual offenders, defective delinquents, and so on, proliferated. The forensic psychosocial services area expanded and both evaluation and long-term client populations increased. The disposition of persons in particular offender categories required special institutional settings that combined maximum security and mental health treatment. During the 1950s individuals designated as psychopathic offenders were either confined with the diverse group of persons designated as "criminally insane" or a special hospital/prison was built to house them. Lima State Hospital in Ohio added new facilities for psychopathic offenders to those already established for the criminally insane.[53] In 1955, the state of Maryland built Patuxent State Institution as a treatment center exclusively for defective delinquents.

Until the 1960s little treatment was the rule in these hospitals for the various mentally disordered offenders. These inmate/patients were generally viewed as resistant to treatment and in a low probability of cure category, so resources in most state hospitals for the criminally insane were mainly used to provide custodial care. The client population increased, but Halleck contends that little change has occurred in the actual institutional treatment of the mentally ill offender since the time when Isaac Ray first called attention to the needs of this group in 1838.[54] In fact, it is a rather well-accepted fact that most mentally ill, even those civilly committed, in state institutions received only minimal custodial care because of a lack of knowledge about effective treatment, a lack of sufficient public funding, and a general shortage of professional mental health staff. Exposés identified inadequate levels of care in institutions for all of the mentally ill well into the fourth and fifth decades of this century.

Although the introduction of psychotropic drugs during the 1950s resulted in some movement out of institutions for civil mental patients, social fears still supported the long-term confinement of mentally ill offenders. Real changes did not occur for them until the 1960s and 1970s, when court cases challenged the constitutionality of the statutes mandating the various types of indeterminate and indefinite confinement of the mentally disabled offender. Both policy and legislation have been changed by a vigorous judiciary led by David Bazelon and Frank Johnson.* The litigation has resulted in a significant revision of procedures for confinement as well as treatment and care during confinement. Cases limiting the length of confinement, mandating confinement in the least restrictive settings, requiring treatment to justify indefinite confinement, and setting standards of minimum care have been most significant.

In response to legal pressures, current inclinations are to hospitalize only as long as necessary and to conduct periodic reviews to determine which persons may be released. Different types of inmates demand different handling. The critical question for the unconvicted in these hospitals is now, "Is the person dangerous to self or others?" If not, he should be released or transferred to a civil rather than forensic mental health facility for care. The current thinking is to treat mentally ill offenders with civilly committed mentally ill persons if they are not convicted and not especially dangerous. Convicted mentally ill may not be kept beyond the maximum sentence for their crime unless additional review and commitment procedures are followed.

In the 1950s and 1960s the recognition of the inefficacy of institutional treatment coupled with the inability of states to financially

---

*David Bazelon has been on the bench of the U.S. Court of Appeals, D.C. Circuit; and Frank Johnson is the judge of the U.S. District Court, Middle District of Alabama.

support institutions with even minimal levels of humane care contributed to the growth of the deinstitutionalization movement in both mental health and criminal justice. While this trend was slower in coming to forensic institutions, by the mid-1970s community clinics were being established in some parts of the country. These clinics are similar to those that flourished in the 1930s, but now the purpose of the clinics appears to be broader, offering more services. The primary focus of earlier clinics was to aid in disposition of convicted criminals. Clinics today are more intensely focused on screening and evaluating for competency to stand trial and for the insanity defense. The clinic is an alternative to a mandatory evaluation commitment in an institution for 30 to 60 days. Some also provide outpatient treatment for offenders on probation or defense.

CURRENT DIRECTIONS

While contemporary practice reflects the humane temper of the courts and advocacy groups, there is substantial conjecture in both mental health and criminal justice circles as to what future directions social values will take in public policy. Public care for the mentally ill, whether in the civil or forensic system, takes a great deal of money. Increased knowledge about mental disease and defect and new hope for treatment, combined with a heightened social awareness of inhumane conditions in institutions, have brought to the public the issue of how and where mentally ill offenders will be treated. Evaluation can be conducted on an inpatient or outpatient basis, and current emphases are on moving from the former to the latter. The trends in long-term care are to shorten the length of stay and return to giving care for the forensic clients in the civil mental health system, excepting those deemed too violent or dangerous for limited security hospitals. The key concerns of security and cost will no doubt have substantial impact on future public policies and programs as this historical review suggests they have in the past. Philosophical and fiscal concerns also affect the temperament of the courts. Recent rumblings of more punitive approaches to criminal behavior may affect the adjudication of criminal responsibility in courts and decrease the numbers of persons acquitted because of insanity.

The historical pattern of care for the forensic client moved from little recognition of the mental illness components in criminal conduct to greater assignment of mental illness explanations for criminal behavior. There are signs today of a resistance to mental health definitions that excuse punishment and of a return to stricter definitions of criminal culpability. Once the offender has been found mentally irresponsible, however, the system of care appears to be moving in a more humane, more treatment-oriented direction following civil mental health programming.

NOTES

1. H. E. Barnes and N. K. Teeters, New Horizons in Criminology, 3d ed. (Englewood Dliffs, N.J.: Prentice-Hall, 1943), p. 327.

2. A. Deutsch, The Mentally Ill in America, 2d ed. (New York: Columbia University Press, (1945), p. 409.

3. Ibid., p. 409.

4. Ibid.

5. Ibid., p. 408.

6. Ibid.

7. W. L. Russel, The New York Hospital: A History of the Psychiatric Service (New York: Columbia University Press, 1945), p. 34.

8. Ibid., p. 33.

9. Ibid., p. 60.

10. Ibid., p. 46.

11. Barnes and Teeters, op. cit., p. 336.

12. D. J. Rothman, The Discovery of the Asylum (Boston: Little, Brown, 1971).

13. Deutsch, op. cit., p. 389.

14. S. Glueck, Mental Disorder and the Criminal Law (Boston: Little, Brown, 1925), p. 126.

15. Ibid., p. 125.

16. Deutsch, op. cit., p. 388.

17. Glueck, op. cit., p. 278.

18. Daniel M'Naghten's Case, 10 Clark and Finnelly 20, 8 Eng. Rep. 718 (1843).

19. M'Naghten Case, House of Lords, 8 Eng. Rep. 718 at 722 (1843).

20. S. J. Brakel and R. S. Rock. The Mentally Disabled and the Law, rev. ed. (Chicago: University of Chicago Press, 1971), p. 380.

21. Ibid., p. 386.

22. State v. Thompson, Wright's Ohio Rep. 617 (1834).

23. State v. Jones, 50 N.H. 369, 9 Am. R. 242 (1871).

24. Durham v. United States, 214 F. 2d 874 (D.C. Cir. 1954).

25. Ibid., at 862.

26. United States v. Brawner, 471 F. 2d 969 (D.C. Cir. 1972).

27. A. Stone, Mental Health and Law: A System of Transition (Washington, D.C.: National Institute of Mental Health, 1975), p. 230.

28. Glueck, op. cit., p. 48.

29. See Com. v. Braley, 1 Mass. 102 (1804) noted in Glueck, op. cit., p. 48.

30. Dusky v. United States, 362 U.S. 405 (1960) (per curiam).

31. Ibid.

32. Stone, op. cit., p. 205.

33. Jackson v. Indiana, 406 U.S. 715 (1972).

34. Ibid., at 738.

35. A. Fink, Causes of Crime (Philadelphia: University of Pennsylvania Press, 1938).

36. S. Halleck, "American Psychiatry and the Criminal: A Historical Review," American Journal of Psychiatry 121 (1965) Supplement, p. v.

37. B. Glueck, "The Psychopathic Delinquent," Journal of Mental Hygiene 2(1918): 119-69.

38. Brakel and Rock, op. cit., p. 342.

39. American Psychiatric Association, Psychiatric Glossary (Washington, D.C.: APA, 1957), p. 38.

40. See Commonwealth v. Cooper, 219 Mass. 1, 106 N.E. 545; Anderson v. State, 209 Ala. 36, 95 So. 171; People v. Moran, 249 NY 179, 163 N.E. 553.

41. Joseph Ulman, A Judge Takes the Stand (New York: Knopf, 1933).

42. Stone, op. cit., p. 181.

43. Maryland Annotated Code, article 31B section 5 (1967).

44. See Tippett v. State of Maryland, 436 F.2d 1153 (4th Cir. 1971); Sas v. State of Maryland, 334 F.2d 506 (1964).

45. Stone, op. cit., p. 186.

46. Ibid.

47. Russel, op. cit., p. 74.

48. Deutsch, op. cit., p. 412.

49. See discussion in E. G. Hoag and E. H. Williams, Crime, Abnormal Minds and the Law (Indianapolis: Bobbs-Merrill, 1923), pp. 75-78.

50. Halleck, op. cit., p. viii.

51. Ibid.

52. Halleck, op. cit., p. xi.

53. Aldo Piperno, "A Socio-Legal History of the Psychopathic Offender Legislation in the United States," (Ph.D. dissertation, Ohio State University, 1974), p. 131.

54. Halleck, op. cit., p. xv.

2

PSYCHIATRY AND
SOCIAL CONTROL:
TWO CONTRADICTORY SCENARIOS

Seymour L. Halleck

My remarks will focus on many aspects of forensic psychiatry, particularly the future of forensic psychiatry, and indeed of psychiatric practice in general, with regard to social control. They will touch on the issues directly and indirectly related to mentally disordered offenders. Many broad issues will be discussed, all centering around the issue of social control. Social control can be defined as efforts on the part of social institutions to minimize behavior that is disruptive and costly to the society as a whole and to maximize behavior that is consistent with the value system of the society. Social control is essentially a peacekeeping function that is designed to benefit not only society but also the individual—though this is not always the case. Those who participate in social-control functions must have some commitment to the value system of the society as a whole, and their efforts, more often than not, will help to sustain the status quo.

Viewed in this light, it is almost impossible to separate the social-control functions of psychiatry from its medical, rehabilitative, or humanistic functions. When the psychiatrist treats the medical problems of a combative schizophrenic and helps him to find a respectable position in his community (if he can), he is participating in a form of social control. When he treats a deprived delinquent youth and helps him to achieve a level of adaptation that allows him to function in society, the psychiatrist is successful in influencing that youth to behave in a manner that meets the needs of society. When the psychiatrist helps any patient learn that it is possible to meet his humanistic or growth needs within the confines of an existing social institution, he is minimizing potential disruptive behavior by helping that person to adjust to the realities of the present. Some element of social control is involved in any psychiatric intervention.

24

I think the social-control functions of psychiatry are most apparent when we deal with involuntary patients, those who are under some restraint of law. When psychiatrists commit an assaultive patient or treat a convicted child molester, they are obviously concerned with protecting society. The social-control functions involved in intervention with voluntary patients are less obvious. The dispensing of medication or provision of behavior modification or some form of psychotherapy are not ordinarily thought of as having social-control functions, yet a careful examination of the consequences of changing people's attitudes, emotions, or behaviors shows that even the most voluntary psychiatric intervention has social-control implications.

Society currently evidences an ambivalent view with regard to allowing the profession of psychiatry to assert social-control functions. In many areas the power of psychiatrists to exert social control is being deliberately attacked and eroded. The majority of these attacks are focused on the treatment of highly disturbed and, as a rule, involuntary patients. At the same time, there have been few efforts to restrain, or even to recognize the need to restrain, the more subtle activities of psychiatrists in the social control of voluntary patients. In effect, we are in a situation in which there are two paradoxical or at least contradictory trends with regard to psychiatry's role in social control. In some areas the psychiatrist's powers are being limited and in other areas they are being extended. I will discuss these trends as they have been emerging over the past two decades and will speculate on how they will continue to influence the profession and the patients. Throughout most of this discussion I will consider the manner in which psychiatry has been reactive to these trends and has accommodated to the forces that impinge upon the profession. In the latter part of the chapter I will speak primarily to psychiatrists, commenting briefly upon ways in which psychiatry must be more active in defining the role the profession should play in the process of social control.

PSYCHIATRISTS AS A CLEAN-UP CREW

At times, some of the social-control functions of psychiatrists have been compared to the activities of the garbage man or janitor. We deal with individuals who create messy, untidy, definitely unpleasant situations for the rest of the society, and who are unlikely to be persuaded to behave differently by rational argument or criminal sanctions. One of my esteemed colleagues, Alan Stone from Harvard, wrote a short article a couple of years ago in which he argued that the forensic psychiatrist was really a garbage man and that his functions were really very similar to those of janitorial work. I thought this was a very clever analogy because I had thought of it too, and I was a little jealous that he said it first.

Amazingly, my colleagues were very upset about this. There were dozens of articles written to our professional newsletter about how he denounces and demeans us so in making this comparison. I also wrote a letter to the newsletter. I said that I had inadvertently let a copy of the article lay around my office and that it had been picked up by the woman who cleans my office. She took it to her boss, and apparently it got to the head of the local janitor's union, and I received a letter that went something like this:

> We noticed that your colleagues are upset at being com-
> pared with janitors. We think if anybody should find this
> comparison odious, it certainly should be we janitors.
> First of all, we have a much longer history than psychi-
> atry. We are certainly more necessary—the world could
> always function without psychiatrists, but certainly could
> not function without janitors. We don't get involved in
> ridiculous squabbles over diagnosis and the method of
> cure that you people do. We don't get involved in mal-
> practice suits, we never abuse the public, and we have
> solved the issues of racism and sexism long before you
> people.

Citing this communication, I signed my letter "yours in cleanliness." The amazing thing is that my colleagues were infuriated with me for having done this. Forensic psychiatrists take themselves seriously.

I do have some concern with this analogy, that it may be dis-couraging to patients, but I don't believe that we, as professionals, should find the analogy odious. There is nothing inherently disgrace-ful about taking care of unpleasant tasks or unpleasant people who can-not be managed by ordinary social institutions as long as this can be done without dehumanizing patients. Psychiatrists have helped count-less patients and have probably helped make a better society by invol-untarily treating severely mentally ill people and by participating in the treatment and care of mentally ill offenders. I know Dr. Szasz, who will address you later, would strongly disagree. If there were no profession of psychiatry, some other social force or institution, probably less rational and probably less benevolent, would be created to deal with the problem.

But today there is increasing concern on the part of many ele-ments in our society as to how much control psychiatrists should be allowed over people who are in compromised positions. Much of the social-control power society once gladly gave to psychiatrists is being stridently questioned and insidiously withdrawn. Our legal system, through litigation and legislation, is constantly putting new restraints on what psychiatrists can do to an unwilling patient. Because the medical and social-control functions of psychiatric practice are sometimes inextricably combined, the new legal onslaught upon psychiatry has not only deprived us of the power to exert control over deviant individuals but has also all too often compromised psychiatrists' capacity to provide what we believe is the best medical care for our patients.

"BELEGALED" PROFESSION

One of my friends and colleagues, Jonas Rapaport, recently referred to psychiatry as a "belegaled" profession. This reminds me of a story that reflects the current relationship of psychiatry and the law. A psychiatrist, a lawyer, and a minister go out fishing in the ocean. After they have gone about a mile or two out, they discover the boat has sprung a leak. The minister begins to pray, the psychiatrist begins to try to think how he can figure his way out of it, and the lawyer says, "The hell with all this obsession, I'm going to jump in and swim to shore." And as the lawyer begins to jump in, the psychiatrist looks into the water and says, "My God, watch out, don't jump, there are sharks all over!" The lawyer does not heed the psychiatrist and jumps in anyway. And lo and behold, as he jumps into the water the sharks form a cordon around him and escort him in to shore. The minister at this point shouts "Hallelujah, it's a miracle!" and the psychiatrist says, "Miracle, hell. That's professional courtesy."

I think this story reflects some of the current tenor of relations between psychiatry and the law. Most of us who engage in clinical practice are being forced to spend more and more of our working day paying attention to legal issues and often do feel belegaled. It might be reassuring to note that we as a profession are not alone. Sometime during the last three decades, trust and respect in many of our institutions of social control, such as the church and the family, have diminished. There is a generalized lack of conviction that social agencies or institutions whose power functions are not precisely defined will do what is best for individuals. There is not space here to elaborate upon the reasons for that breakdown in trust in authority, but it is important to note that in a society in which traditional social institutions do not exert control, more and more issues must be decided in the legal arena. Psychiatry, I would like to submit, is only one of many venerated social institutions (perhaps not as venerated as others) that is no longer being allowed to function in what seems to be an arbitrary manner. The profession is being critically scrutinized by those who distrust psychiatry and by their legal advocates.

TRENDS IN CIVIL COMMITMENT

The most striking change that is occurring is in the area of civil commitment, and much of this is really due to the efforts of Thomas Szasz, who is a seminal figure in this area. Maybe all these changes would have come about without him, but maybe not nearly as quickly. New laws have been enacted in most states that now provide for strict standards for civil commitments and provide the mentally ill patient with a kind of due process very similar to that found in criminal law. Much of this change is welcomed, and indeed many psychiatrists have actively sought such change. But these limitations to the social-control power of psychiatrists have also had unwelcome consequences for psychiatrists, and for many of our patients.

Psychiatrists in most states are now required to present evidence regarding the patient's dangerousness to self or others to initiate a commitment. This is the area Nicholas Kittrie will address in Chapter 3 in more detail, but I believe that dangerousness to self is difficult enough to predict and that dangerousness to others is almost impossible to predict except in very rare situations. The new legal approach to civil commitment has forced psychiatrists to pretend an illegitimate expertise. Psychiatrists cannot predict dangerousness, absolutely, at this point, and they cannot even give reasonable probability statements as to the likelihood of dangerousness. As a result, much of their energy is devoted to assessing predictions that they are incapable of making.

The new laws also hurt patients. In most jurisdictions the new laws are not substantial enough to allow for the involuntary confinement and treatment of an individual who is desperately ill and who would be responsive to treatment but who cannot be treated because there is no proof of dangerousness to self or others. About once a month I sit in on a very, very tragic situation where a particular individual is clearly mentally ill; where the family is on the verge of destroying themselves because they do not know how to deal with this individual; where the family resources are being squandered; and even situations where there is some violence in the home and the family initiates commitment and the psychiatrist concurs, but where commitment is not justified under the law. Under the laws of North Carolina, you need very, very clear evidence of dangerousness, almost physical violence and recent physical violence, before you can commit. So the situation I described occurs; it is a genuine tragedy. Nevertheless, it happens increasingly under the new laws.

An important social-control function has been taken away from psychiatry, and it is quite likely that additional litigation will even further delimit psychiatric power to function in this area. If society continues to see the commitment of the mentally ill as a process similar to the control of criminal behavior, we will eventually see such things as jury trials and patients being instructed that they have the right not to talk to a psychiatrist or not to talk to a psychiatrist without a lawyer being present if there is even remote danger that they might be committed. In North Carolina there currently is an effort to get some litigation out of one of the circuit courts that would give the patient the right to not speak to the psychiatrist in an interview if there is any threat of commitment whatsoever. Can you picture the psychiatrist telling the person that he has the right to remain silent?

INFORMED CONSENT TO TREATMENT

Even though psychiatrists can still commit patients, however difficult it is becoming, their powers to treat a patient who does not want to be treated have been drastically eroded. A recently enacted law in California (Vasconcellos) obviates the use of psychosurgery in certain patients and requires a formidable array of psychiatric evaluations and legal procedures before an unwilling patient can be given electroconvulsive therapy (ECT). A competent patient who refuses ECT can never be given this treatment; also we can surely anticipate increasing limitations on the involuntary use of drug therapy. In most jurisdictions now, drugs cannot be given to a nonconsenting patient unless that patient is committed. It is likely that we will soon have even more rigorous competency hearings and more rigorous evaluations of the individuals' capacity to provide informed consent before we can use these medications with nonconsenting patients.

Lawyers and judges are very familiar with the fact that this whole issue of informed consent opens up an increadible bag of worms. There are many aspects to be considered: the nature of the explanation, whether the explanation is satisfactory with regard to possible risks and possible benefits, how much of the explanation the patient really understands, and whether the patient is competent to deal with the material he is hearing. Doctors are getting very nervous about these things and some are actually videotaping and audiotaping the informed-consent explanations. Some have overreacted, and that leads to interesting things. For example, there's a suit pending in Massachusetts for a surgeon who, wanting to make sure that he gave the patient fully informed consent for open-heart surgery, stressed all the possible bad effects very heavily. The patient refused surgery, went home and died, and the doctor is now being sued for having frightened the patient out of the surgery.

One of the most interesting issues in the area of informed consent is the question of what the patient really hears and how much he really understands. There have been some tests in pre- and postsurgery where they have actually videotaped the instructions to the patients (so we know what was said to the patient), and then asked the patient later what he recalled about the risks and benefits that were mentioned. The average patient score on some of these tests for reasonably intact patients was something like 20 percent. Think for yourself when you go to a doctor or a dentist and he starts telling you "these are risks, these are benefits"; my guess is that you do not hear much of that. I am very much in favor of the informed-consent doctrine, but I think there are some big problems, that it is an enormous area of law, and that it is going to affect medicine in every conceivable area.

There are already important restrictions on the use of behavior modification. Litigation that limits the use of aversive therapy, and even the use of token economies or generalized reinforcers, has already curbed the power of psychiatrists altering human behavior with this particular technique. I do not want to comment here on the social desirability of such limitations, merely to point out that this aspect of psychiatric social control is diminishing and will likely continue to do so.

There are also new restrictions on the use of treatments even with the patient who consents to treatment. In the Kaimowitz case, an individual who was under criminal restraint consented to an experimental psychosurgical procedure that held some slight promise of helping him obtain an earlier release. The courts ruled that an individual under criminal restraint could not consent to such a drastic procedure.

RESEARCH CURTAILED

The Kaimowitz decision has had a chilling effect on psychiatric research in general and particularly on research in prisons, which has been drastically curtailed and for all intents and purposes is dead. I live very close to the new federal correctional institution in Butner. For a time, it was notorious. Everybody felt there was going to be a behavior modification unit and a psychosurgery unit, and before the ground was even broken there were many articles talking about the abuses that were taking place at this institution. I was on the board of directors of that institution and I know that they were not going to do behavior modification and psychosurgery; they were going to test some effects of psychotherapy on a research basis. I had some hopes of being able to study violent offenders, at least through simple things like neuropsychological testing and electroencephalograms. That institution did finally open a year ago and brought patients in, but given the current federal guidelines, it is operating in such a way that there is absolutely no research going on whatsoever worthy of the name. There is some effort to try to deal with one of Norval Morris's systems, but that is not research, and even that has been sabotaged. So, in effect, we have a research institution that was built specifically for that purpose, but that is doing no research. My guess is that there is very little research going on now in any correctional setting in this country.

Drug research in the United States is also seriously limited by restraints based on informed consent, and most of the new drugs are being developed in other countries. Actually, almost all the currently popular drugs are coming in from Europe. They are first developed and tested there, then our drug companies pick them up, and after a while they are marketed here. Certainly if new and more efficient agents for changing behavior are not continuously developed, the social-control functions of psychiatrists will be diminished.

The issue of informed consent may also limit the extent to which interventions that subtly lead to social control can be utilized with voluntary patients. We have not decided if every patient who enters psychotherapy should be warned that some day his confidentiality may be compromised, as indeed it might, if he applies for a sensitive job or an insurance policy. We do not know if we should tell every patient for whom we prescribe a neuroleptic about the wide variety of changes that may be produced in the autonomic and extrapyramidal nervous systems. As the informed-consent doctrine continues to be applied in medical practice, and it certainly will, a certain number of individuals who had previously accepted certain treatments will refuse to do so. Again, as the treatment powers of the psychiatrist are diminished, the social-control powers of the psychiatrist will decrease.

The increased threat of malpractice suits will eventually have an impact on the psychiatrist's willingness to treat certain types of patients. The effect is likely to be most profound in those instances where psychiatrists deal with highly disturbed, seriously ill patients. In California, psychiatrists are currently under criminal, not civil, indictment for failing to provide proper care for highly disturbed patients. (There were some deaths at a state hospital, some of which were related to poor care, some of which were perhaps not related to poor care.) Somebody dug up an old California law that says it is a felony to do harm to a mental patient and several psychiatrists have been indicted and are facing sentences. Again, in California, the State Supreme Court has recently upheld the Tarasoff decision in which a psychotherapist was held liable for having failed to inform a potential victim of the intention of his patient to destroy her. Those who are familiar with that case know that the psychotherapist in this case was a psychologist. He really tried to have the patient committed; he did go to the police, but the police said they would not be able to do anything about it. The patient did kill Tarasoff, whose parents then sued the psychologist for having failed to inform them, and for having failed to inform Tarasoff, about the risk that this man was threatening to kill her. This makes psychiatrists nervous, and some psychiatrists have speculated that such decisions may discourage therapists from working with highly disturbed and potentially violent individuals. I believe there certainly is a risk that this kind of new legalism may have just such a chilling effect.

As a person who works daily with highly disturbed voluntary and involuntary patients, I frequently yearn for the good old days when I saw relatively healthy Yavis patients: Young, Attractive, Verbal, Intelligent, and Single, who willingly pay their bills, who frequently adore me, who are sometimes grateful, and who would never think of being litigious. Given the pressure of my wistful longing, and the realization as well that many other psychiatrists can elect to work primarily with healthy, wealthy, and cooperative patients, I believe it is not too far fetched to predict that the better psychiatrists will increasingly move away from the treatment of highly disturbed patients. I am not saying that our record in investing our energies in the treatment of the most disturbed mentally ill patients has been especially noble up to now, or in the best tradition of Hippocrates. Psychiatry is the only field in medicine where as the patient gets worse or sicker, his care gets progressively worse. If you think about it, we reserve our best efforts for those who are the most healthy, and it is really very, very hard to get psychiatrists to treat sick people. Even then, I think that it is going to get worse. We have certainly not done very well for the severely mentally ill up to now. I conjecture, however, that in the future our involvement with the treatment and social control of highly disturbed and disturbing patients will become far more tentative and far less committed or enthusiastic and this, I would suggest, would be a humanistic tragedy.

INCREASE OF PSYCHIATRIC PRACTICE
IN CRIMINAL JUSTICE SETTINGS

The status of psychiatry's current involvement with the social control of individuals who are convicted or suspected criminal offenders is at this moment blurred and complicated. There is some increased demand for the psychiatrist's service in making dispositional decisions as to which offenders shall be funneled from the correctional system to the forensic system. Suspected offenders who are found incompetent to stand trail or who are not guilty by reason of insanity, as well as sex offenders and some drug addicts, are increasingly referred to diagnostic and treatment programs and hospitals for the criminally insane. Psychiatrists assist the courts in making decisions as to these referrals. They also have some responsibility for the care of offenders who have been so referred.

I recently visited the Florida state system and found out that they are planning to have as many as 2,000 forensic beds in the near future in a state of roughly 6 million people. That's frightening, because there is a real question whether people belong in a forensic system, there is a real question whether this is the best way to treat offenders, and there is a real question whether this is the best way to protect the rights of the offenders. There is also the question of whether diversion into the forensic system is being used for a lot of nasty reasons, like inability to create a good case to convict somebody, to relieve overcrowding in prisons, or to distract attention from the heinous conditions that currently exist in our prisons.

I would also like to say (and I suspect Nicholas Kittrie and Tom Szasz and I are going to agree on this) that I do not think the psychiatrist has a great role in incompetency proceedings, although he currently gets involved. Competency to stand trial is really a legal decision, not a psychiatric decision. Such decisions probably ought to be made by lawyers, perhaps with the assistance of the psychiatrist. I also do not think psychiatrists have anything to contribute to the issue of not guilty by reason of insanity, which fortunately is a rare issue. We can talk esoterically about what is wrong with people; we can describe to the court what may have made a person behave in a certain way; but we have absolutely no capacity to judge responsibility. We have no capacity to say whether by nature or disease or defect the person did not know right from wrong, or whether something was a product of an illness. These are philosophical decisions, not medical decisions, and my advice to psychiatry is usually to stay out of court on these issues. Also, we may have some capacity to figure out who is a sexual psychopath, but even here our energies are expended in the wrong direction. Many people who have sexual abnormalities are not particularly violent people. If we are to have programs that are specialized and indeterminate, I would much rather see them focused strictly on the issue of violence rather than on sexual psychopathology. I think the latter is used primarily because it has prurient interest; it gets the public excited.

There are a number of reasons to anticipate that the commitment of offenders to the forensic system will continue to increase. Our prisons are overcrowded, and diversion of disturbed offenders to specialized treatment centers is viewed as highly desirable by both courts and corrections administrators. As sentences grow more and more lengthy, offenders are sometimes eager to risk the indeterminate aspects of commitment to a forensic program to avoid the certainty of prolonged confinement. It is also likely that as fewer mentally disturbed people are civilly committed, they may become involved in activities that are labeled as criminal and may, once indicted, be referred to the forensic system as incompetent to stand trial. In effect, the law seems to be attempting to decriminalize, at least in name, the status of some mentally disturbed offenders. It should be clear, however, that decriminalization is not the same as deinstitutionalization. Many of the forensic institutions to which these individuals are sent, and most still go to institutions, impose as severe restrictions upon freedom and as hard conditions of confinement as are found in the prisons.

The psychiatrist who participates in the forensic system is lending medical sanction to the social-control function of the criminal law. When the psychiatrist attempts to treat the forensic patient or to take responsibility for the forensic patient's institutional care, the psychiatrist is again a participant in the social-control function. The psychiatrist's power in the latter role, however, may not be great. Within the limits of the patient's right to refuse treatment, the psychiatrist can certainly treat patients. Within the limits of certain guarantees of constitutional rights following such important decisions as Jackson, Baxtrom, and Bolton, the psychiatrist can also exert critical influence in keeping these people incarcerated. As a rule, any negative statement about the offender that the psychiatrist makes to a judicial agency tends to be seized upon as an excuse by the court to keep the offender confined. The psychiatrist has very little influence, however, in gaining the patient's release from the forensic institution. In most jurisdictions, only the court can release the forensic patient or divert him back into the criminal system.

The psychiatrist in the forensic system is in the difficult position of having considerable responsibility for the care and treatment of his patients but little influence in being able to arrange for their eventual release. Many jurisdictions have standards of release that speak of the necessity to cure a patient, but there is often a great disparity between what the psychiatrist considers to be rehabilitation and what the court may think of as a cure. In this setting, the psychiatrist is primarily a pawn in the social-control process, and his medical accomplishments are limited. It should not be too surprising that fewer and fewer psychiatrists are volunteering to work in a forensic setting, where they have great power to retain people but no power to release them. Also it is likely that if the level of care in such settings continues to be inadequate, we might eventually expect legal efforts to divert offenders out of the forensic system and perhaps back into the correctional system, but that might be an unrealistic assumption.

The situation with regard to psychiatrists working in a correctional setting poses a different set of problems. At the moment rehabilitative efforts in our prisons are pathetically and painfully inadequate. Few psychiatrists will work in prisons, and the actual number of psychiatrists available to a given number of inmates is rapidly decreasing. The concept of rehabilitation is in disfavor and our correctional system is increasingly focusing on deterrence and retribution via what I think is irrational, lengthy sentencing.

The current correctional emphasis on deterrence and retribution cannot, in my opinion, work. It is simply too expensive to provide certain and severe punishment to large groups of offenders. Our prisons are already overcrowded, and sooner or later our lawmakers will discover that rehabilitation, even if only marginally effective, is a less-expensive solution than retribution and deterrence. At that point, there may be an effort to divert marginally disturbed criminal offenders to a forensic or mental health system, or there may be an expansion of psychiatric treatment in prisons. The latter trend seems to be more likely. With psychiatrists' new psychotropic medications, with increased understanding of behavior modification, and with a greater understanding of the usefulness and limitations of psychotherapy, psychiatrists may discover or rediscover that criminals can be changed through medical intervention. Prisoners themselves may find advocates who demand their right to rehabilitation just as the mentally ill found advocates who demanded the right to treatment.

Incidentally, the Fourth Circuit Court in Baltimore recently granted prisoners the right to psychotherapy as a part of treatment. The expansion of sophisticated psychiatric services in correctional settings would be fraught with ethical and legal complications. The use of drugs, psychosurgery, and behavior modification in the correctional setting will be as thoroughly scrutinized as it has been in all other settings. Even the use of psychotherapy to change criminal propensities will be challenged. Effective psychiatric service in prisons would also threaten many of the assumptions underlying criminality that buttress the bureaucracy that constitutes our criminal justice system. If it is discovered that psychiatrists can treat criminal behavior, we can anticipate considerable resistance from the correctional establishment regarding efforts to implement such changes.

PSYCHOTHERAPY AND DRUG
PRESCRIPTION AS SOCIAL CONTROL

I think the most interesting expansion of psychiatry's role in social control is now occurring as a by-product of our treatment of voluntary patients—patients who for the most part welcome psychiatric services—and not of involuntary patients. Psychiatric treatment with drugs, with behavior modification, and with psychotherapy is an expanding industry, a multibillion-dollar industry. As more and more members of our population become willing to submit to various forms of psychiatric treatment, psychiatrists will play an increasing role in shaping our society. An expanding use of neuroleptic medication, of major tranquilizers, has an obvious smothering effect upon the disruptive behavior of the mentally ill in our society. Neuroleptic drugs may or may not have direct antipsychotic effect, but they definitely diminish antisocial behavior. It would seem logical to assume that the increased use of these agents will serve to stabilize our society.

This issue can become very complex. We have no way of being assured that psychotic patients will continue to take these drugs once released from institutions. It may be that drug treatment temporarily dissuades therapists in social institutions from dealing with the psychological and social issues that may have played a role in the patient's initial dangerousness. When the patient stops taking the drug he may be especially prone to antisocial or disruptive behavior. I came up with this theory because there is some new research in the last two or three years that indicates that the rate of substantive crime among discharged mental patients is five times that of the normal population. Studies that were done in the 1940s and 1950s indicated that those who were mentally ill have lower crime rates. The studies done in the early 1960s indicate that those who have been hospitalized have slightly higher crime rates.

It should also be apparent that the use of neuroleptic therapy allows more and more psychotic individuals to live outside the hospital. Noninstitutionalized individuals are more likely to have children, and I do not think it is far fetched at all to conjecture that such practices will increase the gene pool for schizophrenia and bipolar depression in the general population, and it may ultimately lead to a higher level of disruptive social behavior. Most of us are convinced these days that schizophrenia and manic depression, whether one calls them illnesses or not, are clearly inherited, and the evidence for that is overwhelming. I am not saying that is all that is involved in these behaviors appearing, but clearly there is a potentiality that is inherited. To the extent that we get these people well enough and out of the hospital to raise children, we are obviously going to increase the number of schizophrenics and manic depressives in our society. It is inevitable every time you cure a disease or help a disease: You disrupt the ecology in ways that have unanticipated consequences.

The antianxiety drugs, or the minor tranquilizers, may prove to have even more powerful effects on social control than the neuroleptic drugs. Valium, I believe, is well on its way to becoming Huxley's "soma." It is used regularly by millions of Americans, and if the rate of its use continues at the present pace, almost every American will be using Valium by the turn of the century. Anxiety is a universal experience and there are many ways to resolve it: sometimes by internal change, sometimes by behavior that changes the environment. It is reasonable to assume that a population of people who regularly deal with anxiety by ingesting a drug that changes their physiology will have less tendency to take abrasive, disruptive, or status-quo-altering actions with regard to the environment. Valium and other antianxiety agents, it would seem, function to cool the society.

VALUE-BASED CRITERIA OF MENTAL HEALTH

Most forms of psychotherapy also serve to sustain the status quo and increase social control. In all forms of psychotherapy an effort is made not only to alleviate the patient's symptoms but also to help the patient to achieve emotional growth and maturity or a state of increased mental health. All of the latter goals are based on value systems, and all the value systems are in large part determined by the prevailing mood of the larger society. Individual therapists may at times influence patients to behave in accordance with their own idiosyncratic value systems, but for the most part the therapist represents a powerful reinforcer of the values of the greater society. By and large, psychiatry and psychotherapy have been reactive in terms of defining its value systems. By this I mean we usually hold the values of mental health that are derived from current social ethos.

Consider how easily so many schools of psychotherapy have adopted the goal of self-actualization as an inherent human need and in so doing have tended to minimize values such as cooperation, interdependence, and the need to serve the community. Bronfenbrenner has noted that a common slogan of the Republic of China is "serve the people" (others have noted that the prevailing slogan in Russia is "never be a bystander") and he notes that the analogous slogan in the United States is "do your own thing." While I believe the majority of American psychotherapists are currently deeply committed to the value of self-actualization, I have little doubt that if our society becomes more socialistic we will soon begin to bombard our patients with messages as to the virtues of community dependence and loyalty rather than individuation or self-actualization. This is one area in which the humanistic function of psychiatry clearly interdigitates with the social-control function. If you wish to help a patient learn to behave in a manner that is best for him, you must try to shape his behavior so that it is most efficient and relevant to the given social milieu. Adjustment to the environment is a requisite goal of any form of psychotherapy if the patient is to achieve his humanistic potential.

In furthering human adjustment, the psychotherapist functions as an agent of social control. Some behavior therapists have argued that their techniques for dealing with mental ills, based on principles of operant conditioning, have limited ethical or social-control implications. They insist that the behavior therapist is not interested in helping the patient to achieve growth, self-actualization, or any of the values that may be used to define mental health, but rather that he is interested in simply getting the patient what he wants. The patient wants to diminish or increase the frequency of the given behavior, and the therapist will simply show him how to do so. I view this analysis as naive. First of all, we are not always willing to help people to achieve goals we do not believe are ethical. Many therapists, for example, would not work very hard to help to relieve a second-story man of his fear of heights. We are more likely to help a person to achieve goals we view as helping him function more efficiently and less disruptively in the community.

A second and often ignored point, something Skinner would appreciate but most of his students have not, is that even in the language of behavior modification the patient's goal in therapy or his motivation to change is itself an operant behavior and is, therefore, largely molded by social influence. Behavior therapists may be simply trying to give patients only what they want, but what the patient wants is more than likely exactly what society expects him to want.

The influence of group therapy in social control is also formidable. Once the group achieves a certain degree of cohesiveness it is a very powerful reinforcing mechanism. More importantly, group therapy deals with an issue of alienation and loneliness in our society. Most of us really do not have the same roots that people 50 or 60 years ago had, and the group does give a kind of intimacy.

I have a lot of problems with group therapy, but every now and then I begin to worry that I may be a latent groupie. About a year ago I went to San Francisco to testify. I used to live there and I started walking around and felt intense loneliness and depression. It had been a day of perfunctory conversations and I really wanted to talk to somebody. I did not want to call any of my friends in the area because it was Sunday afternoon and I did not want to bother them. I finally realized that what I wanted was a group, and I got the fantasy that we ought to have an instant group in every city that we could belong to like a church or Kiwanis. Whenever you go to a town you just look up the group that shares your values and with whom you can feel very comfortable. I tell this story partly to emphasize that the group serves the important political function in our society of obfuscating the alienation we all endure, and at the same time it also obfuscates providing a cure for it.

CONCLUSIONS

I presented all of the above considerations in as provocative a manner as possible in order to make the point that social controls are an inherent aspect of psychiatric practice. Psychiatrists could not resist this role even if they made the most ingenious efforts to do so. And I am arguing that psychiatrists ought to accept this role. There is nothing inherently ignoble or totalitarian or nonmedical about it. The psychiatrist's task is not to avoid social-control functions but to be aware of them, define them, and exercise them in as humanistic a

way as possible. Social-control functions are a medical mandate
that we should stop being apologetic about. On the other hand, we
should not get terribly upset about the legal profession monitoring
what we are doing because most of the decisions we make are too important to be left solely to doctors.

I also think we need to examine with greater intensity the impact
of psychotropic drug treatment on our society. It is conceivable that
modern man should be labeled "drug man," a new evolutionary crea-
ture. And finally, we need to be constantly seeking an open dialogue
between physicians, psychotherapists, and all other members of society as to what values define mental health and the good life. As
long as we are going to be controlling people, we have to have some
system for deciding how to control them, and this must be recognized
as ultimately a question of values.

DISCUSSION

Question: Does what you have to say, especially with regard to
drugs, apply only to physicians and psychiatrists?

Halleck: No, the main point that I want to make is that drugs
are just a tiny, tiny part of social control. I think every time you sit
and talk to a person and try to modify the way he looks at things, you
are trying to change his behavior. Any time you are into changing behavior you are into social control. So what I have to say does not apply strictly to physicians and psychiatrists; it applies to anybody who
works with people who define themselves as in need of help and who
we are trying to change in some way. A lot of people feel that the dan-
gers of social control have to do with psychosurgery, lobotomy, and
intrusive use of powerful medications. I do not think that is true at
all, I think that's a big mistake. I think behavior modification has
really powerful social-control implications. I think psychotherapy
has powerful social-control implications. I think it is illogical to say
that we are not really controlling and influencing people, no matter
what kind of therapy we do.

Question: Social control has its roots in legislation. Do you
feel we as professional psychiatrists, physicians, and other professionals in related fields should take a larger role in influencing the
legislative process?

Halleck: I think as citizens we should, yes. As people who have
ideologies, yes. I think the important thing is to separate your expertise as a professional from your ideology as a citizen. It worries

me terribly when psychiatrists and other professionals go before a legislative body and say, "It is my medical opinion that this law would be good for people," when it's usually not a medical opinion at all, but an ideological opinion. I'm very concerned that we not contaminate our ideologies, which may be based on very humanistic principles, with our medical knowledge. I feel strongly about that in the court-room, too. When a psychiatrist says it is his medical opinion that this person is not responsible for what he did, that's not a medical opinion at all. It happens to be his idealistic opinion or his value judgment, but there's no medical basis to determine whether or not someone is responsible.

Question: Is there one really dominant cultural reality to which individuals should adjust? We should be able to help individuals to adjust to some reality, but it appears that reality is stratified by econ-omy, by politics, by different cultural divisions, and so on. How do we deal with this?

Halleck: Not well. The conflict for me is that I am somewhat on the fringe personally. I don't especially like some of the social institutions in the society and I find myself working to help people ac-commodate to them, as realistically as possible. At the same time I'm politically active in trying to change them. I try to separate those two activities as much as possible and that is not easy. An interesting thing happened four or five years ago when I was teaching some very bright radical students. They were training to be psychotherapists and were dealing with this dilemma: How am I going to be a psycho-therapist in a society I don't like? One of them came up to me and said, "You know, there's really nothing wrong with our being total agents of social control if the society is good." And he went on, "If I could live in Mao's Red China, I would have no problem at all being a psychiatrist. I would have no ethical dilemmas because I would be-lieve fully in the system I was inflicting upon people." I couldn't func-tion in that kind of society, but I think he had a good point. If you really do believe in the prevailing value system, it's much easier for you to do that kind of psychotherapy.

I think you are making another point, too, that the value system is quite variant in our society, quite changable and flexible. What bothers me is I see my colleagues and myself changing our views from week to week with whatever's the current value system. Is it good for a woman to work or is it bad for a woman to work? Should a woman have vaginal orgasms or clitoral orgasms? As recently as ten years ago, my colleagues and I were telling women that if they didn't have vaginal orgasms there was something terribly wrong with them. We don't tell anyone that anymore, but it shows how incredibly fickle we are, how capricious in interpreting the value system. I don't know what to do about that.

Question: How do you relate your conception of social control to the phenomenon of psychic pain?

Halleck: Just that they interdigitate. I think when you're treating psychic pain you have to do something either biological or behavioral to the patient, or you have to get them to accept a different orientation toward life. In the process of relieving their suffering, you end up exerting a social-control function; the two are inseparable. As a physician I would certainly hold the alleviation of pain as my first responsibility, which often gets me into doing more social control than I like to do. For example, with involuntary patients, I still find it difficult to participate in committing somebody and treating them against their will, but on the other hand, the value for me of relieving that person's pain supersedes the value of that person's freedom. You simply have to make a choice on that. Thomas Szasz would take exactly the other stand, that the patient's freedom should supersede any medical value. It's simply an ideological argument, a religious argument. There is no way of deciding if it is a scientific argument.

Question: If you regard dangerousness as either too stringent or too unwieldy a standard for involuntary civil commitment, what would you substitute for it?

Halleck: I'd go along very much with Alan Stone's criteria: Is the patient ill, is there some treatment that might help the patient, and is the patient competent to accept that treatment? Here I've done a 180-degree turn. I initially supported the idea of dangerousness and I initially assisted in legislation to include that in the law. But as I tried to work with the concept of dangerousness for civil commitment, I concluded that it's totally useless and that it has nothing to do with psychiatry. If people want to play around speculating about dangerousness, that's their business. It's useless and corrupt to involve psychiatrists in that process. A few people are beginning to say this; Alan Stone is saying it very eloquently. My guess is that it's going to snowball and you're going to be hearing this from psychiatrists in crescendo.

Question: If psychiatrists don't testify regarding criminal incompetency or insanity, who will? Don't you think it's our professional responsibility to testify in the criminal courts on these matters?

Halleck: I don't believe so. I think there are some facts we have on the one hand, and there are some theological or ideological beliefs on the other. I don't mind going to court and simply talking about what I know factually, or even opinionwise, about what I think is wrong with someone and why he behaves in certain ways. But saying what I think we ought to do with them, or trying to answer questions—are they competent or are they responsible—are really social, theological, and ideological decisions that I think are too important to be left to psychiatrists.

I think one big problem is the ambivalence of both psychiatrists and lawyers as to who ought to be making these decisions, and it works both ways. Psychiatrists often feel they can make these decisions, and then when things get too heavy in court, they want to turn them over to the lawyers. And lawyers do just the opposite. They claim psychiatrists should decide, "since these are medical matters." But if they do not like what the psychiatrist says, then they claim he has no expertise. I think both sides have been extraordinarily ambivalent about whose decisions these ought to be, and it would really help if we decided once and for all. The way I'd like to see it go is that psychiatrists have no power whatsoever to make these final decisions but function simply as providers of information and perhaps as initiators of commitment proceedings since they're in contact with the patient. But psychiatrists certainly should never have the final decision.

3

THE PREDICTION OF DANGEROUSNESS: THE EXPERTS, THE COURTS, AND THE CRIMINAL JUSTICE SYSTEM

Nicholas N. Kittrie

I listened with great interest to my colleague, Doctor Halleck. I must admit that while he was agonized about psychiatrists being taken to court for not reporting dangerous behavior and dangerous patients, I did not share his agony. I think if psychiatrists were a little bit more careful earlier in asserting their ability to predict dangerousness, they would not be sued later for failure to predict danger. Professionals have to be very careful about the skills they profess and what powers and knowledge they claim for themselves, because in claiming a particular power, one is then in the public eye and under duty to perform that function. And indeed, part of what I want to discuss in this chapter is the hazard of claiming that we have the ability to predict dangerousness.

I also noted with great interest an item in one of the reports on the research that led to the conference. Apparently there is pending in Ohio a class-action suit on behalf of the patients in the institution for the criminally insane. In a 1974 Interim Order on this case, the federal court stated that qualified mental health professionals must demonstrate a sufficient degree of proficiency in English to communicate effectively with their patients before they can be considered qualified experts. It took a court to make this enlightened statement. It raises some questions about who we have conducting the evaluation process in many places in this country and whether we really are fooling ourselves in turning over responsibilities to experts who in many instances cannot communicate with their patients.

IDENTIFYING THE DANGEROUS

What I would like to emphasize most in this chapter is the question of who is dangerous and who makes that decision. What is the nature of the interaction between the judge, the lawyer, the family, the patient, the psychiatrist, or any other kind of expert in deciding dangerousness? I would like to address this question of dangerousness from a zero perspective. Who is dangerous? How about a habitual pickpocket? Is he dangerous? How about a 15- to 20-year-old robber or mugger? Is he dangerous? How about a deprived black juvenile without employment skills? Is he dangerous? How about the garage owner with a record of misrepresentations? Is he dangerous? How about a habitual speeder? And then how about somebody who has some kind of mental illness orientation or disorientation? How do we know who is dangerous? Who of all the above is most dangerous?

What concerns me most is that the mental illness label and the mental illness-health sciences seem to serve as extremely important triggering devices for interfering with the lives of people who might be less dangerous than some of the other categories I just listed for you. Let us look at two case studies. You will recall that a man by the name of Lee Harvey Oswald, sometime before the actual crime, wrote a handwritten note to the FBI in which he said, "If you do not stop harassing my wife about my political connections, I am going to do something drastic about it." Nobody did anything about Oswald. The FBI did not take the note terribly seriously. They did not apprehend Oswald to find out if he was dangerous. In fact, the note was placed in some in-basket, and after Oswald was charged with the Kennedy murder the FBI tried to suppress that note. They did not want to seem as though they had not acted with due care and speed. I can assure you that if Oswald had had any mental illness label or any previous connection with the mental illness system, he probably would have been picked up. But the mental illness process and system were not triggered in his case.

On the other hand, let me tell you about my favorite case. In the early 1960s I participated in the drafting of the present mental commitment law in the District of Columbia; Senator Ervin was chairman of the U.S. Senate Subcommittee on Constitutional Rights. We felt at the time that if we could only make commitment tough and provide that somebody could be committed only if he was found to be dangerous, that would be great progress. Indeed, we insisted that nobody be allowed to be committed to a mental institution merely because he was mentally ill or in need of treatment. We gave only one criterion that was permissible for commitment, and that was being "dangerous." I was very proud of that great accomplishment until I witnessed this particular case that I am going to share with you.

The case concerned a veteran of the U.S. Army who lived in Rockville, Maryland, with his mother. Once a week he would get up, take a small suitcase, and come down to one of the Holiday Inns in downtown Washington. He would go in, walk up to the laundry room, open up his suitcase, take out some dirty underwear, take out the quarter, or whatever was required for the machine, and do his laundry. After he did this for about two months, some motel worker noticed him and said, "You look familiar, are you staying in this motel?" And he said, "No, I am not." "What are you doing here?" "Doing my laundry." "Why don't you do it at home?" "Well, I don't like doing my laundry at home."

The motel manager became very concerned. He reported it to the police, and they came down and picked him up. They discovered he had a medical discharge from the U.S. Army, due to some psychiatric problem. A petition was filed to have him committed to Saint Elizabeth's Hospital. I was there throughout the hearing. Two psychiatrists testified that he was dangerous. The logic was something like this: Since he does not belong in the motel and people do not welcome him, this is likely to create a debate, and maybe some violence, and consequently he is dangerous. The enlightened judge decided that since two psychiatrists said he was dangerous, obviously he was dangerous. He was committed to Saint Elizabeth's Hospital.

What I am trying to illustrate with both of these cases is the particular function of the mental illness label. If you have some kind of mental illness label or diagnosis, and if you can couple this with a prediction of dangerousness, that triggers social sanctions. Without that mental illness label, usually there will be no social action.

DEFINING AND PREDICTING DANGEROUSNESS

What is dangerousness? I've looked up the meaning of dangerousness and the decisions of the courts in the District of Columbia. They say that dangerousness means propensity to crime or some lesser hazard. One case in the District of Columbia said that dangerousness means the possibility of a dangerous act in the reasonably foreseeable future. Some cases talk about likelihood of an action, saying that a possibility of injury is not enough. There must be a likelihood. You tell me what the difference is. A possibility is not enough, it has to be a likelihood. Not mere chance, there has to be a virtual certainty. I am not sure what that really means. It sounds very fine and sophisticated, but how do you operationalize it? Let me suggest a hypothetical comparison merely to shock you, not because I recommend it. I would suggest that a young offender with a deprived background and a black heritage in Washington, D.C., is more likely to be dangerous than a mentally ill person, and yet nobody in his sound mind would suggest that you walk down the street, pick up a black youth who has some record of criminality, and lock him up because he is dangerous. Why are we doing it when we attach a label of mental illness?

I will summarize some of the evidence on the prediction of dangerousness in our society, evidence that is very questionable or troublesome. There are a number of studies from different parts of the country on the issue of dangerousness. One was conducted by the California Department of Corrections, and a report was published in 1972. This study of parolees found that 86 percent of those identified as violent did not in fact commit a violent act while out on parole. In a second study, 7,000 parolees were diagnosed as to whether or not they were potentially aggressive, less aggressive, or whatever. The researchers found that of those listed as having the greatest potential for dangerousness, only 3.1 per thousand were later apprehended for some violent behavior. On the other hand, of those listed as not dangerous, as not aggressive, 2.8 per thousand later committed a violation. Another study in California came to similar conclusions. It found that when prediction of dangerousness was based solely on past conduct, 19 false positives existed in every 20 cases. I could go on and on.

I refer you to studies done after the U.S. decision in the Baxstrom case. That was the U.S. Supreme Court decision that said, with regard to those previously convicted and serving sentence for a criminal act, that no extension of the confinement under a claim of mental illness is permissible without the right to the same procedure that applies to civil commitments generally. As a consequence of that decision, large numbers of prisoner-patients were released into the community, patients who were earlier classified as being mentally ill and dangerous. In a 2.5-year study of those who were released to the community, who were earlier classified as being dangerous, only 9 out of 121 released patients had been convicted of any crime. Yet we were willing earlier to pay the social price of keeping all these 121 under lock and key on the grounds that they were potentially dangerous.

At any rate, it is clear that violence, aggressiveness, or dangerousness is always overpredicted, and overprediction will range somewhere between 54 and 99 percent of all the cases involved. So the question really is, "Are we able to predict, are we willing to predict, should we rely on predictions of dangerousness?"

Having dealt with some of these statistics, I will go into some of the policy implications that I see in a system that finds it necessary to rely on prediction of behavior. As my colleague at Harvard, Professor Dershowitz, has suggested, we have two basic models in the United States for dealing with people we consider dangerous or problematic: punishment-deterrence and prediction-prevention. The punishment-deterrence model says that we will want until one has done the overt act. We will wait until he has committed a crime and then punish him, and we hope that that punishment will deter him and deter others. The other model claims that we cannot wait until the overt act is committed.

This model claims: Let us predict the dangerousness and let us prevent it from occurring. The therapeutic or mental health system relies heavily on this prediction-prevention model rather than the punishment-deterrence model. The therapeutic-medical model claims that one ounce of prevention is better than many ounces of a later cure. There is a need to prevent, and it is a good and important goal, but does it function properly when in order to undertake that prevention one has to come up with so many false positives? Clearly this prediction of dangerousness is an issue that raises to me, as a lawyer, and also as a public citizen, many problems of due process, vagueness, denial of equal protection, and so on.

EXPERTS, JUDGES, AND JURIES

We now turn to the role of the expert and his function under this prediction-prevention model. And the expert in this field is not merely the psychiatrist. The expert is usually the mental health practitioner, whatever his or her qualifications are—a social worker, a counselor of some type, a psychologist, or some other specialist. I personally am very much concerned, and I share my concern with my colleagues in the psychiatric fraternity, about the expert who doubles as a therapist and as a keeper of the gate. I think there is a great role conflict between the therapist offering his therapy to a patient who is there voluntarily and the therapist who doubles as an agent of social control.

What are the guidelines the expert uses in deciding who is dangerous? We need to understand the discipline the expert comes from, the basic premises of that discipline, and the guidelines and practices of the discipline. If indeed we allow social intervention in the name of dangerousness, how do different groups define and determine dangerousness? What are the criteria? Are we concerned with danger to the life, limbs, or property of another person? Or it is danger to the life, limbs, or property of one's self? Is dangerousness disturbing the peace? Is dangerousness when one disrupts the general welfare of the family? Is it dangerous when one shows mental cruelty to his colleagues? Is it dangerous when one upsets the sense of aesthetics in a community? Is it dangerousness when one needs treatment? Is it dangerousness when one, in our judgment, will benefit from treatment? Is that dangerousness? I suggest to you that we have never articulated these questions. And certainly we have never debated them.

Indeed, dangerousness could be any one of these things just listed. With regard to which of these criteria are we willing to justify social intervention? And if we decide that the criteria ought to be life, limb, property, or whatever of another, can we predict that dangerousness?

Who can predict? I am troubled by the expert being a predictor. I
am always troubled by predictions. Should we prevent certain people
from driving cars or being airline pilots because, based on their age,
their weight, and their eating habits, we think they are likely to suffer
heart attacks and become dangerous? Are we willing to take the
chances of overprediction? I ask myself, "We do not interfere with
people generally, so why are we willing to do it under the label of mental health?"

The value system of the predictor is very important for us to
understand. The predictors who come from the medical profession
have certain values that determine how they predict. What are these
values? One of the major goals of the physician is to make sure that
everybody who needs care will get care. It is a proper value. It is a
medical axiom that judging a sick person well is more to be avoided
that judging a well person sick. The feeling is: If we are not sure,
let us treat him. If we are not sure, let us give him the medicine. In
the mental health area this fear of judging a sick person well results
in a lot of overprediction. After all, if this man is liable to be trouble
later, it is better if we judge him ill right now.

The tendency to overpredict is especially pronounced in the area
of deviance and crime. If we say that a person is well and he later
does some heathen act, they'll say, "Ha, ha, ha, . . . those psychiatrists let him go"; so it is better to lock him up. There is a fear for the
prestige and social status of the profession, a fear that the standing
of the profession will suffer, and this fear, coupled with the desire to
do "good," results in a drive toward false positives. Indeed, some
recent developments indicate that there is a new public pressure for
the health professional to overpredict, for if he does not overpredict,
he may be sued for not warning society of the potentially dangerous
people.

Where do the judge and the jury fit into this pattern? I am not
really sure. I would like to suggest that if indeed prediction is not
very valid scientifically, and if decisions need to be made as to who
should be locked up and who should not, I would rather leave it to
judges and juries. Dangerousness at this time is not a scientific fact;
it is not a scientific test. Let nonscientists make the decision for the
community. Let judges make the decision of what risks society wants
to take. I think the problem that we face in this area is that we have
gotten rid of one of the earlier myths of mental illness, but we are
still burdened with another. It used to be believed that mental illness
was a crime. But there is another myth still with us—the belief that
the mentally ill are dangerous—and we are forcing experts to participate in the perpetuation of this myth.

It is presumed that mental illness means dangerousness. It is
also presumed that incompetence means dangerousness. You explain

to me how we conclude that somebody who is incompetent to stand trial or who was insane at the time of the crime ought to be locked up in a state hospital. I have an office in Annapolis that overlooks the State House, which was occupied by Governor Mandel. He was held, because of a medical condition, to be incompetent to stand trial. Nobody locked him up. He continued running the state of Maryland. But if that incompetence had been on the ground of mental illness, he would have been sent to a hospital immediately. This is a clear demonstration of the hazards of the mental illness label. All you have to do is add that one phrase, mental illness, and there are automatic sanctions and interventions of the system. You keep that word out and somehow society is willing to be so much more tolerant toward the potentially dangerous.

In conclusion, I would like to suggest that the issue of mental illness should be totally ignored and written off as a factor in understanding or deciding dangerousness. I do not believe that mental illness or incompetency should be a justification for committing somebody on the ground of dangerousness. If we want to lock up certain people because they are dangerous, let us find some other criteria—criteria that are not triggered by and do not depend upon the finding of mental illness or incompetence. Maybe society does not want to take chances with dangerous people; if this is the case, let us decide what the generally applicable test for danger will be. Let us not hide under the label of mental illness. It is a disservice to those in the healing arts to find themselves in the position of being predictors of dangerousness and keepers of prison gates. Let the rest of society, if indeed they want to engage in preventive measures, decide on their own what dangerousness is. It is important that therapists insist on their professional independence, their professional integrity, and the right to do that for which they have been trained. I will conclude with a modified quote from Karl Marx: "You therapists have nothing to lose but the chains that tie you to power." If you would be willing to benefit less from power, if you would be willing to engage more in work and patient service, you probably would do your profession greater justice.

DISCUSSION

Question: Were all of the studies you referred to regarding the prediction of dangerousness based on the offender's past behavior?

Kittrie: No, different studies have used different systems of predictions. Some predictions were based on clinical observations, some on a great number of psychological tests, and some strictly on the basis of past behavior. Even those that were based strictly on past behavior produced a high percentage of false positives, that is, people who were predicted to be dangerous who did not commit a dangerous act. All the various studies show a high percentage of false positives. The question I raise: Should we go on with a social policy based on scientific data that is so troublesome and questionable, or is it our duty to make sure that the social policy be based on valid data? I believe that, in a scientific day and age, it is the duty of government, before they intervene, to demonstrate where the social harm is. And without that demonstration I find social intervention not justified.

Question: It seems that you are arguing that social intervention is not warranted when the prediction of behavior involves a high number of false positives, and also that the mental health laws are unique in this respect. I would like to suggest that that is a myth and, in fact, that many laws are on the books that have to do with the prediction of a certain event and, in fact, perhaps even the majority of laws. I will illustrate. It is not illegal to become intoxicated in the confines of one's own home and it is not illegal to drive a motor vehicle provided one has a license to do so. However, it is illegal to combine the two —to drive a motor vehicle and be intoxicated. Not because there is something intrinsically wrong about doing that, but because the combination of the two has been associated with the likelihood of certain harm. I wonder what the number of false positives are in laws of that kind. The same goes for other crimes—concealing a weapon, possession of safe-cracking tools, and a whole host of other crimes. In theory, I do not see any difference between laws of this nature and laws that have to do with the prediction of dangerousness. Would you also be willing to argue that these laws that I mentioned should be decriminalized?

Kittrie: I think you are asking a very searching and important question. As a matter of fact, as one who teaches criminal law, and who teaches criminal law from a constitutional perspective, this is one of the questions that has troubled me for a long while. Let me answer it in a rather comprehensive way. Yes, I agree that many laws on the books are based on prediction and preventive approaches, and most of them trouble me very much. I will give you an illustration of one that troubles me very much, and I hope it troubles you, too. During World War II, we decided that Americans of Japanese extraction were likely to become spies, saboteurs, or, at the very least, do some other ill. The conclusion was that we might as well put them in some camps. That was a prediction-preventive model. We have done the same with regard to many others. We have provided, for example,

in the Smith Act and in many of the other anticommunist laws, that
Communists may not work in defense establishments, that they may
not hold labor positions, and so on. I want to say here very directly
that I am as much an anticommunist as any of you. I do not believe
in any assurances that the Communists have given up the desire to control the world. Yet, very simply, I am not ready to have a preventive
system with that wide a neck. I would have waited until the particular
Japanese or Communists in fact committed some act of conspiracy or
became spies. Basically and generally, I am very much troubled by
this preventive–predictive approach to public controls. I am committed
to having each instance of this particular model tested, reviewed, and
reduced to a tolerable size. Otherwise, I see too much interference
with the rights of too many innocent people.

Question: In view of your displeasure with dangerousness, would
you comment on the ideal mental commitment law, or do you think
there should be none at all?

Kittrie: When Thomas Szasz first came up with the conclusion
that there should be no involuntary commitment, and he asked me to
join his organization, I said, "Look, I do not agree with your absolute
refusal to commit anybody involuntarily. Still, I will join your organization because we do need to reassess the question of the problem of
involuntary commitment." I guess what I am going to say to you now
will sound ambivalent. It will perhaps sould like I am not ready to
give you a final answer, and the truth is, I am not.

In the mid 1950s I directed a study for the American Bar Foundation on the rights of the mentally ill. At that time I went to England
to look at how they were handling mentally ill patients. The thing that
struck me in England was the fact that only 8 percent of the people in
mental institutions were involuntary commitments at that time. It was
later reduced to 4 percent. So I guess at this particular moment I
feel that there is certainly a need to reduce drastically the categories
of those who are involuntarily committed. Whether I am willing to
take absolutely nobody, I do not know. I certainly will commit somebody who has committed a crime. But I am troubled with the present
state of affairs where fear of future crime suffices to commit, and I
want you to be troubled, too. If England was able to reduce drastically
involuntary commitments, I think we can do the same.

Question: As long as predictions are going to be made, for example, by parole boards, somebody is going to have to make them,
and aren't they going to have to have some standards?

Kittrie: I am not objecting to punishment. I am not troubled
when society agrees that there should be a penalty for an overt act, a

dangerous act. And I am willing to have prediction that reduces the total price of punishment a person has to pay. If, for example, society says that ten years of imprisonment should be imposed for murder, I am not troubled by the parole board saying, "Well, we think on the basis of his progress we will release him a little early." The problem with the mental health area is that we are dealing with sanctions for behavior that otherwise would not be punishable. We are dealing with people upon whom you could not impose criminal sanctions. We say because there is mental illness, we will impose a price on the basis of prediction. So I view the two areas as drastically different. In those areas where we are willing to impose punishment, punishment serves as an outer limit, and to use predictions to reduce that limit does not trouble me at all because the individual gets a bonus. However, in the mental health area, you do not get a bonus. You get special confinement because you are mentally ill. Indeed, under the mental illness model, we punish in situation in which, under the traditional criminal law, intervention could not take place.

Halleck: This year I began teaching law and psychiatry for the first time with a brilliant colleague. Before class he was telling me about his difficulty with the police over parking problems. As we went to class, I observed his behavior as he used the Socratic method of teaching. In the next class, which I was leading, I served commitment papers on him, pointing out the dangerousness of his paranoia, and his delusion that he was an ancient Greek philosopher. I was using this as an illustration to the class that this is deadly serious. It might very well have been possible to commit him on that basis.

Just a couple of comments on Kittrie's talk. The issue of psychiatrists understanding the English language is a serious one. Forty percent of American psychiatrists are foreign medical graduates and on the Eastern seaboard that number is 60 percent. Many foreign graduates are superb psychiatrists, some of our better psychiatrists, but as a rule they have serious problems with the English language. On a site visit to Florida, I actually saw a patient labeled as delusional because she told the psychiatrist at the beginning of the interview that she had butterflies in her stomach. These are serious, real issues. Some psychiatrists who work in our forensic units are superb, but many of them have serious problems with the English language.

One study Kittrie may not have had time to quote was the Livermore and Mill Study, which is a speculative statistical analysis that concludes that if you had a 95 percent certainty test for predicting dangerousness (which is impossible to have), and you applied it to 100,000 people, to catch 95 people who you would then protect from committing a crime, and 5 you would lose, you would have to lock up some 495 people as false positives. So, even with that level of accuracy, you are in big trouble.

Another comment that I want to make is that we learn to predict in medicine—all of medicine is really a matter of predicting. Every time you give a medicine you are predicting that you are going to alter the course of the illness, and you have to make a prediction about what the course of that illness is going to be. The difference between medicine and psychiatry is that in medicine false positives do not do harm. You can order a thousand different tests, you can overdiagnose. As a rule, except for the expense to the patient's pocketbook, you are not hurting the patient, and in medicine a false negative is a tragedy. In psychiatry, it is quite different: A false negative may not be as tragic and a false positive is definitely a tragedy.

4

PSYCHIATRIC DIVERSION IN THE CRIMINAL JUSTICE SYSTEM

Thomas S. Szasz

The phrase "psychiatric diversion in the criminal justice system" refers to any psychiatric intervention that occurs in connection with individuals identified as convicted offenders, with defendants charged with crime, or with persons "accused" of legally permissible misbehavior. Psychiatric diversions from the criminal justice system thus include such diverse interventions as the pretrial examination of defendants for fitness to stand trial, the insanity plea, the insanity verdict, criminal commitment, civil commitment instead of prosecution for a crime, and, last but not least, the judicial imposition of various psychiatric instead of penal sentences on persons formally diverted from the criminal process by treating them as incompetent patients rather than as competent lawbreakers.[1]

Although, in principle, psychiatric diversion is a matter of political philosophy, jurisprudence, and forensic psychiatry, and may therefore be appropriately discussed in the abstract vocabularies of those disciplines, it is, in practice, a brutal fact of everyday life and hence must also be discussed in the ordinary language of everyday life. I shall do so, to begin with, by citing and briefly commenting on contemporary American examples of psychiatric diversion.*

---

*Examples from the past and from other countries abound. I will not consider them here, save for a few allusions to Soviet psychiatric practices, as my emphasis in this chapter is on the incompatibility between the principles of the free society in contemporary American thought and the practices of psychiatric diversion in the present-day administration of American criminal justice.

CASES OF PSYCHIATRIC DIVERSION

A recent article, revealingly titled "Presidential Assassination: An American Problem," by Edwin A. Weinstein, a professor at Mount Sinai Medical School and an acknowledged expert on such matters, begins with the following two sentences: "Assassinations of Heads of State of foreign countries have usually been carried out by organized political groups seeking to overthrow the government or change its policies. In the United States, on the other hand, Presidential assassinations have been the work of mentally disturbed individuals."[2]

To demonstrate the depravity of this sort of writing, let me rephrase these sentences from the point of view of a hypothetical Soviet mental health expert: "Emigrations from capitalist countries have traditionally been the acts of poor and persecuted people seeking better opportunities for themselves elsewhere. Emigrations and attempts at emigration, from the Soviet Union, on the other hand, are the acts of mentally disturbed dissidents."

Clearly, Weinstein's account implies that those persons who have killed foreign heads of state had valid reasons for doing so, whereas those who have killed American heads of state lacked such reasons. My sarcastic Soviet modification of it implies that it is reasonable to leave capitalist countries, but not communist countries. Certain classes of acts and actors are thus diverted, literally with the stroke of a pen, from matters of moral, political, and judicial discourse into matters of psychiatric diagnosis and disposition.

Ironically, when psychiatric diversion is now practiced in the Soviet Union, it provokes indignant condemnation by Western observers and by Aleksandr Solzhenitsyn. For example, in his Warning to West, Solzhenitsyn writes: "In Odessa, Vyacheslav Grunov has been arrested for possessing illicit literature and put into a lunatic asylum."[3]

If we replace illicit books with illicit drugs, and change the scene to the United States, Solzhenitsyn's sentence reads: "In Chicago, John Jones has been arrested for possessing illicit drugs and put into a lunatic asylum."

Of course, many thinkers—Ludwig von Mises among them[4]—have suggested that books are more dangerous than drugs. Hence, if it makes sense for the government to ban dangerous drugs, it makes even more sense for it to ban dangerous books—and to incapacitate the persons who disagree with such policies. I do not see how we can have it both ways: that is, how we can support the proposition that the American use of dangerous drugs constitutes a form of mental illness and that those who use such drugs may appropriately be controlled by means of psychiatric sanctions and at the same time oppose the symmetrical Soviet proposition about dangerous books. Yet it is precisely this sort of inconsistency that characterizes the position on psychiatric diversion of the foremost American intellectuals, including those who otherwise support market mechanisms and the rule of law.

So much for hypothetical cases of psychiatric diversion. Probably the most famous actual victim of American psychiatric diversion is undoubtedly Ezra Pound. Pound, it may be recalled, lived in Italy during World War II. Allegedly he made some broadcasts over the Italian radio that were treasonous. After the war he was arrested and charged with treason. However, instead of being tried, he was declared to be schizophrenic and hence unfit to stand trial. As a result, he was locked up at Saint Elizabeth's Hospital in Washington, D.C., for 13 years. [5]

The chief characteristic of psychiatric diversion, as of all departures from the rule of law, is capriciousness. Pound was incriminated and punished by means of it. The woman whose brief story I shall next cite was exonerated and allowed to go unpunished by means of it.

On April 11, 1976, Melissa Morris killed her three-month-old son by beating him to death. She claimed she did it to rid him of the devil. On September 15, 1976, she was released from a Maryland mental hospital "after a judge found 'no clear and convincing evidence that she presents a danger to herself or society.' The decision by a Montgomery County Circuit judge, John Mitchell, followed a murder plea of not guilty by reason of insanity by Melissa Morris, 19, of Wheaton. "[6]

I am focusing deliberately on the capriciousness of the judgments that go into decisions to psychiatrically divert or not divert a case, since, as Hayek has emphasized, it is arbitrariness, rather than brutality, that is the hallmark of a totalitarian system of criminal law. [7] Accordingly, I shall next cite the case of a man who not only acted crazy and committed a crime, but who nevertheless escaped both psychiatric and legal punishment, while his victim, on whose freedom he infringed, was punished (through his insurance company). On the night of July 4, 1975, Robert Henry went bar-hopping with friends on Long Island. Off Montauk Highway, he stripped naked, "finding it [according to the judge] a fine night for a stroll." The police sighted him, started after him, and shouted to him to halt. Instead of obeying that order, Henry started to avoid arrest by dashing across the highway. As a result, he was hurt by a truck driven by Richard Rusillo. Henry sued for damages, and a Long Island judge upheld an award of $2,030 to him and $525 to his lawyer, payable by the Great American Insurance Company. [8] In this case, then, "streaking" (that is, running around naked), crossing a highway illegally, obstructing traffic, and resisting arrest all went unpunished and unpsychiatrized.

The above case stands in sharp contrast to television star Louise Lasser's recent encounter with psychiatric law. Lasser was apprehended for possessing cocaine, a criminal offense. Unlike Henry, Lasser harmed no one. Her act—that is, possessing cocaine—was quintessentially private. Nevertheless, she could have been legally punished for it. But she was not. In fact, she was not even tried. Instead she was "placed in a drug diversionary program, consisting of seeing her psychiatrist. . . . In ordering the program [explained the newspaper story of the case], which is common for first-time drug offenders instead of trial, Beverly Hills Municipal Court Judge Leonard Wolfe set December 1 for Miss Lasser's return to court. Charges could be dropped at that time."[9] That is psychiatric diversion in pure culture.

SUICIDE: A HISTORICAL EXAMPLE

Having offered an overview of the anatomy of psychiatric diversion, I shall continue with some brief remarks about its physiology, that is to say, its function. How and why has psychiatric diversion come into being and why is it now so popular?

Commitment to the rule of law places a heavy moral burden on the citizens of a free, or would-be free, society. Indeed it does so for two reasons, one of which has received much more attention than the other. First, such a commitment implies that the majority of the citizens, through the government, will eschew infringing on the freedom of those of their fellows who obey the law, even if the latter annoy or offend the sensibilities of their neighbors. That, essentially, is what we have come to mean by the phrase, "the rule of law."

The rule of law has, however, another implication as well, which constitutes an important additional burden for those who commit themselves to it. That burden has to do with the enforcement of the laws and with the dilemma of the citizen—especially as legislator, judge, district attorney, or juror—faced with laws he regards as stupid, unjust, or evil. I refer here to the obvious, but often neglected, fact that the rule of law requires not only that the innocent be left at liberty, but also that the guilty be punished. This often makes those entrusted with implementing the law feel guilty. Thus arises the question: What can a people, and especially its law enforcement authorities, do when they are confronted with acts or actors that they do not want to punish at all? Actually, they have only a few options. They can look the other way. They can acquit. They can repeal the offensive law. Each of these options is used in the administration of the criminal law. But each suffers from a serious defect, namely, that it impairs the collective sense of security that the impartial administration of the law is supposed to provide. It is precisely at this point that psychiatric diversion comes into play: It provides a mechanism that simultaneously allays the citizens' guilt for punishing certain acts and actors and satisfies their need for security by depriving certain acts of their legitimacy and certain actors of their liberty. A historical example illustrates this core function of psychiatric diversion. The example I shall use, namely, the crime of suicide and its punishment in eighteenth-century England, reveals not only the true function of psychiatric diversion but also the fact that this procedure actually antedates psychiatry (in its modern sense).

To set the matter before us in its historical context, I want to remark briefly on the history of the legal status of suicide and madness in English law. According to Henry Fedden, the secular prohibition of suicide in England can be pinpointed quite accurately, as follows:

> Bracton, the legal authority of his time, writing in the thirteenth century, does not rank suicide as a felony. Thus fifty years after the Magna Carta, the suicide was not yet legally a criminal in England. His fate, however, was in the melting-pot. Many of Bracton's contemporaries had not agreed with him, and by the middle of the next century, in spite of Bracton's ruling, the person who intentionally took his life had become guilty of <u>felo-de-se</u> (self-murder). [10]

Suicide, which had long been considered to be a sin against the church, thus became a crime against the crown as well, and the penalty for it was accordingly very severe: The deceased person's body was buried without Christian rites at the crossroads of a public highway, perhaps with a stake driven through it, and his "movable goods" were confiscated and went to the crown.

With respect to insanity, the starting point from a historical point of view is the ancient position that did not regard insanity as having any bearing upon criminal guilt. According to Rollin M. Perkins, "Principles of criminal liability dating prior to the Norman Conquest persisted into the thirteenth century and a 'man who has killed another by misadventure, though he deserves a pardon, [was considered to be] guilty of a crime; and the same rule applies . . . to a lunatic.'"[11] In the thirteenth century the issuance of such a pardon to lunatics who committed homicide came to be granted "as a matter of course."[12] In the time of Edward III (1327-77), "madness became a complete defense to a criminal charge."[13] Inasmuch as suicide was considered to be a species of murder, lunacy was, after the fourteenth century, a complete defense against it also. However, it appears—

although the records concerning this matter are sketchy—that such a verdict was issued quite rarely in cases of suicide before the seventeenth century.

The earliest reliable records concerning deaths by suicide in London go back to 1629. From then on we can trace the incidence of both "suicide in nonlunatics" and "suicide in lunatics." They reveal that by the seventeenth century the traditional penalities against the offense had not been rigidly enforced, the body often being buried privately or at least without indignities. In the early part of the eighteenth century there seems to have been an increase in the incidence of suicide in England, and with it there occurred an important change in the behavior of the persons who sat on coroners' juries.

"The rise in suicide in 1721"—according to Sprott's fine study of English suicide "From Donne to Hume"—"may have been occasioned by the bursting of the South Sea Bubble in the previous year; in the eighteenth century financial failure probably became one of the common 'entrances' into the deed. . . . At the same time [as suicide increased] coroners' juries brought in more and more verdicts of lunacy."[14] Uncontaminated by modern psychiatric doctrines, Sprott describes the process of "discovering" that the person dead by suicide was insane as a phenomenon that points to what went on in the minds of the jurors rather than in the minds of those destined to be posthumously diagnosed as lunatics:

> In the eighteenth century juries increasingly brought in findings of insanity in order to save the family from the consequences of a verdict of felong; the number of deaths recorded as "lunatic" grew startlingly in relation to the number recorded as self-murder, whereas in the previous century, according to a modern legal authority, ninety percent of self-killers sat on by coroners' juries had been returned as having made away with themselves. Devices were employed to save or bestow the goods of the deceased, and by the 1760's confiscation of goods seems to have become rare.[15]

The more heavily the punishment of suicide weighed on the shoulders of the jurymen who had to bring in the verdict, and the more brazenly they discarded the burden by declaring the diseased person a lunatic, the more passionately clergymen denounced suicide as a sin, and the more earnestly legal scholars denounced posthumous diagnoses of lunacy on the part of suicides as subversions of the rule of law. John Wesley, for example, recommended that the suicide's body be gibbetted, and Caleb Flemming declared "'suicism' unnatural, depraved, impious, and inhuman . . . [an] act of high treason against the laws of human society."[16] To deter suicide, Flemming recommended that "the naked body [be] exposed in some public place: over which the coroner should deliver an oration on the foul impiety; and then the body, like that of the homicide, be given to the surgeons."[17] To be sure, not all clergymen were so sanguine, some supporting the tactic of declaring the suicide non compos mentis as moral progress. According to Sprott, the earliest instance of clerical support for this strategy was John Jortin's endorsement of it in 1772:

> In all dubious cases of this kind, it is surely safer and better to judge too favourably than too severely of the deceased; and our Juries do well to incline, as they commonly do, on the merciful side, as far as reason can possibly permit; and the more so, since by a contrary verdict the family of the dead person may perhaps suffer much.[18]

Such psychiatric bootlegging of humanism carried a very high price, however, Veritably, eighteenth-century Englishmen sitting on coroner's juries diagnosing suicides as lunatics sowed the wind, and we are reaping the whirlwind. They had laid the legal foundations for a forensic-psychiatric maxim that has, for obvious reasons, become dear to the hearts of modern mad-doctors—namely, that a person suspected of lunacy is insane until proved otherwise. Put that way, it is obvious that such a legal-psychiatric rule is the very opposite of the legal-punitive rule that a person accused of crime is innocent until proved guilty. Nevertheless, for two centuries people in English-speaking countries have been puzzled by the so-called abuses of institutional psychiatry and have sought, vainly, to remedy them. But the abuses of our psychiatric system flow as inexorably from the claim that a person is crazy unless he can prove to his diagnosticians that he is not, as flow the abuses of the inquistorial criminal systems from the claim that a defendant is guilty unless he can prove to his prosecutors that he is not.

These evasions of the law punishing suicide were, of course, too obvious to deceive legal scholars. For example, Blackstone realized at once that if a finding of lunacy could be contrived to nullify the laws against suicide, it could just as easily be contrived against every other crime.[19] That, of course, is precisely what men like Karl Menninger and Ramsey Clark have done, believing all the while that they have "discovered" that crime is mental illness and that criminals ought to be treated rather than punished.[20]

Clearly, psychiatric diversion has actually very little to do with psychiatry. It is not the result of, and does not depend on, the modern understanding of the mind or of mental diseases, as its contemporary proponents claim; instead, it is the result of, and depends on, its psychosocial utility, especially in a free and democratic society, for managing the guilty conduct of certain persons and the guilty consciences of those who sit in judgment on them.

THE YOUNG, THE OLD, AND THE INSANE

Psychiatric interference with the rule of law in the name of individualized justice and therapy is precisely the sort of thing that, as we might expect, would appeal to statists of all persuasions—as the contemporary literature on "psychiatric justice" in fact reveals.[21] However, the fact that psychiatric justice is also embraced by antistatists—by classical liberals, conservatives, and even libertarians—is, on the face of it, rather surprising. Because Ludwig von Mises is justly considered to be the pioneer recreator, in its contemporary version, of free-market economics and of the moral philosophy on which it rests, I shall illustrate the capitulation of antistatists before the onslaught of modern psychiatry by remarking briefly on his comments relevant to our subject.

The crux of Mises's mistake about psychiatry is simple: He accepts that there exists a class of persons whom certain medical experts, called "psychiatrists," can reliably identify as insane, and that such persons cannot be treated as moral agents. Mises writes:

> The anarchists overlook the undeniable fact that some people
> are either too narrow-minded or too weak to adjust them-
> selves spontaneously to the conditions of social life. Even
> if we admit that every sane adult is endowed with the
> faculty of realizing the good of social cooperation and
> of acting accordingly, there still remains the problem
> of the infants, the aged, and the insane.[22]

Mises here places the very young, the very old, and the very odd in the same class—all characterized by their supposed inability to cooperate with their fellow human beings. What is wrong with this? Everything. I will show this by examples, rather than by exposition. The argument I shall construct might be a little simplified, but it is, I believe, entirely accurate.

A month-old infant cannot cooperate. It cannot contract for care, but can only feel hunger or pain, scream, and thus coerce relief. The same goes for a senile person, especially if he is a bedridden invalid, who is, save for one big difference, much like an infant. The difference is that whereas the helpless infant "waits" to live and others wait for him to live, the helpless old person "waits" to die and others wait for him to die.

How does an insane person resemble them? The answer depends on what one means by an "insane person." If one means an individual whose brain has been destroyed by syphilis, who is demented with paresis, then what is true for the old invalid is also true for the insane. But it is inconceivable that in 1949 this is what Mises meant by insanity. It is more likely that by insanity he meant the sort of (mis)behavior that psychiatrists call schizophrenia, exemplified by the "patient" declaring that he is Jesus. Such a person, I contend, is not incapable of cooperating and contracting; he chooses, instead, to coerce by means of dramatic, deceptive, and self-aggrandizing claims about himself. He is more like a counterfeiter than like a child. He is defiant, rather than defective. [23] Mises completely ignores that possibility, treating the "insane" person as if he were utterly incapable of cooperating.

"We may agree," continues Mises, "that he who acts antisocially should be considered mentally sick and in need of care." [24] Mises here compounds the confusion between bodily defect and personal defiance, medical disease and moral deviance. It is distressing, too, to see someone like Mises use a vague and potentially vicious term like "antisocial" so cavalierly. How could he so casually psychiatrize the protestor as psychotic and consign him into the crushing embrace of the psychiatrist? There can be only one answer: by accepting the principles and practices of psychiatry as intellectually valid and morally sound. This conclusion is borne out by his next statement: "But as long as not all are cured [of insanity], and as long as there are infants and the senile, some provision must be taken lest they jeopardize society." [25]

Mises keeps persisting with his catastrophic classification of infants, invalids, and the insane as members of the same class. Of course, I agree with Mises that infants, children, very old persons, and those disabled by incapacitating illness require special protection, and they represent special problems that threaten the well-being of those members of society who support the very existence of that society. That is why, on the one hand, such persons receive special protections from society, and, on the other hand, are excluded—either by law, as are children, or by biology, as are invalids—from many of the rights and privileges granted to the healthy, adult members of society. However, I disagree strongly with Mises about his placing insane persons in the same class with infants and invalids, and about the sort of societal response that would, in a free society, be most appropriate for dealing with them.

Infants, incapable of caring for themselves, are also incapable of rejecting the protections offered them. Whether so-called insane persons are capable of caring for themselves is, sometimes, debatable; that they are capable of rejecting the help offered them—indeed, that they often go to extreme lengths to reject it—is, however, painfully obvious. Mises suggests that in the face of such behavior, psychiatric coercion is a legitimate and necessary societal option. I believe it is neither legitimate nor necessary. If so-called insane persons refuse the protection that is offered them, a right that no society can deny them and remain free, then I believe we should adopt a moral perspective and a social policy toward such persons that are more consistent with the principles of the rule of law than is recourse to psychiatric coercion. I propose that we regard "insane" individuals as deviant or defiant persons rather than as diseased or demented patients; that we treat them the same way we treat the so-called normal members of society, that is, by leaving them alone so long as they obey the law, and by prosecuting and punishing them if they break it.

THE RESPONSIBILITY TO PUNISH

The sort of psychiatric diversion from the criminal justice system that characterizes our present American situation constitutes a genuinely fresh historical danger to individual liberty, which calls for appropriate new correctives.

Traditionally, societies have been tyrannical. Those who wished to secure liberty or to enlarge its scope were thus occupied with efforts to curb the powers of the rulers, whether they were theocratic, aristocratic, or democratic. From Montesquieu and Jefferson to Mises and Hayek, the magic formula has been limited government. That made sense in the context of its underlying premise: The rulers wanted to do too much, especially in the way of coercing others; hence the thing to do was to make it difficult or impossible for them to do certain things, especially in the way of coercing others not guilty of lawbreaking. Thus was constitutional government born.

However, in contemporary American society that classic premise is no longer valid or is not valid in its original form.* The

---

*It is important to reemphasize that psychiatric classification and constraint is basically compatible with, and is indeed exceedingly suitable for, political systems that debase individual liberty in favor of equality (of condition) and collective security. In other words, psychiatric diversion is perfectly suited to the Soviet style of social control, whether exercised by a czarist or a communist autocrat. Mutatis mutandis, it is completely incompatible with the American style of social control, which repudiates paternalism and is committed to the principle of treating each person as a moral agent entitled to both the protections and punishments of the rule of law.

American government is now a threat to the freedom of its own people, not because it punishes the innocent, nor because its punishments are too harsh, but rather because it does not punish the guilty. One result is an ever-increasing army of thiefs and thugs, muggers and murderers, abroad in the land, preying on a people unprotected by their own police and judiciary. Another result is an ever-increasing tendency not to punish those who are evil and who commit evil acts but instead to treat them for nonexistent illnesses. I only state the obvious when I say that our personal liberty is as easily threatened by a desperado as by a despot, by a mugger as by a monarch. We all know that. Why, then, do we keep asking stupid questions, such as: Why is crime increasing? Why do so many people rob and kill?

One answer to these questions lies in inverting the patently false adage that "crime does not pay." Crime indeed pays, and in more ways than one; that is, it pays not only for the criminals but also for the criminologists (by which term I refer here to all those who make a living confining, diagnosing, treating, rehabilitating, and otherwise managing and studying offenders). And it pays each of them both economically and existentially, that is, by putting money in their pockets and meaning into their lives. We cannot reduce crime until we recognize these facts. And even when we do recognize them, we shall be able to reduce crime only in proportion to either making noncriminal pursuits more attractive for would-be criminals, or making criminal activities less attractive for them, or both. We are not likely to do any of these things so long as we look to professional criminologists (and other statist reformers) to solve a problem of which they themselves are so important a part.

In summary, it seems to me that however complex the nature of our present crime problem in America might be, it has at least one obvious cause, for which there is at least one obvious remedy. That cause is the unwillingness of the American people, as individual citizens and as members of the government at every level, to shoulder the responsibility for punishing men, women, and children who deprive other individuals of their life, liberty, or property. And that remedy is to reject the ethic of a fake psychiatric therapeutism masquerading as the rehabilitation of offenders and to reembrace the ethic of a truly dignified system of criminal sanctions consisting of minimal but fitting punishments meted out as inexorably and as fairly as possible. I believe that such a system of criminal justice is no more utopian than is a system of constitutional government. In proportion as limited government has been realized, people have been safe from tyranny. In proportion as a decent punitive penology would be realized, people would be safe from crime.

DISCUSSION

Question: Do you think that no matter how ill a person is, he still has a guilty mind? How does your system of punishment deal with the concept of mens rea?

Szasz: I am not opposed to the concept of mens rea. I am opposed to the psychiatrization of the concept. Let me give you some examples to explain what I mean. Let's take the case of the driver of a car apprehended for killing a pedestrian. The pedestrian is dead. The question is: Why did the driver hit him? Did the pedestrian jump in front of the car? Was he walking in the middle of the road on a dark and rainy night dressed in dark clothes? Or was the pedestrian a well-known underground figure and the driver of the car a hitman for a rival gang who ran the victim down with his car while the latter was walking on the sidewalk? These are the sorts of questions a jury should consider. The answers to these questions form our concept of the driver's mens rea. In short, mens rea should be determined commonsensically, not psychiatrically.

You might ask me, What about mens rea in the case of a person who claims that he is Jesus or that God is telling him to kill his wife or neighbor? In my opinion, such a claim ought to be treated not as an extenuating circumstance, but as an aggravating circumstance. Now we say that such a person is mad, psychotic, that he is not as responsible for his evil deed as is a person who says he killed someone because he hated him or wanted his money. I don't like that. I think that by so doing we reward dishonesty. The man who kills and is honest about it we now say has mens rea, so we punish him severely. Whereas the man who kills and is dishonest about it, by producing "psychotic" explanations of why he killed, we now say has no mens rea, so we punish him less severely than we do the honest killer. I think that's stupid. It may be one of the reasons why we have so many "crazy" criminals.

Question: How do you feel about the controversy of environmental influence on a person's behavior and on his value system? Might not the relationship between their actual behavior and the behaviors from which they have to choose constitute some degree of mitigating circumstances?

Szasz: You raise a very complicated and sticky question. I don't mind trying to answer it, but I cannot do so if it's framed so abstractly. Could you give me an example?

Question: Imagine a person from a very deprived, limited background who has had very little chance of gaining any education, any type of vocational skills, or, for that matter, any real work ethic from his family or from his social group or peers, and suppose he becomes involved in some type of minor theft behavior. This person is as guilty of committing a crime as anyone else; there's no question about that, but what I'm basically asking is: Don't the circumstances and his opportunities have to be taken into account as far as any punishment that is meted out? I get the impression that you are saying that those circumstances make no difference.

Szasz: You articulate a view that is widely held today, namely, that poverty causes crime. It is one of those "facts" that's simply wrong. It is not true. Fifty years ago there was more poverty in America, but there was less crime. Lower-class crime has more to do with envy than with poverty. Furthermore, rich people steal, too. They embezzle and defraud, instead of committing theft by stealth or violence. In short, my answer to your question is "no": I do not believe that poverty should count as an excuse for crime for poor people, just as I don't believe that mental illness should count as an excuse for it for rich people. Nearly everyone who deprives others of their lives, liberty, or property has an excuse for it—an "explanation" for why he did it justifiably.

Question: Earlier you said that what other people call psychosis you call lies, for example, when a person says a voice told him to kill someone. Would you address the following example: A person goes to a psychiatrist and says, "I hear voices telling me to kill my wife, and I don't want to do that."

Szasz: That's what psychiatrists call "ambivalance." He both wants to and doesn't want to kill his wife. I am not sure what else you have in mind asking that. How the psychiatrist can help such a person, or whether he can do so, depends on a prior clarification of what the ostensible patient wants and is willing to do and what the therapist is willing to offer and do.

Question: If the patient declines hospitalization—

Szasz: Why should he be offered hospitalization? He's not sick. Killing someone is not an illness. Wanting to kill someone is not an illness. It's an indication that he doesn't like her. He's saying, loud and clear, "I don't like her." If you don't want to hear that, I can't help it.

Question: Would you say he's consciously lying?

Szasz: I'm not concerned with conscious/unconscious, that's Freud's problem.

Question: All right, but he's saying he's hearing the voices before the act; he's not lying to cover the act. You said people lie to cover nasty acts.

Szasz: Yes, he's covering his conscience; obviously he feels guilty. You could ask him: "Why kill her? Why not divorce her?" You could talk about it. That's what I do with people. They don't talk about voices telling them to kill their wives because they can talk about it in plain English. If they talk in terms of "voices" they don't get to my office.

Question: That's why you don't see these problems?

Szasz: I do see these problems, on the telephone. I believe it's very important how you talk to people. I see problems like this, but I don't let people like this come to my office. People who talk like this are not decent persons. I don't want them in my office.

Question: If a person does kill someone, and he's determined to be "mentally ill," what is the responsibility of correctional agencies in dealing with his mental state? Don't we have some responsibility in the correctional system?

Szasz: Sir, this is again too abstract. Can you tell me, in concrete terms, how do you know that this person is mentally ill?

Question: I guess what you're really saying is that everyone is responsible for their actions?

Szasz: I am saying exactly that. I believe in free will. That's very old-fashioned—just as old-fashioned as punishment. They go hand in hand. But, you see, I also believe in helping such a person. Let's assume that he says: "I have problems with my mother. And with my brothers. And I don't get along with other prisoners. And I'm scared when they put out the lights. I would like to talk to somebody." I would ask: "Who would you like to talk to—a rabbi, a priest, a psychologist, a psychiatrist?" If the state wants to pay for this, okay. I'm all for helping him on his terms. Not on the state's terms, not on the psychiatrists's terms. On the prisoner's terms. He's already being punished. That's all the punishment he's supposed to have. He's not supposed to be involuntarily psychiatrized on top of it.

Question: How does the philosophy you've articulated here today deal with mental retardation? What about the mentally retarded
in the criminal justice system?

Szasz: What I have said applies equally to mental retardation.

Question: You're saying, then, that you don't believe in mental
retardation?

Szasz: No. I believe in mental retardation. But I believe that
someone who is sufficiently unretarded to commit a crime is sufficiently unretarded to be punished for it.

Question: What criteria do you use in defining "sufficiently unretarded"?

Szasz: It's quite difficult to plan a bank robbery. If somebody
can plan and execute a bank robbery, even unsuccessfully, then I
would say he's "unretarded" enough to be tried and punished for it.

Question: A child can light a fire. Is that arson?

Szasz: There is a gray area everywhere. And yes, it may be
arson, although the culprit may be a "juvenile." You know what's
happening in New York City? Kids 11 and 12 years old are driving
around in Cadillacs. They're making thousands of dollars a day by
trafficking in drugs. Why are they trafficking in drugs? Because if
you're over 16 and you do that, you go to jail for 200 years, but if
you're under 16, then nothing happens to you. Eleven-year-olds can
be champion chess players. What's childhood? I think we have over-
sentimentalized childhood. Children are in jail, anyway; it's called
the public school system. They're really being punished without doing
anything. I would set them free from the schools and punish them for
their crimes.

Question: In Italy they differentiate between the criminally insane and the insane criminal. One goes to jail and the other goes to
the hospital. This is a well-established practice, dating back 500
years. Are they way off base or what?

Szasz: This is an illustration of what I have called the literalized metaphor. Literalized metaphors are what religions are made
of, so they are not something to sneeze at. Some of them are 2,000
years old. Criminality is a literalized metaphor. People have come
to believe that someone who has committed a criminal act has, in

addition to what he has done, something—like a liver or a kidney—
called criminality. But there is no criminality. There are only criminal acts and criminal actors. Please keep this in mind: There is no
such thing as criminality. Did the Japanese-Americans have some
secret quality in them that was discovered by Chief Justice Warren
and Franklin Roosevelt? No. Did the Jews have some quality that
Hitler discovered in 1933? No. There is no mental illness, and there
is no criminality. There are people who annoy or upset other people.
That's a fact.

Question: I would like to draw your attention to a situation a
couple of years ago in Texas in which a young man went to a psychologist or a counselor saying that he had this urge to get up on a tower
and shoot people, but he didn't know why he had it and he didn't want
to have it. Before anyone could help him, he did get up on the tower
and shoot people at random, and he shot his wife and his mother and
finally himself. The autopsy showed that he had a large brain tumor.
If he hadn't shot himself, would you say that this man was responsible
for his behavior that he had tried to prevent?

Szasz: Let me make a moral statement first and then a neuro-
physiological statement. I feel much more competent as a moralist
than as a neurophysiologist. Morally, obviously he could have shot
himself first; then he could not have killed the other people. To me
that is self-evident: He had that moral choice. Physiologically,
there is, as far as I am concerned, no evidence that any kind of brain
lesion causes crime. Crime is not like albumin in the urine.

Question: How do you distinguish between punishment and
treatment?

Szasz: I distinguish between punishment and treatment on the
basis of the subject's choice or consent. That's why my views are so
much at odds with the views of conventional psychiatrists who say that
the basis for distinction lies in the "science of psychiatry." That's
rubbish and vicious rubbish at that. It explains, however, why, only a
few years ago, locking people up in mental hospitals was widely accepted as a treatment, and why kicking people out of mental hospitals
who want to be there is now widely accepted as a treatment. I'd want
to give the patient a choice about whether he wants to go to a hospital
or not; and once he has been in for a long time, when that's his only
home, I'd give him a choice about whether he wants to stay or not. But
that's anathema to psychiatrists. In a totalitarian system, whether political or psychiatric, the last thing you want to do is give the citizen or
the patient a choice. The commissars don't give the Soviets a choice
about whether they want to live in the USSR or not. The psychiatrists
don't give the patients a choice about what they want. In short, I reject

the whole notion of involuntary psychiatric treatment; if it's involuntary, it's punishment.

As far as I am concerned, every deprivation of liberty imposed on someone who doesn't want it is punishment. If someone wants to get rid of his liberty, it's not punishment. If you want to go to the USSR and live there, that's okay; but if you took me there by force, that would be punishment. If you want to join a Trappist monastery, that would be fine for you; if you were locked up in one, that would be punishment. It's as simple as that. Control is the crucial issue.

Halleck: I agree with Dr. Szasz and I often comment in my own practice that whatever the patient wants we don't give him. We are often in the situation of forcing antipsychotic drugs upon people, and if somebody asks for them we are really shocked. At the same time, we are often in the situation of trying to refuse people antianxiety drugs like Valium, which people love, and we're always trying to give the patient exactly what he isn't asking for.

In terms of disagreements, Dr. Szasz doesn't really know that these people are lying, and I don't really know if they're telling the truth. The only thing I can say is that if hearing the voices is just simply lying, it's a form of lying that's inherited—the evidence for that I think is overwhelming. I don't know what that means, but it's something worth considering.

Another point I want to make is that I don't think we any longer commit people quite as readily as we used to do; we're much more careful about that. While I agree that there's great diversion in most areas, I don't think that diversion in civil commitment is growing, but rather that it's decreasing. I happen to have had a couple of resident M.D.s from Syracuse who, believe me, really worked me over on that issue constantly. I'd still like to hold out for the view that some people who try to kill themselves, or do kill themselves, do so for irrational reasons, and I still feel that if there is a way society can prevent them from doing this, these people may later be grateful.

This is strictly a value issue. I'm simply arguing that health values or survival values should in some situations take precedence over freedom values, and I know Szasz takes exactly the opposite position. I would just hold that sometimes it's better to be alive with less freedom than to die with your rights, as one of my colleagues has very pithily stated.

Many of these things could be resolved if we did some very simple research. I went back to teaching forensic psychiatry this year, and in reviewing all the arguments on whether commitment is good or bad for people, I discovered that nobody anywhere in the literature has done a systematic study asking patients how they feel about commitment afterward. It would be very simple to ask the patients, not

psychiatrists. I'm going to ask them at the time of commitment how
they feel about it, ask them three months later, six months later, one
year later, and two years later. I don't know how it will come out.
For me, if the majority of these patients said that it was a horrible
experience, I would stop trying to commit people.

Szasz: As to my point about lying, of course I was half-joking.
But I was half-serious, too. If someone says he hears voices, of
course I can't know whether he is lying or not. But if he says he is
Jesus, then I can be much more confident in my judgment that he is!
There's a margin of error, I suppose, but it's very small. Patients
no longer say they are Napoleon, and they don't yet say they are Car-
ter.

As to the business about the resident M.D.s. Naturally, they
work you over about suicide because they know that you're openminded.
But I travel around enough to know that there are plenty of facilities
in which resident M.D.s cannot mention the civil rights issue except
at great peril to themselves.

You are quite right, of course, that civil commitment is used
much less than formerly. However, my impression is that while
fewer people are now being sentenced to psychiatric jails, many more
are being sentenced to a kind of permanent psychiatric parole in out-
reach programs and are on thorazine. They may never be in a hospital,
or they may be in a hospital only for three days or a week, but then
they are on psychiatric parole in a halfway house or at home. So they
are free only in the sense that they are not in a mental hospital. This
is an improvement. It is better to be on parole than in jail. I am not
trying to be puristic about this. I am merely emphasizing that such
persons are not really being treated without psychiatric-legal sanctions. They are not left alone by psychiatry-and-the-law.

Let me comment on Halleck's last point. Whether health values
or civil rights should prevail is, indeed, a value judgment. Personally, I believe that civil rights, that individual liberty and dignity, are
more important than health values, than psychiatric diagnoses or treatments. However, in addition to this moral issue, there is also a practical or prudential issue that is raised once the proposition is accepted
that there are some people who commit suicide for so-called irrational
reasons and that it is socially desirable and permissible to interfere
with their decisions and acts. What is that problem? It is the same
problem that has bedeviled psychiatry all along—namely, that creating
such a category of individuals requires that we also create a category
of experts authorized to decide who falls into the category of irrational
would-be suicides and who does not. But if we know anything about
people and psychiatry and power, we know—or so I submit—that such
a determination cannot be made fairly or correctly. It is bound to be

"abused." People will be categorized as irrational would-be suicides because they annoy others or because others want their money or want to punish them or whatever. Once you let someone put his foot in this metaphorical door, he'll break the door down. You can be sure of it. It is impossible to limit civil commitment to those cases where the subject is subsequently genuinely grateful for having been "protected." I grant that there are such people. But I am loathe to endanger the liberty and rights of everyone in order to afford them the dubious "therapy" of protecting them from themselves. This is an example of what I mean when I say that sometimes we must choose between liberty and therapy: that is, I reject the proposition that giving "therapy" to some justifies endangering the liberty of all.

NOTES

1. See, generally T. S. Szasz, Law, Liberty, and Psychiatry (New York: Macmillan, 1963); Psychiatric Justice (New York: Macmillan, 1965); Ideology and Insanity (Garden City, N. Y.: Doubleday, 1970); and Psychiatric Slavery (New York: The Free Press, 1977).

2. E. A. Weinstein, "Presidential Assassination: An American Problem," Psychiatry 39 (August 1976): 291.

3. A. Solzhenitsyn, Warning to the West (New York: Farrar, Strauss and Giroux, 1976), p. 118.

4. L. von Mises, Human Action (New York: Farrar, Strauss and Giroux, 1976), p. 118.

5. See Szasz, Law, Liberty and Psychiatry, chap. 17.

6. "U.S. Woman Is Freed in 'Exorcism' Murder," International Herald-Tribune, September 17, 1976, p. 5.

7. F. A. Hayek, The Constitution of Liberty (Chicago: University of Chicago Press, 1960), especially pp. 12, 152-53.

8. "Court Award to Injured Streaker," New York Times, September 24, 1976, p. A-23.

9. "About People," Syracuse Herald-Journal, June 9, 1976, p. 2.

10. H. R. Fedden, Suicide: A Social and Historical Study (London: Peter Davies, 1938), p. 137.

11. R. M. Perkins, Criminal Law (Brooklyn, N. Y.: The Foundation Press, 1957), p. 738.

12. Ibid.

13. Ibid., p. 739.

14. S. E. Sprott, The English Debate on Suicide: From Donne to Hume (LaSalle, Ill.: Open Court, 1961), p. 99.

15. Ibid., p. 121.

16. Ibid., pp. 136-38.

17. Ibid., p. 138.

18. Ibid., p. 140.

19. W. Blackstone, Commentaries on the Laws of England: Of Public Wrongs (Boston: Beacon, 1962), pp. 211-12.

20. See, for example, T. S. Szasz, "Justice in the Therapeutic State," Indiana Legal Forum 3 (Fall 1969):14-34; and "The ACLU's 'Mental Illness' Cop-out," Reason, 5 (January 1974): 4-9.

21. See, generally, Szasz, Psychiatric Justice; and Psychiatric Slavery.

22. Mises, op. cit., p. 149.

23. See T. S. Szasz, The Myth of Mental Illness (New York: Hoeber-Harper, 1961); The Second Sin (Garden City, N. Y.: Doubleday, 1973); Schizophrenia: The Sacred Symbol of Psychiatry (New York: Basic Books, 1976).

24. Mises, op. cit., p. 149.

25. Ibid.

5

INTEGRATION AND
FUTURE DEVELOPMENTS

INTEGRATION

Halleck, Kittrie, and Szasz have touched on a wide range of issues. Halleck, a psychiatrist, argues that social controls are an inherent aspect of psychiatric practice, but that there is nothing inherently ignoble, totalitarian, or nonmedical in the role of social control agent. What psychiatrists must do, he says, is stop apologizing for playing this role and get on with the more important business of playing it in as humanistic a way as possible. In addition, psychiatrists should remain continually alert to the serious implications of their activities and thus not resent being monitored by the legal profession.

On the other hand, many of Halleck's arguments suggest that the legal scrutiny of psychiatric practice has recently gone beyond what he would call reasonable. The introduction of strict standards and procedures for civil commitment has made unfair demands on psychiatrists, he says, and has also resulted in very sick patients going untreated. Insistence upon patients' provision of informed consent to treatment has raised a myriad of complex issues and has already resulted in some precedents that Halleck finds frightening.

One of the unfair demands currently being placed on psychiatrists, in Halleck's view, is the legal mandate to predict dangerousness to effect civil commitment. The new legal approach to civil commitment, he says, has forced psychiatrists to pretend an illegitimate expertise. Kittrie, however, as a lawyer, sees this issue from a different perspective. Psychiatrists, says Kittrie, should have thought of the difficulties involved in predicting dangerousness before they claimed the ability to do it. In fact, anybody pondering the prediction of dangerousness should recognize that a variety of problems quickly arise. How, asks Kittrie, is dangerousness to be defined?

Can degrees or gradations of dangerousness by identified? Who shall be responsible for defining dangerousness?

Psychiatrists are understandably prone to overpredict dangerousness, Kittrie claims, and the resultant generation of "false positives" raises profound questions of preventive detention. Thus a prediction of dangerousness is a new and questionable device for effecting commitment. The old questionable device, Kittrie says, was to attach a label of mental illness.

No one, of course, has more of a reputation for taking issue with the mental illness label than does Szasz. In line with his countless earlier arguments, Szasz's presentation in Chapter 4 focuses on the abuses incumbent upon diverting criminal justice cases into the psychiatric realm. Advocates of these diversionary practices claim that they follow logically from a modern understanding of the mind and mental diseases. This is not really the case, Szasz says. Psychiatric diversion in the criminal justice system thrives, he argues, because it provides a mechanism that simultaneously allays the citizens' guilt for punishing certain acts and actors and satisfies their need for security by depriving certain acts of their legitimacy and certain actors of their liberty. What Szasz recommends in contrast is that the American people shoulder their responsibility for punishing people—men, women, and children—who deprive other individuals of their life, liberty, or property. To do otherwise, he says, is to endanger constitutional government and individual liberty.

On balance, Halleck bemoans restrictions on psychiatry and Szasz bemoans expansions of psychiatry. The juxtaposition of these articulate advocates cautions against hastily choosing up sides. Their differences of opinion on some issues are related to very basic differences in values, as they have both eloquently elaborated.

While the differences in general perspective between Halleck, Szasz, and Kittrie should not be obscured or belittled, the similarities in their orientations are equally notable. All agree that the clinical promise to the criminal justice system has been overstated or the clinical inroad overextended. All acknowledge that critical problems surround attempts to meaningfully articulate the criminal justice and mental health systems, whether philosophically or in actual practice. Indeed, all are themselves trying to define the appropriate role of legal variables in the mental health system and/or the appropriate role of clinical variables in the criminal justice system. Generally speaking, Szasz and Kittrie argue for separation of the two systems, while Halleck seeks closer working relations, albeit with more clear-cut role expectations.

The points and counterpoints contained in the analyses of Halleck, Kittrie, and Szasz are but one example of the expanding dialogue between clinicians and jurists. The problems that arise at the intersection of the mental health and criminal justice systems are currently under intense appraisal and reappraisal. This is reflected in both recent trends in the management of perennial issues (for example, incompetency to stand trial and the insanity plea) and in the emergence of new issues (for example, right to treatment).

Incompetency to Stand Trial

Reassessments of the incompetency-to-stand-trial issue have lately challenged the motives of those invoking the procedure and the procedure itself. Critics are contending that a latent goal of the incompetency procedure is to serve as an "easy way in" to institutionalization, especially for an indefinite period of time. This goal is described as an odious denial of the constitutional right to trial and tantamount to preventive detention. Furthermore, from the initial raising of the question through confinement in institutions for mentally disordered offenders, the procedure itself has been decried as a mockery of justice.

While the definitional criteria of competency to stand trial have been widely agreed upon, confusion nonetheless surrounds the application of the test, both in statute and in actual practice. Many statutes lump the incompetency issue together with the not-guilty-by-reason-of-insanity issue. Thus court requests for evaluation on the former cannot be distinguished from requests for evaluation on the latter, resulting at best in an unnecessary expenditure of resources on performing both evaluations. Furthermore, clinicians are often not well versed on either issue (including their distinguishing characteristics) and are inclined to define capabilities and incapabilities in mental health and mental illness terms. As a result, requests for evaluation on the incompetency issue often solicit reports containing only psychiatric diagnoses or other clinical assessments of the defendant's affliction with psychiatric disorders.

This misguided orientation is one of the reasons the need for psychiatric expertise in applying the incompetency criteria has itself been challenged. Generally speaking, criteria for competency include an understanding of the criminal charges, an understanding of the nature and object of the criminal procedure, and an ability if not willingness to assist defense counsel. In what sense is clinical psychiatric training, knowledge, or insight necessary in assessing this understanding, ability, and willingness?

Efforts to clarify this issue have produced some checklists and screening instruments for assessing an accused's mental competency. Bukatamin, Foy, and DeGrazia have proposed the following sorts of questions be asked in a screening interview: Who is your lawyer at this time? What is your lawyer's job? What is the purpose of the judge? What does the jury do? What will the prosecutor do? What are the charges against you? What do they mean to you? Why were they made against you? What is the difference between guilty and not guilty? And so on.[1]

Another assessment instrument was developed in a major study conducted under the auspices of the Harvard Medical School's Laboratory of Community Psychiatry.[2] A sampling of the questions contained in this instrument includes the following: What are you charged with? Is that a major or a minor charge? Do you have confidence in your lawyer? Do you think he's trying to do a good job for you? If you're found guilty as charged, what are the possible sentences the judge could give you? If you're put on probation, what does that mean? The argument is that no psychiatric expertise is needed to ask these sorts of questions, to interpret the accused's responses, and to arrive at a conclusion regarding his understanding of the criminal procedure and his posture toward defense counsel.

The widespread practice of automatically institutionalizing persons found incapable of standing trial has also come under assault. Critics contend that the criteria for being incompetent and those for needing hospitalization are not synonymous. The suggested reform is court consideration of disposition as a separate question. Similarly, the widespread failure to provide treatment directed toward sumption of competency has been condemned. Treatment should be administered expeditiously, it is argued, for the longer the trial proceedings are suspended, the weaker the case for both defense and prosecution.

Statutory confusion of incompetency and insanity and the biases of the clinical perspective once again become issues at the point of restoration of competency and resumption of criminal proceedings. If incompetency is best designated as the absence or impairment of the accused's understanding, ability, and willingness discussed above, then competency is best designated as their return or improvement. But instead, statutes calling for a "recovery of sanity" typically result in evaluation reports citing such variables as the defendant's renewed appreciation of the difference between right and wrong. Similarly, clinical personnel of institutions holding the incompetent routinely consider restoration in terms of achievement of a level of mental health sufficient to return to the community setting an inappropriate standard, since return to the courtroom is what is at issue.

The degree to which courts have allowed these compromised versions of justice to prevail is evidence of the latent goal of incompetency proceedings referred to earlier: to serve as an "easy way in" to institutionalization, especially for an indefinite and often interminable period of time. That a finding of incompetency has in fact traditionally functioned as a final disposition was highlighted by the recent landmark case in this area, Jackson v. Indiana,[3] which requires the release or civil commitment of defendants who are judged not likely to regain competency within a "reasonable period of time."

The need for periodic review of incompetency cases is evident. Other various and sundry problems that have been cited regarding the incompetency issue include denial of bail, violation of the Fifth Amendment, institutionalization absent any actual conviction, and institutionalization that is not credited against a subsequent sentence, that is "dead time."

In Chapter 2 Halleck argued that competency to stand trial is a legal decision, not a psychiatric decision, and that it ought to be made by lawyers, perhaps with the assistance of psychiatrists. Szasz's invective against diversion from the criminal justice system into the psychiatric system includes the pretrial evaluation of competency. Elsewhere, Szasz has discussed this specific form of diversion in detail (Psychiatric Justice, Macmillan, 1965). The essence of Szasz's argument is that the question to be considered is whether or not an accused can play the role that is expected of him in the court proceedings. Competency is equated with the ability to play the role, incompetency with inability. Whether or not he is mentally ill, Szasz says, is essentially irrelevant. Szasz's recommendation is that the responsibility for examining the defendant and for deciding his fitness to stand trial be placed in the hands of a judge or a panel of judges, a lawyer or a panel of lawyers, or a lay jury.

Robert Burt and Norval Morris have argued "that the incompetency doctrine as such should be abolished and that mental incompetency should no longer be a bar to criminal trial but merely one appropriate ground for authorizing time-limited trial continuances."[4] Under this proposal, which provides for a preliminary hearing, periodic review, and an individualized treatment plan, the criminal procedure would be postponed no longer than six months even if competency as such were not restored.[5] Alan Stone has also proposed "a specific statutory limit to the length of time a person may be confined for return to competency purposes."[6] The Harvard Medical School project referred to above lends indirect support to these proposals for time limitations, since one of its findings was that incompetency to stand trial is usually quickly responsive to treatment.[7]

Criminal Responsibility

Many have noted an irony in the fact that the insanity defense is rarely employed but widely discussed. Especially since the Durham rule was articulated in 1954, debate over tests for assessing insanity, over concepts within tests, and over definitions of concepts within tests has been intense. Some stand adamantly behind the M'Naghten rule, others behind Durham, and others behind the American Law Institute Model Penal Code test. Still others argue that there are really no substantial differences among the various tests or that any there may be are lost on the jury. Thus Weihofen (back in 1933) asked:

> Is there anyone who seriously thinks that the jurymen in even an appreciable minority of cases decide the question of sanity or insanity by a dispassionate and judicial application of the test given them by the judge? Whether a jury will return a verdict of guilty or not guilty by reason of insanity depends primarily upon the dramatic quality of the offense charged—whether it was a brutal and atrocious act arousing public indignation or repugnance, or an act arousing public sympathy or condonation; upon the personality and appearance of the defendant, his lawyer, and the prosecutor; upon the nationality, religion, or color of the defendant and the jurymen; upon wholly extraneous matters, such as the existence of a recent "crime wave," and a resulting belief by the jury in the need for drastic punishments; upon a thousand and one legally irrelevant facts appealing to the jury's "common sense"; and— usually less important than any of these—upon the instructions of the court. [8]

In an interesting experimental analysis, Rita Simon found evidence that jurors exposed to no test would acquit on the basis of insanity in greater proportion than jurors instructed according to M'Naghten or Durham. She also found, however, that the criteria for criminal responsibility as defined under Durham is closer to a jury's "natural sense of equity" than is the M'Naghten rule. [9] This represents irony upon irony, of course, since Durham is no more, and the jurisdiction in which it was propounded is now part of a trend toward the Model Penal Code test. Parenthetically, statutory confusion between insanity and incompetency, and all the problems associated with the clinical evaluator's ignorance of and antipathy toward legal criteria, should be recollected at this juncture.

It is often suggested that there is a close relationship between the insanity plea and capital punishment. The insanity defense is merely a ploy, some say, for avoiding infliction of the death penalty. To the extent this statement is true, the use of the insanity defense is currently in a state of disarray. The national confusion regarding capital punishment is having repercussions throughout the criminal courts and corrections agencies, and its impact on the insanity plea is only one of many examples.

While many debate the merits of the respective tests of insanity, others advocate outright abolition of the defense altogether. The latter are, however, by no means a homogeneous group. Alan Stone notes that rejection of the insanity defense comes from all sectors of the political spectrum.

> It is attacked on one side because it excuses too many, and on the other because it excuses too few. One abolitionist [Seymour Halleck] claims that it is unfair because it is only available to the rich. Another [Thomas Szasz] claims it is applied only to the poor and minorities as a stigmatizing weapon of oppression. Former President Nixon is concerned that the insanity defense allows dangerous criminals to go free, while others argue that the blameless mentally ill are confined longer than criminals.[10]

Some say that to call the insanity plea a defense is dubious. While the defendant is technically acquitted, he is routinely committed to an institution for an indeterminate length of time. Critics complain that the indefinite commitment often runs longer than the maximum criminal sentence for the offense in question. The inordinately long hospitalizations are one rationale for a two-stage process that is proposed by some as a substitute for current procedures. In the first stage, guilt or innocence of the criminal charge would be ascertained through a regular criminal trial. In the second state, disposition of those found guilty would be decided by a panel of experts. The panel, comprised of specialists in the social and behavioral sciences, would take any mental health needs of the offender into account in their individualized dispositions. Opponents of this proposal question, among other things, the abilities of experts to perform in this fashion and the advisability of placing so much power in their hands.

The notion of "partial responsibility" or "diminished responsibility" has also been suggested as an alternative. The general purpose of these approaches is to reduce either the seriousness of the charge or the severity of the punishment in light of a mental disorder. While the concept of diminished responsibility has been widely accepted in cases involving intoxication, most jurisdictions have been hesitant to expand the notion beyond these instances. The subsequent limitation of the doctrine distresses some clinicians who see it as a realistic reflection of gradations in intent and motivation. From the psychiatric perspective, behavior is rarely as categorical as the insanity defense implies.

In a similar vein, but with more far-reaching implications, is the contention that mental illness is only one of a variety of problems that should be considered in assessing the capacity to formulate criminal intent. C. R. Jeffrey has phrased it well:

If the argument is that certain persons are exempted from responsibility because they behave in a bizarre manner and therefore they cannot control their behavior, then it must be noted that behavior is also determined by slum areas, poverty, racial discrimination, and other sociological variables. Why does the lawyer believe in psychic determinism as put forth by the psychiatrist, and not believe in environmental determinism as put forth by sociologists and experimental psychologists?[11]

The same Robert Burt who (along with Norval Morris) recommends abolition of the incompetency-to-stand-trial doctrine supports retention of the insanity plea. While acknowledging some reservations about both the defense and his position regarding it, Burt suggests that the courtroom ritual surrounding the defense "may be central to preserving the ethical integrity of the criminal justice system" since it brings "into focus the grand issues of moral responsibility underlying the imposition of criminal norms and punishments." Burt also states: "Retaining the ritual for its own sake might be justified by the same reasoning that occasionally moves agnostics to attend religious services: to acknowledge strong attachments to the past and to hedge bets for the future."[12]

A similar line of reasoning is taken by Stone, who recommends retention of the defense as an "escape hatch" to use when confronting "a case so bizarre and so incongruous that all the premises of criminal law, including free will, seem inappropriate." Using the escape hatch not only avoids embarrassment, Stone says, but also implies obversely that all other defendants do have free will. "Thus, the insanity defense is in every sense the exception that proves the rule. It allows the court to treat every other defendant as someone who chose 'between good and evil.'"[13]

Clearly, the insanity defense is a charade to some, a sacred ritual to others, and an escape hatch to still others. In large measure because of its juxtaposition of free will and determinism, the insanity plea highlights as no other issue the strain between the mental health and criminal justice systems, between the clinician and the jurist. As the articulation of these two systems has lately been analyzed in greater depth, the problems surrounding the insanity defense have been underscored. And the more carefully these problems are scrutinized, the clearer it becomes that they are not just medical and not just legal but, in fact, as Halleck observed in Chapter 2, philosophical in nature.

Sexual Psychopathy

Some of the most condemning indictments in recent forensic literature have addressed the statutes and procedures governing what is variously known as psychopathy, sexual psychopathy, defective delinquency, and sexual dangerousness. The statutes are described as vague, arbitrary, and discriminatory, and the implementing procedure as a travesty of justice.

The most basic problem is the inability to precisely define the terms "psychopathy," "defective delinquent," and so on. The variations in definitions from jurisdiction to jurisdiction certainly suggest a degree of conceptual fuzziness. But this is a less-insurmountable problem than the very real possibility that the fuzziness reflects the absence of any identifiable syndrome whatsoever. The question is whether or not any actual conceptual or behavioral phenomenon is designated by the terms "psychopath," "defective delinquent," and so on. Correlatively, critics ask, how can this class of offenders be clearly defined as a separate class from all other offenders? These challenges have not been successfully met.

The purpose of the law in defining special categories, of course, is to provide special handling of those contained within. But the absence of any effective treatment for those labeled psychopaths is another one of the major criticisms. In <u>Millard</u> v. <u>Cameron</u>, the U.S. Court of Appeals for the District of Columbia extended the right to treatment to a person confined in Saint Elizabeth's Hospital as a sexual psychopath, contending that such confinement is justifiable only upon a theory of therapeutic treatment.[14]

The blatant absence of procedural safeguards in the processing of psychopaths was addressed by the U.S. Supreme Court in <u>Specht</u> v. <u>Patterson</u>.[15] The court held that sexual psychopath proceedings are subject to both the equal protection clause and the due process clause. Rights that the court then specifically enumerated included the defendant's presence with counsel and his opportunity to be heard, confront witnesses, and offer evidence.

The sexual psychopath statutes represent both a fear of the dangerousness of sexual offenders (for which there is no empirical support) and a desire for a legal net broad enough to catch all manner of socially undesirable persons. As such, they are intimately related to social values, including what Halleck calls "prurient interest" in sexual psychopathology. Oddly enough, all the interest still has not led many to the realization that definitions of sexual deviance are relative in time, place, and among different groups of people. And given the fact that clinicians in contemporary America cannot even agree among themselves about what constitutes sexual deviance, or antisocial reaction, or psychopathic personality, or antisocial personality, a matter of relativity becomes no matter at all.

Citing "procedural ills, erratic applications, abuses, . . . constitutional infirmities, . . . erroneous assumptions, [and failure] to serve their ostensible purposes," Stone has recommended the abolition of sexual psychopath laws.[16] Burt concurs in this recommendation, calling the laws "pure obscenities, at least in the sense that they are utterly without redeeming social value."[17]

Right to Treatment, Informed Consent, and Right to Refuse Treatment

As the definition and management of incompetency, insanity, and psychopathy have been undergoing change, so too have new issues emerged from recent critical analyses of the mental health and criminal justice systems. Perhaps the most significant is the articulation of the right to treatment. In a landmark 1966 decision, the U.S. Court of Appeals for the District of Columbia held in Rouse v. Cameron that the purpose of involuntary hospitalization is treatment, and that absent treatment a hospital is turned into a penitentiary.[18] In 1971 an Alabama court found that treatment is a constitutional right for persons involuntarily committed to mental institutions as a quid pro quo for confinement. Said the court: "To deprive any citizen of his or her liberty upon the altruistic theory that the confinement is for humane and therapeutic reasons, and then fail to provide adequate treatment violates the very fundamentals of due process."[19] Adequate treatment was defined to comprise three elements: a humane psychological and physical environment and facilities, a qualified staff in numbers sufficient to administer adequate treatment, and individual treatment plans.

The issues that have since evolved around the provision of the right to treatment are many and complex. Not the least sensitive issue is the question of who shall be held liable for the absence of treatment and with what sorts of punitive sanctions.

Closely related to the right to treatment is the issue of informed consent. The requirement for consent is based on the idea that a patient has the right to understand what treatment will be given him and the ramifications of accepting such treatment. In Kaimowitz v. Michigan Department of Mental Health, the court stated that "consent is not an idle or symbolic act; it is a fundamental requirement for protection of the individuals' integrity."[20] The court in Kaimowitz specified the necessary elements of informed consent as a capacity to give consent (competency), thorough and clear information of consequences (knowledge), and freely given assent without coercion (voluntary). An extremely important point is raised by Kaimowitz, namely, the suggestion that it may be impossible, by definition, for an incarcerated person to give voluntary consent. On the one hand, the atmosphere of the institution encourages obedience and cooperation. On the other hand, the inmate, with freedom uppermost in his mind, is likely to cooperate with those he perceives as having power over his release, regardless of the consequences.

It is the Kaimowitz decision that Halleck claims has had a "chilling effect on psychiatric research in general and particularly on research in prisons." Halleck raises a number of issues to be considered under informed consent, including whether the explanation given the patient is satisfactory with regard to possible risks and benefits, and how much of the explanation the patient understands.

The law with regard to informed consent in psychiatric settings has apparently only begun to crystallize. Meisel, Roth, and Lidz describe a state of affairs that would encourage clinicians to record their informed consent interviews, as Halleck says they are:

> What constitutes a valid consent today may not remain so tomorrow; what constitutes a valid consent in one juris-diction may not be an accurate representation of the law in a neighboring jurisdiction; and what constitutes a valid consent in one branch of medicine may be a less than wholly accurate guide to a valid consent in another branch of medicine.[21]

The next obvious question to ask, and it is being asked more frequently of late, is whether there is a right to refuse treatment. Wyatt v. Stickney touched on this issue in relation to informed consent when it said, "Patients have the right to not be subjected to treatment procedures such as lobotomy, electro-convulsive treatment, adversive reinforcement conditioning , or other unusual or hazardous treatment procedures without their express and informed consent after consultation with counsel or interested party of the patient's choice."[22]

The issue of the right to refuse treatment is logically most often discussed in relation to the more extreme or high-risk treatments. Stone suggests that any patient protesting the administration of these treatments should be granted a full judicial hearing. The treatments he is referring to include psychosurgery, convulsive therapy, aversive therapy, inhalation therapy, and the administration of highly ad-dictive substances.[23]

When the treatment in question has as its purpose the change of the mind or thought processes of the recipient, the right to refuse treatment has been argued from the basis of the First Amendment right to free speech. The First Amendment has been interpreted to support the right of an individual to "mind freedom" and "privacy of the mind." In rejecting an involuntarily confined patient's consent to psychosurgery, the court in Kaimowitz said:

> There is no privacy more deserving of constitutional pro-
> tection than one's mind. . . . Intrusions into one's intel-
> lect when one is involuntarily detained and subject to the
> control of institutional authorities is an intrusion into one's
> constitutionally protected right to privacy. If one is not
> protected in his thoughts, behavior, personality and iden-
> tity, then the right to privacy is meaningless. [24]

Efforts continue to find a reasonable balance between right to
treatment and right to refuse treatment. In a proposal for the federal
regulation of psychosurgery, the Harvard Journal on Legislation
raises objections to both prohibition and imposition. "Any statute,"
it is argued, "must balance freedom from the medical and social hazards of psychosurgery against the possibility of freedom from the de-
bilitation of mental illness."[25] While a case is made against compelling a person to undergo psychosurgery against his wishes, a provocative argument maintains that it would be wrong to prevent a
person from choosing the treatment if the choice does not threaten
others.

> There would be a contradiction in the government's pro-
> tecting its citizens from the dangers of psychosurgery by
> prohibiting them from obtaining it—insuring autonomy by
> denying autonomy. Deciding whether to consent to psy-
> chosurgery is an unimpeded exercise of free choice—a
> value in itself with which it is prima facie wrong to inter-
> fere. It enables persons to experiment—even with living
> —and to discover things valuable both to themselves and
> to others. For the victim of mental illness, it is a part
> of the search for full humanity. [26]

When is something treatment; when is it punishment? When
should the state be obliged to do something; when should it be obliged
to do nothing? When should a patient have the right to be treated;
when should he have the right to be left alone? These are extremely
difficult questions, and Szasz humbles our efforts to answer when he
reminds us that only a few years ago, locking people up in mental
hospitals was widely accepted as a treatment, but now kicking people
out of hospitals who want to be there is widely accepted as a treatment.

FUTURE DEVELOPMENTS

Incompetency, Insanity, and Psychopathy

It is questionable whether the incompetency-to-stand-trial procedure, the insanity defense, and the sexual-psychopath statutes

indeed <u>have</u> a future. But the numerous calls for abolition are accompanied by calls for reform short of abolition. Perhaps this reflects no more than the difference between those taking long-range and those taking short-range assessments of the situation. On the other hand, an eye to the historical ebb and flow of punishment and treatment orientations within the criminal justice system suggests that a good deal of the disenchantment behind pleas for both abolition and reform is with the excesses of these statutes rather than the principles upon which they are based.

Widespread adjustment in procedural abuses would quiet much of the controversy surrounding the incompetency-to-stand-trial issue, and these adjustments are underway and should continue. The most significant developments to be anticipated include a decline in the use of the procedure as an "easy way in" to indefinite commitment (for either especially heinous offenders or nuisance misdemeanants), a declining role for clinical criteria and personnel in the assessment of competency, and the implementation of a full range of procedural safeguards, especially periodic review or some system of time constraints. In all, it is likely that the procedure will be invoked less frequently, that it will function much like other postponement procedures, and that incompetent defendants routinely will be restored to competency within a reasonable period of time or remanded either back to the criminal justice system or on to the civil mental health system.

The insanity defense is a more complicated issue, and future developments likely will reflect this fact. Debates probably will continue over the various tests and criteria. The Model Penal Code test is having its day in court, but the <u>M'Naghten</u> criteria have a long history and continue to hold strong. In a sense, the debates are academic and of meaning only to jurists and clinicians, which in no way demeans their philosophical import. On a practical daily basis, however, much of this import seems lost on juries. That juries may be operating from some lay, commonsensical notion of justice is not inherently distasteful either.

In any event, and as in the incompetency procedure, clinical concepts and personnel show signs of declining influence in the insanity defense. (And more and more psychiatrists are withdrawing from this arena not by force but by choice.) Other developments on the horizon include the provision of treatment and of safeguards such as periodic review for those adjudicated insane. Use of the statute should itself decline, especially if capital punishment is effectively abolished.

With both incompetency and insanity, much of the criticism has been directed toward the general absence or compromising of due process, the indefinite commitment without review, and the overextended role of clinical variables and personnel in test assessments. Significant adjustments along these lines would so radically transform the incompetency procedure that it would satisfy the major demands of the most discontented critics and yet preserve the principle upon which the procedure is based. This principle is that a person in some way out of touch with the trial procedure should not participate. Or, as Szasz would have it, incompetency is nothing more nor less than inability to play the expected role.

Similar developments with the insanity defense would also transform much of the procedure but not the principle behind it. Many complaints would be satisfied, but by no means all, especially since the principle itself is defined as problematic by some. This principle was well articulated by Judge Bazelon when, in the Durham decision, he stated that "our collective conscience does not allow punishment where it cannot impose blame."[27] While Szasz might agree technically with this statement, he would likely go on to suggest that we resume blaming criminals for their conduct and stop diverting them to the psychiatric system via the insanity defense. To many, of course, this proposal is objectionable. Debate between these perspectives stands at the crux of contemporary developments in criminal justice and mental health.

If a reduction in clinical involvement, an implementation of due process, and a reduction in indefinite commitment are applied to the sexual psychopath statutes, as in all likelihood they will, the statutes will be effectively abolished. That is, to remove the excesses of these statutes is to remove the statutes themselves. All sexual psychopath laws are is an attempt to use clinical perspectives to circumvent due process for the purpose of effecting indefinite commitment.

Right to Treatment, Informed Consent, and
Right to Refuse Treatment

The impetus for restricting the role of clinical concepts and personnel is the failure of clinical efforts to date to impact significantly on the crime problem or the administration of criminal justice. Clearly this is one of the major messages of Durham. As these shortcomings have come to light, the right to treatment has emerged as a major issue. Traditionally, one of the justifications for creating separate categories of offenders as "criminally insane" and for consigning them to special "institutions for the criminally insane" has been to provide them with treatment for this condition. The treatment has not been provided, and the courts are beginning to mandate that from now on it must be if these special categories and institutions are to remain.

A court order on right to treatment is a two-edged sword. On the one hand, the courts have clearly stated that concepts of adequate care can be defined, operationalized, and implemented within the current state of the psychiatric arts. Thus, for example, patient/staff ratios could be improved, individualized treatment plans could be developed, and established treatment modalities could be employed with greater numbers of patients. Furthermore, some of the improvements needed to provide adequate treatment could be effected in part by a custodial staff—for example, the provision of a humane physical environment. In a nutshell, the courts are telling institutions that they can and will move from nineteenth-century to twentieth-century standards of care.

On the other hand, for some institutions the roots in substandard care are literally a century deep, and the necessary alterations in physical structure, staffing, and orientation are therefore enormous. In these circumstances, right-to-treatment orders are actually functioning to close the institutions.

As therapies that are tantamount to behavioral engineering become ever more finely tuned, the right to refuse treatment gains in relevancy. This right is an especially sensitive issue in the criminal justice system, though it is an issue in the civil system as well. With crime rates soaring, with recidivism rates high, with institutions overcrowded, and with the poor track record of earlier clinical endeavors, many advocate, and many fear, accelerated efforts to employ all manner of behavior engineering techniques on convicted offenders. There is evidence that this has already happened, and it will likely continue to happen. On the other hand, Halleck noted in Chapter 2 that there are also countertrends, some of which, in their zealous protection of offenders' rights, may stifle sophisticated research.

As the risks and ramifications of new treatment procedures heighten, informed consent becomes an issue. Some argue that the way to deal with the sticky ethical questions of behavioral engineering is to leave the entire matter up to the individual offender's choice. Make the procedure available to him and let him decide if he wants it. But as the Kaimowitz decision highlighted, being incarcerated and giving informed consent may be a contradiction in terms.

The difficult issues continue to spiral. To make any coherent plan for action in the future, there are a number of questions that must be addressed. What rights, if any, does an individual have upon conviction or incarceration? What rights, if any, does the state have to impose its will on convicted offenders? Under what circumstances can an offender be forced to submit to a treatment? Under what circumstances does the offender have a right to demand the state provide a treatment? What is needed is a clarification of the relationship between rights and responsibilities.

Mental Health-Criminal Justice Relations

While it is discouraging that we still flounder on such basic and perennial questions as those just enumerated, Ochberg and Brown suggest that "the problems with which we struggle now are to a large extent the problems of our successes."[28] Significant strides have been made, especially in the last few decades, in both the mental health and criminal justice systems. The general trends, in fact, have been remarkably parallel between the two systems, not only recently but well back into the nineteenth century. As the historical review in Chapter 1 indicated, both relied heavily on "total" institutions for many decades, but both have recently made major efforts to develop less-restrictive settings and to implement community-based programs on an unprecedented scale. Furthermore, the rights of those defined as mental patients and criminals have lately been carefully scrutinized and elaborated in each of the two systems.

There is evidence (some of it in the research findings presented in Part II of this book) that the similar trends in mental health and criminal justice are more than just coincidental and in part reflect a common client base. In what resembles a pattern of "musical clients," there is movement back and forth between the two systems. When the rolls in one system are full, clients are shunted to the other. It is as if there is a pool of people who will be labeled deviant at any one time, and their definition as "mental patients," or "criminals," or "criminally insane" depends as much on current constraints in the deviance management systems as on their behavior.

This situation has serious implications for policy making and service planning. It raises the question of whether separate facilities and programs should be maintained for each of the three groups or whether services should be dovetailed whenever possible. Currently, conflicting arguments are being made, as the following items indicate:

The Special Committee of the Association of the Bar of the City of New York has proposed that defendants found incompetent to stand trial be treated as civil patients. Both prisons and institutions for the criminally insane are considered inappropriate dispositions since no criminal conviction has occurred.[29]

In part of a larger argument to abolish the category of "the criminally insane," since those so designated are especially likely to be victimized by the "new correctional biotechnology," Burt contends:

it would solve nothing to confine mentally ill prisoners in civil mental hospitals with the hope that they would be treated indistinguishably from all patients. . . . Because of their peculiar involvement with the criminal justice system, the

hospital authorities would be sensitive to public fear of
these patients in particular and, among other adverse effects, would see special need to ensure against their escape
and to hold them for long terms. Mentally ill prisoners
can by protected from seriously adverse discriminations
only by keeping in high visibility the proposition that they
are not very much different from all prisoners. [30]

A study group in Massachusetts has recommended high-security
treatment centers for both civilly committed noncriminal and mentally
ill criminal offenders. These centers would be distributed across
the state (one per specified region), and each center would serve between 10 and 20 patients. They also recommend that each center operate a halfway house. The study group conceives of these centers
not as miniprisons but as intensive treatment facilities. [31]

The latter proposal reflects the recent emphasis in both the mental
health and criminal justice systems on dangerousness as the critical
variable for involuntary confinement. There is a logic to focusing on
dangerousness (to others, that is) that fits nicely with correlative
emphases on the tolerance of differentness and the rights of the different. Thus, Kittrie (who has, in fact, authored a book entitled The
Right to Be Different[32]) reports having been proud of his involvement
in legislation that prohibits involuntary commitment merely on the
basis of need for treatment and permits it only on the basis of dangerousness. In like fashion, Halleck reports that he also earlier
supported this rationale and assisted in its legislation. Since then,
the enormous problems involved in the prediction of dangerousness,
including the generation of intolerable numbers of false positives, have
become evident, and Kittrie and Halleck (like most others) have ad-
justed their positions accordingly. It is regrettable, however, that
subsequent challenges to predict dangerousness and confessions of inability to do so too often lose sight of the logic in focusing on dangerousness that lured us down its path to begin with.

In any event, the criteria according to which we divide up and
manage the deviant population is in need of clarification and reassess-
ment. Where mental illness and criminality are somehow combined,
priorities must be addressed. Many clinical personnel prefer to deal
with mental patients as mental patients, regardless of any criminal
involvement. But others argue for dealing with criminals as criminals, whatever their mental status.

Two Models

Kittrie noted in Chapter 3 that Dershowitz has identified two
models used in the United States for dealing with deviants: the pun-

ishment-deterrence model and the prediction-prevention model. Szasz's presentation in Chapter 4 is clearly in line with the punish- ment-deterrence model (as in Kittrie's discussion), and Halleck's re- marks in Chapter 2 reflect the prediction-prevention model. While Halleck's sympathies with the prediction-prevention model are evi- dent, he nonetheless notes that trends are currently running in the other direction. Giving Szasz much of the credit for this, Halleck elaborates on the resultant restrictions that have recently been placed on involuntary commitment within the civil mental health system.

In the criminal justice system, as Halleck again notes, the same sort of trend toward the punishment-deterrence model has lately be- come manifest. This orientation surfaced (or, more accurately, re- surfaced) with the publication of Lipton, Martinson, and Wilks's study of the effectiveness of correctional treatment that more or less con- cluded that nothing tried so far has worked very much at all.[33] This study has been so enthusiastically (if sometimes begrudgingly) re- ceived that there can be little doubt that it was catalytic. Professionals in the criminal justice system were primed for it, many after years of frustration in trying to realize the rehabilitative ideal.

It is now becoming fashionable to be categorically cynical toward treatment in corrections. The climate is one of admitting limited capabilities and dropping pretenses of effecting change. Open demands for retribution are giving vent to previously repressed resentment toward offenders for not being more responsive to rehabilitative ef- forts. The utilitarian principles of the classical school are being resurrected in calls for calculated rationality in the assigning of pun- ishments.[34] In a nutshell, the trend is toward blaming criminals and toward punishing them. This is precisely what Szasz recommends.

These developments could have serious implications for the management of mentally disordered offenders. The emphasis on blame might cast mental aberrations as loopholes for avoiding pun- ishment. Thus greater interest might be directed toward tightening up tests for assessing criminal responsibility and even criteria for competency to stand trial. On the other hand, less interest might be directed toward the identification and treatment of special categories of offenders (like psychopaths and defective delinquents) whose men- tal status has been defined as questionable yet who nonetheless have been held criminally responsible. Perhaps courts will decide that justice is best served by assuming that all persons should be punished for criminal deeds regardless of their mental status. Such an extreme outcome appears unlikely, however, since it would require legal phi- losophy to relinquish its long-standing commitment to the concept of mens rea as a component of crime.

In any event, we are witnessing nothing less than a reassertion of the notions of free will, choice, responsibility, and accountability

in the administration of criminal justice. The return to the punishment-deterrence model appears to represent a kind of existential
backlash against the failure of the prediction-prevention model to deliver on its promises. The limitations of the deterministic orientation are reflected in the gross inadequacies of the extant system in
both its theoretical efforts to understand why people engage in criminal behavior and in its practical efforts to stop them.

The Politics of Therapy and Criminal Justice

In a book aptly titled <u>The Politics of Therapy</u>, as well as in his
presentation in Chapter 2, Halleck makes the point that the therapeutic enterprise both reflects and reinforces its social context.[35] The
mental health system supports established social values. Generally
speaking, what society calls good and bad, psychotherapists call good
and bad. And as these values undergo change in society at large,
they concurrently undergo change in psychotherapy. Halleck poi-
gnantly underscores this point by noting that American psychotherapy
focuses on self-actualization and minimized cooperation, interdependence, and other communal values. If the society becomes more socialistic, he predicts, psychotherapists will begin bombarding their
patients about the virtues of community dependence and loyalty. Another example Halleck cites is less hypothetical. Ten years ago, he
notes, therapists were telling women that there was something wrong
with them if they didn't have vaginal orgasms.
The mental health system generally defines health in terms of
adjustment to established life-styles. In so doing, as Halleck, Szasz,
and others have explained, the mental health system functions as an
agency of social control. The deviant, the maladjusted, those who
don't fit are defined as having personal pathologies. The possibility
that the established order is itself pathological and that the maladjusted are the healthy is not addressed. Nor is attention directed
toward the <u>origins</u> of many personal problems <u>in</u> social problems. To
the degree that therapists patch up the individual personal casualties
of an ailing social system, they divert attention from the roots of personal problems. In the final analysis, this diversion indirectly perpetuates the larger social ills by disguising them as individual pathologies. As Szasz says, psychiatric diversion actually has very little
to do with psychiatry but a lot to do with politics.
Within the criminal justice system, a school of thought that is
very politically oriented has been coalescing in the last few years.
Variously known as "new," "radical," "critical," or "socialist" criminology, it analyzes crime and the administration of criminal justice
in terms of macroscopic structural variables such as class, status,

and power. This perspective takes issue with traditional criminology and its focus on such variables as the family histories of ordinary criminals. The new criminology does not abide by the prediction-prevention model.

On the other hand, and more important, radical criminology also stands in opposition to the trend toward the punishment-deterrence model. One of the major spokesmen of the school, Richard Quinney, argues that the return to the rational utilitarian dispensing of justice ignores the social reality of inequality and justifies further oppression within the established order. The resurrected and revamped punishment-deterrence model "dispenses justice (i.e., punishment) for the purpose of preserving the capitalist social order. . . . Crime has come to symbolize the ultimate crack in the armor of the existing social order. And given the modern pessimism that social problems cannot really be solved—without drastically altering the established order—controls must be instituted to protect 'our society.'"[36]

To Quinney, the punishment-deterrence model now gaining sway in criminal justice is a "revised social theory for advanced capitalist society" propounded by those desiring to preserve that society. To the radical criminologist, however, the established order _is_ the ultimate problem behind crime. They contend further that awareness of this fact has not escaped the powers-that-be who have subsequently popularized the myth that society can't be changed and have reinstituted the punishment-deterrence model of criminal justice. Blaming the offender has become officially sanctioned, but to the radical criminologist, this is really blaming the victim. The task ahead, in the words of Quinney, is "to attend to a socialist sense of justice."[37]

A good example of applied radical criminology is a recent analysis of the relationship between schools and juvenile delinquency conducted by Liazos.[38] Social scientists have maintained, says Liazos, that schools contribute to delinquency by their failure to prepare students properly for later life. Thus, the solution typically proposed is better schools and better education. Liazos argues that schools create delinquents because of their success, not their failure. That is, under the present economic system the job of the schools is to prepare youths, especially lower-class youths, for alienated work and lives. Those students who resist this precast mold, who rebel against the demands for obedience to authority, who refuse to fit are by definition delinquent.

Given the shortage of decent jobs, Liazos argues, truly liberating schools would create social misfits. He concludes, therefore, that the schools are neither the problem nor the solution; what is needed are changes in the larger society, the economy, and the ruling groups.

Work, work training, and manual labor are not inherently degrading and destructive. Organized differently, so that all people may use their minds and release their creativity, work is beneficial to body and spirit. What causes alienation today is (1) the limit on well-paying decent jobs, (2) the relegation of dead-end jobs to the lower classes, (3) the degradation attached to manual labor, and (4) the planning and control of work by a small number of persons. . . .

We must work together to create a new society which will allow and encourage all to lead decent, full, and creative lives. . . .

Such a society would eliminate most crime by abolishing the conditions underlying crime and delinquency.[39]

CONCLUSIONS

Juxtaposed, the prediction-prevention model, the punishment-deterrence model, and radical criminology pose questions of power, of conflict, and of values. As Halleck and Szasz both conclude, many of the differences between them are ultimately based on opposing priorities between health values and freedom values. For Halleck, health values take precedence over freedom values: "I would just hold that sometimes it's better to be alive with less freedom than to die with your rights." Szasz responded, "Personally, I believe that civil rights, that individual liberty and dignity, are more important than health values, than psychiatric diagnoses or treatments. . . . sometimes we must choose between liberty and therapy [and] I reject the proposition that giving 'therapy' to some justifies endangering the liberty of all."

The prediction-prevention model appeals to our scientific ethos. In conjunction with the rehabilitative ideal and the medical model, it appeals to our Messianic hopes for correction and cure (that is, most of us feel sympathy for the blatantly mad). The punishment-deterrence model appeals to our Puritan heritage and our fear of the approach of 1984. Many of us feel hostility for the blatantly bad. Radical criminology appeals to our sense of equality, freedom, and fair play. Some of us feel indignation for those who have been blatantly had.

Perhaps, as Szasz cautions, we cannot have it all ways. But hopefully we can achieve some sense of balance. The history of both the mental health and criminal justice systems has too often been one of leaping from bandwagon to bandwagon. Two recent publications are both humbling and stimulating in this regard. The first is an article by John Monahan entitled "Prediction Research and the Emergency Commitment of Dangerous Mentally Ill Persons: A Reconsideration." In this article Monahan says:

> A careful reading of the prediction research reported to date does not support the unqualified conclusion that the accurate prediction of violence is impossible under all circumstances or that psychiatrists, psychologists, and others will invariably overpredict its occurrence by several orders of magnitude. . . .
>
> Rather than demonstrating that all forms of violence prediction are "doomed" (as I have previously stated), a more discerning reading of the existing research suggests that it demonstrates the invalidity only of predictions made in one context that an individual will be violent in another, very different context.[40]

The second reference is an article by Judith Wilks and Robert Martinson entitled "Is the Treatment of Criminal Offenders Really Necessary?" In it the authors state:

> The suggestion that we have perhaps reached the point of diminishing return in regard to treatment, should not be taken to mean that the only alternative to be pursued if we seriously intend to reduce the crime rate is mandatory incarceration. This is not the only logical alternative to treatment. And a pox on those who speak as if it is.[41]

The ebb and flow go on, seeking balance rather than opposition between the criminal and the mental patient, the offender and the state, punishment and treatment, free will and determinism, rights and responsibilities, and health and freedom.

NOTES

1. B. A. Bukatamin, J. L. Foy, and E. DeGrazia, "What Is Competency to Stand Trial?" American Journal of Psychiatry 127 (1971): 1225-29.

2. Laboratory of Community Psychiatry, Harvard Medical School, Competency to Stand Trial and Mental Illness (Washington, D.C.: National Institute of Mental Health, 1973).

3. Jackson v. Indiana 406 U.S. 715 (1972).

4. Robert A. Burt, "Of Mad Dogs and Scientists: The Perils of the 'Criminal-Insane,'" University of Pennsylvania Law Review 123 (1974): 273-74.

5. Robert Burt and Norval Morris, "A Proposal for Abolition of the Incompetency Plea," University of Chicago Law Review 40 (1972) 66-95.

6. Alan Stone, Mental Health and Law: A System in Transition (Washington, D.C.: National Institute of Mental Health, 1975), p. 212.

7. Laboratory of Community Psychiatry, op cit., p. 4.

8. Henry Weihofen, Insanity as a Defense in Criminal Law (Fairlawn: Oxford University Press, 1933), p. 9.

9. Rita Simon, The Jury and the Defense of Insanity (Boston: Little, Brown, 1967).

10. Alan Dershowitz, "Abolishing the Insanity Defense: The Most Significant Feature of the Administrations Proposed Criminal Code—An Essay," Criminal Law Bulletin 9 (1973): 435, note 4; Group for the Advancement of Psychiatry, Pennsylvania Criminal Responsibility and Psychiatric Expert Testimony, Report 5, 1954; Robert Waelder, "Psychiatry and the Problem of Criminal Responsibility," University of Pennsylvania Law Review 101 (1952): 378; Seymour Halleck, Psychiatry and the Dilemmas of Crime (New York: Harper & Row, 1967); Thomas Szasz, Psychiatric Justice (New York: Macmillan, 1965); Dershowitz, op. cit., note 4; Katz and Goldstein, "Abolish the Insanity Defense—Why Not?" Yale Law Journal 72 (1963): 853; As quoted in Stone, op. cit., 218-19.

11. C. R. Jeffrey, Criminal Responsibility and Mental Disease (Springfield, Ill.: Charles Thomas, 1967), p. 278.

12. Burt, op. cit., p. 282-83.

13. Stone, op. cit., p. 222.

14. Millard v. Cameron, 373 F.2d 468 (1966).

15. Specht v. Patterson, 386 U.S. 605 (1967).

16. Stone, op. cit., p. 192.

17. Burt, op. cit., p. 286.

18. Rouse v. Cameron, 373 F.2d 451 (1966).

19. Wyatt v. Stickney, 325 F. Supp 781 (M.D. Ala. 1971), 344 F. Supp 373 (1972), 344 F. Supp 387 (1972), p. 785.

20. Kaimowitz v. Michigan Department of Mental Health, 42 L. W. 2064.

21. Alan Meisel, Loren Roth, and Charles Lidz, "Toward a Model of the Legal Doctrine of Informed Consent," American Journal of Psychiatry 134, no. 3 (1977): 288.

22. Wyatt v. Stickney, 344 F. Supp 373, at 380.

23. Stone, op. cit., p. 105.

24. Kaimowitz v. Michigan Department of Mental Health, 42 L. W. 2063.

25. Statute, "Beyond the Cuckoo's Nest: A Proposal for Federal Regulation of Psychosurgery," Harvard Journal on Legislation 12(1975 627.

26. Ibid.

27. Durham v. U.S., 214 F. 2d 862, 876(D. C. Cir. 1954), quoting Holloway v. U.S. 148 F. 2d 665, 666-67(D. C. Cir. 1945).

28. Frank Ochberg and Bertram Brown, "Mental Health and the Law: Partners in Advancing Human Rights," University of Pennsylvania Law Review 123 (1974): 507.

29. S. Brakel and R. Rock, The Mentally Disabled and the Law (Chicago: University of Chicago Press, 1971), p. 416.

30. Burt, op. cit., p. 289.

31. Ochberg and Brown, op. cit., p. 506.

32. Nicholas Kittrie, The Right to Be Different (Baltimore: Johns Hopkins University Press, 1971).

33. B. Lipton, R. Martinson, and J. Wilks, The Effectiveness of Correctional Treatment (New York: Praeger, 1975).

34. See Franklin Zimring and Gordon Hawkins, Deterrence: The Legal Threat in Crime Control (Chicago: University of Chicago Press, 1973); Norval Morris, Future of Imprisonment (Chicago: University of Chicago Press, 1974); Ernest van Den Haag, Punishing Criminals: Concerning a Very Old and Painful Question (New York: Basic Books, 1975); and Andrew Von Hirsch, Doing Justice: The Choice of Punishments, Report of the Committee for the Study of Incarceration (New York: Hill & Wang, 1976).

35.. Seymour Halleck, The Politics of Therapy (New York: Science House, 1971).

36. Richard Quinney, Class, State, and Crime (New York: David McKay, 1977), p. 13.

37. Ibid., p. 23.

38. Alexander Liazos, "School, Alienation, and Delinquency," Crime and Delinquency 24, no. 3 (1978): 355-70.

39. Ibid., p. 369.

40. John Monahan, "Prediction Research and the Emergency Commitment of Dangerous Mentally Ill Persons: A Reconsideration," American Journal of Psychiatry 135 (1978): 198-201. See also John Monahan, "The Prevention of Violence" in Community Mental Health and the Criminal Justice System. ed. John Monahan (Elmsford: Pergamon, 1976), pp. 13-34, 198, and 199.

41. Judith Wilks and Robert Martinson, "Is the Treatment of Criminal Offenders Really Necessary," Federal Probation 40 (1976): 3-9.

II

THE OHIO
EVALUATION
PROJECT

INTRODUCTION

Part II of this book reports the findings of the Ohio forensic services evaluation project and discusses the impact of the research in program planning. In Chapter 6, Dee Roth, chief of the Office of Program Evaluation and Research of the Ohio Department of Mental Health and Mental Retardation, relates events that led to the evaluation project. She also discusses the ensuing conference and outlines policy and program changes in forensic services implemented subsequent to the research.

Chapter 7 describes the design and methodology of the evaluation. The findings of the project are discussed in Chapters 8 and 9, and the conclusions are presented in Chapter 10. In all, the data support the development of community-based programs for mentally disordered offenders, but they suggest that numerous problems continue to confront professionals and administrators attempting to articulate mental health and criminal justice services. It should be noted that the findings are presented here as they were formulated at the time the project was completed.

The final chapter of the book is the conference presentation of Timothy Moritz, director of the Ohio Department of Mental Health and Mental Retardation. In the context of the recent history of forensic services in Ohio, Moritz addresses existing trends and plans for the future in both service delivery and legislative reform.

6

COMMUNITY-BASED
MENTAL HEALTH SERVICES FOR
THE CRIMINAL JUSTICE SYSTEM:
THE OHIO EXPERIENCE

Dee Roth

The research described in Chapters 7 through 10, and the subsequent course of action by a state mental health department discussed in Chapter 11, represents the best kind of interaction between science and public policy. The 1960s and early 1970s saw two separate lines of development in the Ohio Department of Mental Health and Mental Retardation that finally coalesced in the launching of a massive study into an entire segment of the service delivery system. One line of development was in forensic psychiatric services, where a number of forces were pushing toward a more community-based system of treatment. The second line of development was taking place in research, where there was a shift in focus from basic science to studies of a more applied nature.

In 1972 the Ohio Department of Mental Hygiene and Corrections was split into two entities, the Department of Rehabilitation and Correction and the Department of Mental Health and Mental Retardation, with the latter, through its Division of Forensic Psychiatry, bearing responsibility for diagnostic and treatment services to mentally disturbed offenders. The major setting for forensic services was Lima State Hospital, the facility for the "criminally insane," in which almost all evaluation, treatment, care, and custody for forensic clients took place. When the 1960s came to an end, Lima State Hospital was overpopulated, understaffed, and very expensive, both for the state and for courts and communities that sent individuals there for evaluations.

National trends at this time were moving toward community-based services as an alternative to institutionalization for almost all service needs, and Ohio borrowed from the experience of other states and established its first community forensic center in 1971. By early

1974, six state-supported community forensic centers were in operation, with a variety of funding structures. Early indications from those most closely involved with the centers were that they were successful in meeting their goals and in serving the needs of both clients and courts.

At the same time that new approaches were being developed in forensic psychiatry, a quiet revolution was taking place in the department's research program. In the 1960s the flourishing of basic research at the state level reflected the national priority and prominence of basic research. At the beginning of the 1970s, however, we took a critical look at our research program and decided that it was having little impact upon what we were attempting to do in the areas of patient care and client services. At that time we were in the middle of several new thrusts: services were being developed in local communities for general mental health as well as forensic clients; hospital populations were dropping, although recidivism was increasing; and we were experimenting with various structural arrangements to better administer an array of services in a large and diverse state. However, the existing research program offered no answers to assist us with the plethora of dilemmas of a mental health system entering the 1970s.

After substantial deliberation and a statewide research needs-assessment study, the decision was made to phase out the basic science program and replace it with one that focused on questions of applied mental health. In 1972 the Office of Program Evaluation and Research (OPER) was created within the Division of Mental Health out of the dual concern that relevant research be pursued and that ongoing evaluation be developed that would become an operating part of every level of the system. OPER subsequently promulgated a set of research guidelines that indicated ten areas of priority funding—one of which was forensic psychiatry—and that established a procedure of exhaustive technical and administrative review for the competitive awarding of research grants. Over the next biennium a wide-ranging program of applied mental health research became operative within the division.

In 1974 the department had a general sense that the new community forensic centers were functioning well, but we lacked the kind of systematic knowledge that would enable us to evaluate the centers' performances as individual units and to assess their impact on the overall forensic services delivery system. In that year OPER began a series of discussions with the Ohio State University Program for the Study of Crime and Delinquency (PSCD) around the possibility of a systems analysis of the delivery of forensic services throughout the state. PSCD was awarded a contract for a multiyear, multipurpose study that included separate analyses of individual centers as well as an integrative comprehensive analysis of the total state system, with direct implications for future program planning, development, and administration at the state level.

Systematic evaluation reports on six community forensic centers were presented to OPER by the end of 1975, along with an overall version, The Forensic Centers of Ohio: An Integrative Report. These reports were shared with the administrators of centers that were studied, with officials responsible for the forensic area, and with district managers, who are the chief administrative officials responsible for the overall planning and delivery of mental health services within ten geographic regions of the state. In the spring of 1976 the researchers presented OPER with the overall analysis of the forensic system, An Analysis of the Forensic Psychiatric Services Delivery System in Ohio: A Final Report.

The final report was widely disseminated throughout the state and was reviewed by the top administrative staff of the department. In addition to its confirmation of the utility and success of the community forensic centers, the research highlighted a number of issues that remain problematic, including the provision of services in the least restrictive environment; the adequate definition of the dangerousness level of clients; the appropriate domains of the civil mental health, forensic, and criminal justice systems and their coordination; and the efficacy of various types of treatment.

In order to further disseminate the results of the study, and to address the problems highlighted, the forensic centers' research became the subject for discussion at an all-day conference in Columbus in May 1977. The conference brought together three nationally known experts and drew an overflow crowd of more than 400 of Ohio's professionals in mental health, criminal justice, and the forensic system, including administrators, psychiatrists, psychologists, social workers, judges, attorneys, probation officers, parole officers, and academicians. This audience heard Thomas S. Szasz, Seymour L. Halleck, and Nicholas J. Kittrie discuss the structural and clinical problems inherent in the area of forensic psychiatry and suggest possible solutions. Department Director Timothy B. Moritz described the future plans for the development of forensic services in Ohio.

Since the execution of the research project and the dissemination of its findings, a number of new developments have occurred in the forensic service delivery system that were directly recommended by the final report. As of August 1978, Ohio has a network of 16 community forensic centers across the state. The primary developmental funding source for these centers has been the Law Enforcement Assistance Administration, but the centers are being picked up by state and local funding as their federal budgets are phased out. The existence of the centers has had a significant impact on their clients as well as on Lima State Hospital, since referral to Lima is no longer necessary from any part of the state. Active communication among the centers is being maintained through the center directors' association and through a coordinator in the Division of Forensic Psychiatry.

Landmark legislation (Sub. H.B. 565), which incorporates several policy recommendations made by the research, was made final and signed in August 1978. The legislation repeals Ohio's Ascherman Act, which allowed for the indefinite commitment of individuals designated as psychopaths. Sub. H.B. 565 also designates for the first time the community forensic centers, rather than Lima State Hospital, as the mandated setting for court-ordered evaluations for competency to stand trial and for not guilty by reason of insanity. Lima will now do inpatient evaluations of clients only upon referral from a forensic center, after an outpatient evaluation has already been performed. The legislation also designates the Department of Mental Health and Mental Retardation as the licensing agent for forensic centers, and the Division of Forensic Psychiatry is currently assembling a task force to develop an implementation manual for the legislative and administrative rules for the certification of community facilities.

Over the long term, the department plans to phase out Lima State Hospital and build smaller institutional forensic psychiatric units on the grounds of existing state hospitals. Architectural plans have been drawn up on three such forensic units, and the facilities' programmatic components are in the active planning stage.

From an administrative perspective, we feel that research is a viable and necessary tool in our mandated tasks of treatment and prevention. By bringing the rigor of good research methodology to bear on the kinds of pressing problems facing us as a mental health system approaching the 1980s, we can develop new knowledge that will enable us to improve current treatment, to develop new strategies and techniques, and to achieve a better understanding of the patterns of mental illness and mental health. The study outlined in this book, and the larger issues it highlights, provides an excellent example of successful public policy research and its applications.

7

COMMUNITY VERSUS INSTITUTIONAL CARE: AN EVALUATION PROJECT

Whenever people gather together to live in communities, it becomes necessary to control those who would do harm to themselves or others in the group. As this country has grown it has developed complex systems of regulations and regulators to deal with those who seriously violate group norms. These violators come in all varieties, but for the most part they are identified as either mentally ill or criminal and are then handled by the system devised for their care and control. Not infrequently, however, the question arises as to whether the violating individual is mentally ill or criminal or both. This question is an extremely important one because it helps determine what system of processing and disposition the individual will encounter. Since the distinction is significant, it is not surprising that society has devised a social structure to deal with this special problem area as well.

Recent years have witnessed an accelerated interest in the mental health and criminal justice fields and especially in their common ground, which has been known most widely as "forensic psychiatry." Particularly noticeable have been the following developments:

1. There has been a growth in research and theoretical debate surrounding the definition and management of criminal insanity, incompetency, and sexual psychopathy. While insanity statutes have been in existence in the United States since the introduction of the M'Naghten rule in 1843 (and indeed were preshadowed by an irresistible impulse clause introduced into Ohio law in 1834, [1] it was not until the midtwentieth century that dissatisfaction with the variants of M'Naghten-Irresistible Impulse rules resulted in the development of new tests of criminal responsibility. In a 1954 decision, Judge

David Bazelon established the <u>Durham</u> rule in the U.S. Court of Appeals for the District of Columbia, which was closely followed by the American Law Institute Model Penal Code test in 1962.[2] But perhaps the best indicator of the intensity of the dilemma is the fact that the <u>Durham</u> rule survived only 18 years, reversed in June 1972, ironically by the same court (D.C. Circuit) that originally defined it.[3]

While rules for criminal incompetency originated in common law and have come down through the years almost wholly unchanged, critical analysis of their definition and use has recently emerged. A good deal of criticism has been directed toward many issues, ranging from the misuse of criminal incompetency proceedings for avoidance of trial, or for finding an "easy way in" to institutions, to the development of checklists for determining incompetency.

The sexual psychopath laws are relatively recent on the national scene, gaining general support in the United States during the middle and late 1930s. Like the <u>Durham</u> rule, however, sexual psychopath statutes were not in existence very long before they came under serious criticisms. Debates have often focused on the definition of psychopathy, the relationship between psychopathy and sexual deviance, and the indeterminate commitment to institutions for the criminally insane incumbent upon conviction under sexual psychopath laws.[4]

2. There was the emergence in the 1960s of a strong interdisciplinary emphasis in the social and behavioral sciences. Psychologists, sociologists, social workers, and others have since been stressing the importance of crossing over into one another's fields in both "pure" theorizing and "applied" research and fieldwork. Especially visible in the literature is the conceptualization of both criminality and mental illness under the rubric of "deviance." Students of deviance have been devoting a great deal of attention to identifying commonalities and differences among the various "deviance definition and management systems," especially the mental health and criminal justice systems. These latter two systems interface in the arena of forensic psychiatry, and thus it is not too surprising that emerging studies in deviance have often focused on this arena. A recurrent theme coming out of this work is that the philosophies and practices of the mental health and criminal justice systems are frequently contradictory. This realization has moved many professionals in the forensic area toward cooperative endeavors.

3. There was the crystallization in the 1960s of a deep disenchantment with institutionalization as a deviance-management technique and a subsequent espousal of community-based services as a viable alternative. The community mental health movement has been the vanguard of short-term intensive-care hospitalization and only as a last resort to treatment in the community. Similarly, community-based corrections have advocated the replacement of incarceration,

whenever feasible, by halfway houses, furlough programs, and, of course, probation and parole. While the limitations of community-based services have lately received attention, the rationale for alternatives to institutionalization continues to appear valid.

4. There has been renewed debate in the criminal justice system between proponents of a rehabilitative orientation and advocates of a punitive approach. Until recently, the trend for decades had been a general movement from the latter to the former. Evidence in the near past includes the "decriminalizing" and "medicalizing" of various forms of deviant behavior (such as drug and alcohol abuse, prostitution, and homosexuality) and the increasing representation of clinical personnel in the process of administering criminal justice. On the recent scene, however, rehabilitation has been conceptualized by some as an invasion of mental, physical, or environmental integrity, and calls have been issued for an offender's "right to punishment."

5. There has been the increasingly frequent suggestion that "dangerousness" and "probability of repeating" should be the states' main barometers in defining and managing deviants. Disenchantment with the results of previous corrective and curative efforts, plus growing sociolegal concern with constitutional rights of institutionalized persons, led in the 1960s to a focus on the deviant's "threat to the community." This turning of attention from intrapsychic to behavioral variables in large part gained momentum with recent court decisions guaranteeing the "right to treatment," and at the same time (perhaps in response) the right to refuse treatment has also emerged as a critical issue.

Until quite recently most states have met the need for psychiatric evaluation and treatment of the criminal offender by establishing a forensic institution that is usually identified by a label like "state hospital for the criminally insane" or some equally ominous nomenclature. It appears, however, that now some alternatives are being tried. A final trend that logically derives from the above-identified developments (indeed to many professionals the most significant development of all) is the recent emergence of community-based court clinics or forensic psychiatric centers. In various sectors of the nation, community-based clinical services have been designed to meet the mental health evaluative and treatment needs of the criminal justice system, from pretrial through presentence to probation and parole. While such programs were established as early as 1909,[5] and an interest in clinics was evident in the 1920s and 1930s, they have not been a major part of forensic services until rather recently. A national survey of court psychiatric clinics conducted by the eminent forensic psychiatrist, Manfred Guttmacher, was published in 1966. Just a decade ago it identified only 27 court clinics in the United

States.[6] Although only a few states moved in this direction, an indicator of developments between 1966 and the present is that, by 1974, the state of Massachusetts had 30 court clinics in operation.[7]

While three clinics listed in the 1966 Guttmacher survey were in Ohio, these were funded and operated as a part of the local court system they served. In 1971 state mental health officials in Ohio also began to experiment with the community clinic as an alternative forensic service delivery unit. Studies published in 1976 and 1977 indicate that the state of Tennessee has also been piloting such clinics.[8] Although there is no recent national survey to document the size of the trend, the indicators suggest that the clinic approach is being tested at least in some areas of the country.

COMMUNITY CENTERS ESTABLISHED

Until recently in Ohio, evaluation and treatment of the mentally ill offender have been largely conducted at Lima State Hospital. This institution was opened in 1914 and subsequently became the evaluation center for mentally disabled offenders throughout the state.[9]

In line with contemporary thinking, however, in 1971 the Ohio Department of Mental Health and Mental Retardation, Division of Forensic Psychiatry, inaugurated a program to support community-based forensic centers. Although the study reported in this book includes only six of the earliest established centers, those in Akron, Cincinnati, Columbus, Dayton, Hamilton (Butler County), and Toledo, other centers have been opened since the evaluation project. All of the centers have been funded to a greater or lesser extent through the state of Ohio Division of Forensic Psychiatry with monies provided by local, state, and federal sources.* Like their counterparts across the nation, Ohio's forensic psychiatric centers have been designed to ease many of the problems in the articulation of mental health and criminal justice systems. More specifically, it was anticipated that the forensic psychiatric centers would:

supplement the evaluative and treatment services of Lima State Hospital (LSH);
improve the quality of evaluations and treatment conducted at LSH by virtue of lightening its caseload;

---

*The major impetus for the development of the centers came from the availability of federal money from the Law Enforcement Assistance Administration distributed in Ohio through the Administration of Justice Division of the Ohio Department of Economic and Community Development.

provide evaluations to the court in a shorter period of time than required by LSH;

provide more thorough and comprehensive evaluation reports than can be provided by LSH by virtue of greater accessibility to offenders' families, friends, employers, and other social agencies;

prevent the negative impact upon the offender and his family of institutionalization at LSH;

prevent the need to reintegrate offenders released from institutional care;

negate the costs incumbent upon institutionalization at LSH;

prevent the social, psychological, and economic disruption to the offender, his family, and the community incumbent upon uprooting him from his home and job;

ease the time and monetary problems incumbent upon expert testimony in court;

provide evaluations, recommendations, and outpatient treatment for probation and parole departments;

provide emergency intervention and consultation services for local detention facilities;

educate and train local social agents in the identification and management of mentally disordered offenders;

identify dangerous or potentially dangerous offenders for the criminal justice system; and

reduce recidivism via accurate evaluations and appropriate recommendations and treatment.

Although these are ambitious goals, the forensic psychiatric centers were designed to meet them as Ohio experimented to find more efficient and economical as well as more humane methods for the management of the mentally disordered offender.

THE EVALUATION PROJECT

From 1972 through 1975 the Ohio Division of Forensic Psychiatry and the Office of Program Evaluation and Research of the Ohio Department of Mental Health and Mental Retardation contracted with the Ohio State University Program for the Study of Crime and Delinquency to evaluate the newly established centers.* The first

*Separate contracts funded this evaluation. The first contracts were negotiated with the Division of Forensic Psychiatry of the Ohio Department of Mental Health and Mental Retardation in 1972 and 1973 to evaluate the Dayton and Toledo centers. Another contract granted

evaluation to be completed was that of the Toledo center; the report was delivered in April 1974. The Dayton report followed in September 1974. The model for evaluation developed by the research team for use in these two earlier reports was duplicated in late 1974 and 1975 at the Akron, Cincinnati, Columbus, and Butler County centers. Each center evaluation produced a separate report and the project was completed with an integrative report that discussed all of the centers. A report that presented an analysis of the total state forensic services delivery system was made final in 1976.* In order to maximize the policy-making impact of the research, in the spring of 1977 the research team presented a statewide conference on forensic issues to foster discussion of the problems in forensic service delivery that were identified in the evaluation study.

The purpose of the evaluation project was to compare the services delivered in local centers with those available to the center communities through previous arrangements with the state institution, LSH. The study was designed to describe the centers' operations and determine if they were meeting the goals identified by the state in its program plan. The model selected for the study compared the centers with each other and with the state institution. Research questions addressed included:

What kinds of clients were being served? How did they differ from those served in the institutional setting? What clients were best served in each setting?

Who referred clients to the centers?

What professional staff were involved in the variety of diagnostic and treatment services? Was there an optimal mix of disciplines for meeting service needs? What were the qualifications of staff members?

What services were provided by community centers? Were these services perceived as adequate by referral agencies?

What were the costs and benefits of using community rather than institutional settings for evaluations?

What coordination and cooperation were necessary to facilitate the most efficient operation of the total state forensic system?

---

through the Office of Program Evaluation and Research of the Ohio Department of Mental Health and Mental Retardation in 1974 funded the study of the other four centers.

*A complete list of the reports prepared in this project is in the Preface.

DATA-COLLECTION PROCEDURES

The project team developed multiple measurement instruments to gather data for and about the various relevant groups: clients, staff, consultants, referral agents, and administrators. A comparative descriptive design was developed that included the following procedures:

1. The collection of hard data on all clients served at the centers along the following dimensions: demographic characteristics; status within the criminal justice system (current charge, court status, prior juvenile and adult record); history of involvement in the mental health system; referral source and reason for referral (psychopathy, competency/sanity, and so on); processing within the center (types of evaluations, for example, psychometric testing, psychiatric interviews, social case histories); evaluations and recommendations of the center; and court disposition. These data were gathered from center files and from municipal and county police, probation department, and court records.

2. The collection of hard data on variables similar to those listed in the first paragraph for a sample of those individuals admitted to LSH for evaluation from the same geographical area served by the center for a period of time encompassing both the lifespan of the center since receipt of state funds and a representative period prior to that time. These data were gathered directly from LSH case records.

3. The collection of objective and attitudinal data through questionnaires and/or interviews of selected center staff members, judges, and probation/parole officers. The staff schedule gathered information on length of employment at the center; distribution of time devoted to administration, evaluations and recommendations, and treatment; and perceptions of the goals and performance of the center, of working relations with referral agents, of typical referrals, of the relation of the center to LSH, and of the strengths and weaknesses of the center. The schedules used with judges and probation/parole officers focused largely on perceptions of the goals and performance of the center.

4. Computer analyses of the above data to determine the comparative statuses of the centers with one another and with LSH with regard to client profiles and cost effectiveness.

5. The formulation of policy recommendations to the Department of Mental Health and Mental Retardation based on the above analyses.

SAMPLING

The study sample included the total forensic client populations of each center from the time of the center's becoming a part of the state program (identified by the receipt of support from the state) to the data collection point.* The number of cases and the period sampled varied from center to center. The total study reviewed 1,799 cases from community centers. The center samples ranged in size from 155 to 536. Data from these centers reflected differing lengths of time in the operation of each center as well, ranging from ten months to 2.5 years (see Table 8.4).

The client samples from each center were compared with a sample of the most recent cases from each center county evaluated at the institutional setting (LSH). The LSH samples ranged in size from 53 to 95. The samples were drawn over four- to five-year periods.

This sampling plan allowed the study to compare a total of 1,799 center clients with 393 LSH clients and also allowed comparisons of each center with the other centers and with an LSH client sample from its own service area.

In addition, samples of center staff, consultants, and referral agents were included in the study. Almost all full-time staff were interviewed in each center. Project personnel were involved in informal discussions with staff throughout the months of data collection. Part-time and consulting staff psychiatrists and psychologists were sampled where appropriate. In each center city, judges, police, detention facility personnel, and a sample of probation and parole officers were contacted.

To provide data for statewide analysis of significant factors in the criminal justice and mental health systems, questionnaires were sent to the following groups: all municipal, common pleas, and county court judges; all superintendents of state mental health institutions; all superintendents of state correctional institutions; all supervisors of state mental health and mental retardation districts; and all county sheriffs who are in charge of county jails.

SOME TERMS

Prior to presenting the findings of the evaluation study it is necessary to define some terms and phrases that will be used in the discussion of mental disability and the criminal law. Some of these terms are common to forensic practitioners across the country; others are unique to Ohio law and its practitioners.

---

*Typically, receipt of state funding is coincidental with the opening of the center. The Cincinnati center is an especially unique exception since it was opened in 1957 but did not begin to receive state monies until 1973.

Competency/Incompetency to Stand Trial

In general the current criteria are those stated in <u>Dusky</u> v. <u>United States</u>.[10] They are basically a restatement of long-standing interpretations in criminal procedures. This opinion says the relevant questions are "whether he has sufficient ability to consult with his lawyer with a reasonable degree of rational understanding, and whether he has a rational as well as factual understanding of the proceedings against him."[11] It is important to note that these criteria allow for the interpretation of what constitutes a reasonable degree of understanding.

Most critics of the court find little fault with the criteria themselves; however, great misinterpretation occurs in the proceedings to determine competency and the disposition of those declared incompetent to stand trial. The issues of who raises the question of competency, how it is determined, how much understanding is necessary, and what provision is made for those incompetent to stand trial are all serious concerns of current jurisprudence and forensic psychiatric practice.

At the time of the project Ohio statutes* provided for incompetency by allowing the issue of "insanity" to be raised before or after trial.[12] The courts interpreted competency by the common criteria; however, the statutory use of the word insanity was confusing to mental health professionals conducting court evaluations.

Not Guilty by Reason of Insanity

The criminal law, strongly rooted in the concept that an individual is culpable when he performs an evil deed of his free will, has made provision for diminished or lack of capacity to freely choose between good and evil with the insanity defense. While statutes vary from state to state, the major tests of insanity provide that at the time the offense was committed the defendant was impaired in one or all of the following ways:

---

*Ohio revised this statute in Amended Substitute House Bill 565 (effective November 1, 1978). The new law provides clearer criteria and procedures for determining competency and evaluating individuals pleading not guilty by reason of insanity. It also repeals the Ascherman Act and establishes new procedures for the transfer of prisoners, parolees, and probationers to the Department of Mental Health and Mental Retardation.

The M'Naghten test: This is the most common standard and basically it says, "the party accused was labouring under such a defect of reason, from disease of the mind, as not to know the nature and quality of the act he was doing; or if he did know it, that he did not know he was doing what was wrong."[13]

The irresistible impulse test: This is not the sole test in any state but is used in conjunction with M'Naghten in many. The idea of irresistible impulse as defined in Davis v. United States[14] is that the defendant is insane if "though conscious of the nature of his act and able to distinguish right from wrong, . . . yet his will, by which I mean the governing power of his mind, has been otherwise than voluntarily so completely destroyed that his actions are not subject to it, but are beyond his control."[15]

The product rule, or the Durham test:[16] Although not currently accepted in most jurisdictions, this standard has had impact on judicial thinking. It holds that "an accused is not criminally responsible if his unlawful act was the product of mental disease or mental defect."[17]

The American Law Institute test: Prepared as a part of the Model Penal Code, the ALI test is gaining wide application. It combines the thinking of the others to some extent. It states: (1) a person is not responsible for criminal conduct if at the time of such conduct as a result of mental disease or defect he lacks substantial capacity either to appreciate the criminality of his conduct or to conform his conduct to the requirements of the law and (2) as noted in the article, the terms "mental disease or defect" do not include an abnormality manifested only by repeated criminal or otherwise antisocial conduct.[18]

The insanity defense allows a court to find a person who has committed an evil act not criminally responsible for the deed and therefore not subject to criminal sanction; while not legally or theoretically necessary, in most jurisdictions the individual is mandatorily confined for treatment of the excusing mental illness or defect that is presumed to have continued.

At the time of the project, the same Ohio statute that covered competency provided for the insanity defense. At that time Ohio courts applied a test of insanity that had the elements of both the M'Naghten test and irresistible impulse. In addition another statute stated the presumption that insanity at the time of the offense continued and mandated commitment.[19]

Psychopathic Offender

The majority of states have statutes that mandate special evaluation and disposition of persons who commit certain crimes; these are usually sex offenders, but the statutes frequently are extended to others identified as habitual or psychopathic offenders.

The term psychopath is imprecise and difficult to apply. While many mental health professionals hedge on the use of the term, the law has utilized it. Psychopaths are persons characterized by Cleckley in 1964 as being superficially charming, intelligent, untruthful and insincere, egocentric, lacking in good judgment, unable to form interpersonal relationships or love, and lacking remorse or shame.[20] Cleckley made the point that these individuals look and behave like the average person; however, the psychopath is ungenuine. Even though Cleckley felt he had identified the syndrome, both mental health and legal critics currently consider the term "too vague for judicial use."[21]

The effect of these laws is to redefine criminals to a special mental health status in order to hospitalize them for indefinite periods of time. These statutes vary greatly in their definition and implementation; however, they are all to a great extent based on the assumption that psychiatric or psychological treatment can effect a cure in the offender. Implicitly they have resulted in the long-term confinement of offenders who are particularly fearful to the public.

Ascherman Act

The Ascherman Act (2947.25 of the Ohio Revised Code) was the psychopathic offender statute in Ohio at the time of the project.* Named for the legislator who is mainly responsible for fostering its passage, this law provided for a psychiatric examination before sentence to determine the individual's mental condition. If the court found, after the report from examining experts, that the person was mentally ill, mentally retarded, or a psychopathic offender, it could order the individual committed to the jurisdiction of the Department of Mental Health and Mental Retardation for an indefinite period.

NOTES

1. State v. Thompson, Wright's Ohio Rep. 617 (1834).
2. Durham v. United States, 214 F.2d 862 (D.C. Cir. 1954); American Law Institute, Model Penal Code 4.01 (1962).

---

*The Ascherman Act was repealed by Am. Sub. H.B. 565, effective November 1, 1978.

3. United States v. Brawner, 471 F.2d 969 (D.C. Cir. 1972).

4. Aldo Piperno, "A Socio-Legal History of the Psychopathic Offender Legislation in the United States" (Ph.D. diss., Ohio State University, 1974).

5. In 1909 William Healy opened an advisory court clinic in the Cook County Juvenile Court of Chicago. The first adult court clinic was established in the magistrate's court of Chicago in 1914. See M. Guttmacher and H. Weihofen, Psychiatry and the Law (New York: Norton, 1952), p. 261.

6. Manfred Guttmacher, "Adult Psychiatric Court Clinics," in Crime, Law and Corrections, ed. Ralph Slovenko (Springfield, Ill.: Charles Thomas, 1966), pp. 479-93.

7. Paul Lipsitt, "The Screening and Assessment of Competency to Stand Trial," seminar on the Mentally Ill Offender: Incompetency and Insanity, Cleveland, February 1974.

8. See Joyce K. Laben and Lona Davis Spencer, "Decentralization of Forensic Services," Community Mental Health Journal 12 (1976): 405-14; Joyce K. Laben et al., "Reform from the Inside: Mental Health Evaluations of Competency to Stand Trial," Journal of Community Psychology 5 (1977): 52-62.

9. Fifth Annual Report of the Ohio Board of Administrators (State of Ohio, 1916), p. 15.

10. Dusky v. United States, 362 U.S. 405 (1960)(per curiam).

11. Ibid.

12. Ohio Revised Code, Sec. 2945.37.

13. Daniel M'Naghten Case, 10 Clark & Fin, 200, 210-211, 8 Eng. Rep. 718, 722-723 (1843).

14. Davis v. United States, 165 U.S. 373.

15. Ibid., at 378 (1897)(Federal Rule).

16. This test was originally formulated in a New Hampshire case, State v. Jones, 50 N.H. 369, 9 Am. R. 242 (1871).

17. Durham v. United States, op. cit.

18. American Law Institute, Model Penal Code (proposed official draft), 1962, 4.01.

19. Ohio Revised Code, Sec. 2945.39.

20. Hervey Cleckley, The Mask of Sanity (St. Louis: Mosby, 1964), pp. 362-64.

21. A. Stone, Mental Health and Law: A System in Transition (Washington, D.C.: National Institute of Mental Health, 1975), p. 183.

8

FINDINGS:
THE COMMUNITY FORENSIC CENTERS

Data were gathered on six community forensic centers in the
state of Ohio. All of the centers are located in major metropolitan
areas. Two are in the northern part of the state (Toledo and Akron),
two are in the central section (Dayton and Columbus), and the remaining two are in the southwestern corner (Butler County and Cincinnati).

Three of the centers—Butler, Cincinnati, and Toledo—provide
services solely to their home counties, although the Toledo center
also provided services to an adjacent county during its early days of
operation. The Columbus center serves one county in addition to its
home county, and the Akron center serves two additional counties.
The Dayton center provides services to the largest geographical area,
an eight-county region.

The Toledo center has been the longest in operation, first receiving clients in July 1971. The Butler center has the shortest lifespan, having opened in February 1974. The Akron center began taking
clients in November 1972, and both Columbus and Dayton in January
1973. The Cincinnati center is unique since it has served municipal
court referrals since 1957 but common pleas cases only since July
1973. All the following data regarding the Cinncinati center are restricted to the common pleas referrals seen since that time.

CENTERS' OPERATION AND SERVICE

Funding for the establishment and operation of the six centers
has in large measure derived from the Law Enforcement Assistance
Administration (LEAA). In Ohio the state planning agency responsible
for dispersing these monies is the Administration of Justice Division

of the Department of Economic and Community Development. Typically, funds for the forensic centers flow from the Administration of
Justice Division through the Ohio Department of Mental Health and
Mental Retardation. Some of the centers are funded solely by LEAA
monies, while others receive substantial monetary support at the local level. The latter pattern is more characteristic of the older
centers.

Generally speaking, the centers are mandated to provide services to a wide variety of criminal justice agencies including common
pleas, municipal, and county courts; common pleas and municipal
probation departments; parole authorities; and local detention facilities. Some also provide services to juvenile courts, mayor's courts,
probate courts, and federal district courts. Most center directors
define their target populations very broadly, and most maintain that
the centers receive few inappropriate referrals. Referrals include
pretrial, presentence, and postsentence cases. Reasons for referral
cover the gamut, though they can be roughly categorized into two
groups: evaluation and treatment. Referrals for evaluation include
evaluation of competency to stand trial; of sanity at the time of alleged
commission of the act; of candidacy as a mentally ill, mentally retarded, or psychopathic offender; of drug dependency; of dangerousness; of probability of repeating; of probation risk; of amenability to
treatment; plus many others. Evaluation for candidacy as a mentally
ill, mentally retarded, or psychopathic offender is legislatively mandated for persons convicted of a variety of personal offenses, especially sexual offenses and offenses against children. Such an evaluation can also be ordered at the judge's discretion for persons convicted
of any other offense. The statute governing these evaluations is commonly known in Ohio as the Ascherman Act, after the senator who
sponsored the legislation.[1] To avoid the unwieldiness of the phrase
"evaluation for candidacy as a mentally ill, mentally retarded, or
psychopathic offender," these evaluations shall hereafter be referred
to simply as Ascherman evaluations.

All six centers are processing this broad spectrum of evaluation types, though in differing proportions. The procedures employed
in conducting evaluations also vary somewhat but are basically very
similar. Most centers compile social histories, conduct clinical interviews, and perform psychological testing on the bulk of their clients. Psychological testing includes assessment of intellectual
functioning, personality tests, and measures of neurological dys-
functioning. Some vocational testing is also employed. Evaluations
are conducted both in the offices of the centers and their consultants
and in detention facilities. Some centers have large full-time staffs
and are very team-oriented in their approach, others rely heavily on
consultants who function very independently. All six centers compile

written reports regarding their evaluation results for the referral agents. Expert testimony in court is the exception rather than the rule at all centers.

Some center directors express a serious need for inpatient facilities of some sort for their more severely disturbed clients. On the other hand, other directors express little if any desire for institutional beds. Correlatively, some centers occasionally employ local civil inpatient facilities, while others do not. Perceived needs for and actual use of local inpatient facilities do not differ simply on the availability of such units. The issue is much more complex and is intimately related to endemic hostilities between the criminal justice system and the mental health system. The majority of centers are having or have had problems with the unwillingness of civil mental health facilities to accept forensic clients. Time and again the research team was told by center personnel that "civil mental health won't touch clients involved in the criminal justice system with a ten-foot pole."

There is considerable debate among the staff members of the various centers about the appropriate role of treatment (as opposed to evaluation) services. Some directors believe that the provision of treatment services is equal in importance to conducting evaluations. Others believe that treatment is a legitimate activity for the centers but assign it a much lower priority than evaluation services. Still other directors believe that treatment is not appropriately included in the mandate of the centers. This disagreement is in some degree the result of differing interpretations of the provisions of state funding contracts. As local funding sources are generated to replace decreasing federal support, it can be anticipated that centers will offer services that respond to local definitions of desirable ones. In the meantime, one center's caseload is 50 percent evaluation and 50 percent treatment, while another center treated only 4 of 300 clients seen in a 17-month period. The treatment that is being conducted includes both individual and group psychotherapy.

Besides evaluation and treatment, the centers are also designed to provide emergency intervention services to local detention facilities and consultation and education to all sectors of the local criminal justice system. All centers have been performing these services, though to greater or lesser degrees. At some centers consultation and education are largely informal and narrow in scope; at others formal training programs dealing with a broad spectrum of forensic issues have been developed.

Staffing patterns at the six centers are diverse. The directors of the Butler, Dayton, and Toledo centers have master's degrees in social work (M.S.W.) and the directors of the Akron and Columbus centers have M.A. degrees in psychology. The Cincinnati center is administered by an M.D. clinical director and an M.S.W. clinic co-ordinator. The total number of professional employees ranges from 20 at the Cincinnati center to 7 at the Columbus center. With the exception of Toledo, consultants and part-time employees are greater in number than full-time personnel. Full-time personnel are com-prised of psychologists and social workers, especially the latter. The bulk of psychiatric input is on a consulting basis.

CLIENT CASELOADS

One of the most significant findings of this study is that the community forensic centers have experienced steady increases over their lifespans in the number of clients served. The caseload data are presented in Table 8.1, which includes both the actual number of clients and the rate per 100,000 of the center's home-county popula-tion. Although some centers serve additional counties, the population figures are restricted to the home counties since the vast majority of clients seen to date at all six centers are from the local county.

The decline in caseload for the Toledo center between 1974 and 1975 is more apparent than real. As indicated in Table 8.1, the To-ledo figures for the last three years do not include treatment cases, yet the director reports that these cases had risen by the spring of 1975 to comprising 50 percent of the total caseload. In any event, the Toledo center overall displays the highest rate of clients per 100,000 of the population. The lowest rate, on the other hand, is found at the Cincinnati center. Between these extremes, the other centers' rank order from high to low is Butler, Columbus, Dayton, and Akron.

To fully interpret these data, they must be analyzed within the larger context of the total forensic psychiatric service delivery sys-tem in the state of Ohio. While this analysis is presented in detail in Chapter 9, a preview of some of the findings will give a better per-spective to the caseload data in Table 8.1. Of special interest is the impact of the centers on the state institution for mentally disordered offenders, Lima State Hospital (LSH); which prior to the establishment of the centers provided both evaluation and long-term treatment/con-finement (indefinite commitment) services for the whole state.

The number of examination referrals and indefinite commitments to LSH from the six center counties between 1968 and 1974 are con-tained in Table 8.2. The most notable finding presented in this table appears to be the dramatic shift in the relative percents of evaluation referrals and indefinite commitments for all center counties combined between the 1968-71 time frame and the period 1972-74. Between 1968 and 1971, examination referrals outnumbered indefinite commit-ments approximately two to one. This situation was in part due to the

TABLE 8.1

Client Frequencies and Rates per 100,000 Population for the Six Forensic Centers, 1971–75

Center and Home-County Population	1971		1972		1973		1974		1975[a]	Projected Total, 1975	
	Fre-quency	Rate	Fre-quency	Rate	Fre-quency	Rate	Fre-quency	Rate	Fre-quency	Fre-quency	Rate
Akron (November 1974) 553,371	—	—	3[b]	.54[c]	98	17.71	198	35.78	130	260	46.98
Butler (February 1974) 226,207	—	—	—	—	—	—	124	54.82	80	160	70.73
Cincinnati (July 1973) 923,205	—	—	—	—	60	6.50	156	16.90	142	284	30.76
Columbus (January 1973) 833,249	—	—	—	—	194	23.28	306	36.72	224	450	54.00
Dayton (January 1973) 608,413	—	—	—	—	162	26.63	283	46.51	162	324	53.25
Toledo (July 1971) 484,370	71	14.65	268	55.33	400[d]	82.58	433[d]	89.39	184[d]	368	75.97

[a] January–June.
[b] Number of clients.
[c] Rate per 100,000 population.
[d] These figures do not include the treatment cases, which average approximately 75–100 per month.

Source: Compiled by the authors.

123

TABLE 8.2

Admissions to Lima State Hospital by Commitment Type and Calendar Year for Center Counties, 1968–74

Center	1968 Exams	1968 Indef-inites	1969 Exams	1969 Indef-inites	1970 Exams	1970 Indef-inites	1971 Exams	1971 Indef-inites	1972 Exams	1972 Indef-inites	1973 Exams	1973 Indef-inites	1974 Exams	1974 Indef-inites
Akron (November 1972)														
Number	59	34	52	29	41	28	29	20	9	19	3	19	10	20
Percent	63	37	64	36	59	41	59	41	32	68	14	86	33	67
Butler (February 1974)														
Number	36	9	33	13	48	16	32	8	8	6	10	5	2	4
Percent	80	20	72	28	75	25	80	20	57	43	67	33	33	67
Cincinnati (July 1973)														
Number	50	40	70	43	42	28	39	40	15	24	21	33	21	34
Percent	56	44	62	38	60	40	49	51	38	62	39	61	38	62
Columbus (January 1973)														
Number	59	35	53	23	54	35	43	29	3	33	3	39	4	34
Percent	63	37	70	30	61	39	60	40	8	92	7	93	11	89
Dayton (January 1973)														
Number	57	25	63	25	52	26	47	24	13	24	23	31	15	27
Percent	70	30	72	28	67	33	66	34	35	65	43	57	36	64
Toledo (July 1971)														
Number	49	52	45	29	48	31	29	21	10	11	3	14	6	22
Percent	49	51	61	39	61	39	58	42	48	52	18	82	21	79
Total														
Number	310	195	316	162	285	164	219	142	58	117	63	141	58	141
Percent	61	39	66	34	63	37	61	39	33	67	31	69	29	71

Source: Compiled by the author.

124

TABLE 8.3

Admissions to Lima State Hospital by Commitment Type and
Calendar Year for Noncenter Counties, 1968-74

| Year | Exams | | Indefinites | | Total |
	Number	Percent	Number	Percent	Number
1968	354	59	245	41	599
1969	408	67	200	33	608
1970	383	62	231	58	614
1971	281	60	190	40	471
1972	128	49	132	51	260
1973	156	50	153	50	309
1974	159	51	151	49	310
Total	1,869	—	1,302	—	3,171

Source: Compiled by the author.

fact that, in 1971, LSH adopted an extremely restrictive admissions
policy in the wake of severe overcrowding at the institution. A comparison of the respective center opening dates with the 1968-74 admission trends for each of the six center counties suggests, however,
the possible impact of the centers as supplements or alternatives to
LSH.

The suggestion that the centers are in fact accounting for a part
of the reduction in admissions to LSH is buttressed by the data regarding admissions to LSH from noncenter counties. These data are
presented in Table 8.3, which indicates that indefinite referrals to
LSH outweigh evaluation referrals only in 1972, and then only by a
very slight margin. That is, while post-1971 referrals to LSH from
the center counties have been more than two indefinite commitments
for every evaluation, referrals from the noncenter counties have been
almost evenly split between evaluation referrals and indefinite commitments. The centers appear to be providing some of the evaluation
services previously provided by LSH.

USER SATISFACTION

The project research team interviewed or distributed questionnaires to a large number of center staff members and local referral
agents. Overall, successful contacts were made with 51 percent

(N = 52) of the 102 judges solicited and 71 percent (N = 89) of the 126 probation/parole officers. Almost all center staff members were contacted at all six centers; numerous formal and informal discussions occurred during the many months of data collection.

For comparative purposes, variations of the same questions were asked of center staff members and referral agents. Overall responses were very similar at all six centers. When asked about the goals and purposes of the centers, most referral agents revealed an accurate understanding and also the opinion that the centers were essentially achieving their purposes. Similarly, center staff members felt that referral agents generally understood the goals and purposes of the centers. Judges, especially of the common pleas courts, were accorded the greatest understanding and parole officers the least. Mutual perceptions of the quality of working relations followed this same pattern.

With regard to evaluations performed by the centers, referral agents were asked a variety of specific questions that tapped the overall quality of evaluations, whether or not evaluation reports addressed questions posed in referrals, whether evaluators understood statutory questions, whether evaluations were completed in time, and whether evaluation reports were helpful in decision making. The overwhelming majority of responses from referral agents were positive on all these dimensions at all six centers. Referral agents also claimed that the centers' reports were superior in quality to those emanating from LSH. The centers' reports were described as more detailed and comprehensive and easier to understand. In addition, center evaluators were said to be of higher professional caliber and to treat both clients and other professionals with greater respect and courtesy. The questionnaires completed by staff members of the centers conflicted with one of these contentions. Staff members' comments about the legal questions inherent to the basic types of examinations indicated widespread confusion regarding the statutory criteria for Ascherman and competency/sanity candidacy.

Overall, the judges were quite emphatic in their endorsement of the local centers. One judge said, "I have been in this court prior to the formation of our clinic. It took three or four months to get evaluations. Now we get them in 30 days or less. This has been the biggest improvement in our criminal justice system since I have been here." Said another: "I am pleased particularly by the great effort made by the director and his staff to learn about our problems and how they can serve us better."

Less-categorically positive findings came from questionnaires mailed to the sheriffs and superintendents of all local detention facilities in the centers' home counties. To begin with, there were no returns from one county and no responses from the sheriffs of two other counties. Of the three remaining sheriffs, two responded affirmatively when asked if the opening of the local center had resulted in a reduction in transports of offenders to LSH. On the other hand, when asked to check the various resources they employ to deal with mentally disturbed inmates, only 4 (17 percent) of 24 responses referred to the local center. The modal category of responses indicated use of state civil mental hospitals (N = 10, 42 percent). Detention facility personnel were then asked if their needs for psychiatric services were currently being met; 58 percent (N = 7) said no, 42 percent (N = 5) said yes, and 75 percent (N = 9) had the impression that the percentage of offenders in need of psychiatric intervention was increasing. And, finally, when asked if the opening of a court clinic in their area had assisted them in their need for psychiatric intervention services, six (55 percent) answered negatively and five (45 percent) responded affirmatively.

The studies of three of the six centers included attempts to solicit information from potential referral agents who had not in fact used the centers. These nonusers, identified by center records and by conversations with center personnel, were asked to indicate why they had not utilized the available services of the centers. Of the 48 total reasons returned, 29 percent (N = 14) said they had never heard of the center; 23 percent (N = 11) replied that they did not have many cases needing the services provided by the center; another 17 percent (N = 8) reported that the center was too far away (seven of these eight worked in counties adjacent to the centers' home counties). Only five (10 percent) claimed either having heard bad reports or having had bad firsthand experience with the centers.

CLIENTS AND THEIR MOVEMENT THROUGH THE SYSTEM

The research team gathered data from the files of the six centers on all clients whose cases had been completed between the time of the opening of the respective center and the time of the evaluation project. Data were also gathered on samples of evaluation referrals to LSH from the same geographical areas served by the centers; these samples tapped time periods encompassing both the entire lifespan of the respective center and a time frame of equal or greater length immediately prior to the center's opening. Table 8.4 depicts the time frames and the client numbers for all six centers and their corresponding LSH samples.

Demographically, all samples were overall very similar in composition. Data indicated that clients tended to be young, white, male, unmarried, and to have a low level of education and employment.

TABLE 8.4

Project Data Collection Periods and Client Numbers for All Six
Centers and Corresponding LSH Samples

	Center		LSH	
	Time Frame	Client Numbers	Time Frame	Client Numbers
Akron	March 1974– December 1974	156	January 1971– December 1974	55
Butler	November 1973– February 1975	155	January 1970– December 1974	55
Cincin- nati	July 1973– December 1974	218	November 1971– February 1975	53
Columbus	January 1973– December 1974	536	October 1970– December 1974	54
Dayton	January 1973– July 15, 1974	301	January 1971– June 1974	81
Toledo	July 1971– December 1973	433	January 1968– December 1973	95

Source: Compiled by the author.

More specifically, no less than 82 percent of any one sample were
male. In all samples the modal age category was 21–30 years, which
included no less than 41 percent of any one sample. Furthermore, in
seven of the 12 samples, the second highest category was under 21
years of age.

The percentages of whites ranged from 40 to 85, but only two
samples included less than 50 percent, and five samples were at least
74 percent white. While this distribution obviously includes a dispro-
portionate number of blacks compared to the general civilian population, so too does the general criminal justice population from which
these persons were drawn. No more than 40 percent of any one sample were married, and the remaining samples included 32 percent or
fewer married.

Regrettably, no definitive conclusions could be reached concerning histories of prior involvement in the criminal justice and
mental health systems. Although LSH records often include FBI and
local "rap" sheets, unverified self-reports were typically all that were
contained in center files. Data were obtained, however, on clients'
current offenses. "Current offense" is defined as the most recent

offense; in some cases the individual had only been charged with the offense; in others he had been convicted of the offense. Offenses were coded into the following six categories: sexual, nonsexual personal, property, drug, public order, and miscellaneous other.

When clients charged with the first three categories of offenses are combined, they comprise over 90 percent of the LSH samples from five of the six center counties. In contrast, these three categories include no more than 82 percent of any one center sample and as few as 65 percent. Furthermore, the modal category among these three categories is property offenses for five of the six centers, and the sixth center is bimodal between property and sexual offenses. Again in contrast, three of the LSH samples have the modal category of clients under sexual offenses, two under property offenses, and one under nonsexual personal offenses.

These data suggest that, generally speaking, LSH is receiving clients charged with or convicted of more serious offenses than those being referred to the centers. This finding likely reflects a number of variables including the inpatient-outpatient distinction between the facilities and a tendency of referral agents to send less-serious cases to the centers until the latter have established satisfactory "track records."

While the vast majority of the LSH clients are referrals from common pleas courts, referrals to the centers include sizable proportions from municipal courts, probation departments, and (to a lesser extent) parole authorities. There is, nevertheless, considerable variation among centers; the sample from the Dayton center, for example, included 70 percent from the common pleas courts compared with 37 percent of the Butler center sample. Even in the latter instance, however, as in the other five centers, common pleas referrals were the modal category of referrals.

The data regarding reason for referral reveal a similar pattern: the centers overall receive a greater diversity of evaluation requests than does LSH, but substantial variation exists among centers. Thus the referrals to LSH were almost exclusively for Ascherman or competency/sanity evaluations, while reasons for referrals to the centers include varieties of other pre- and postsentence evaluations, evaluations of drug dependency and treatability, general evaluations, and emergency interventions.* Table 8.5 presents the percentages

---

*Evaluations for competency to stand trial and for criminal responsibility at the time of alleged commission of the act cannot be separated in the data since the same statute governs both and since

TABLE 8.5

Percentages of Ascherman and Competency/Sanity Referrals for Six Centers and Lima State Hospital Samples

	Center		Lima State Hospital	
	Percent	Number	Percent	Number
Akron				
Ascherman	17	26	60	33
Competency/sanity	16	24	40	22
Butler				
Ascherman	14	22	75	41
Competency/sanity	9	14	25	14
Cincinnati				
Ascherman	17	38	51	27
Competency/sanity	13	28	49	26
Columbus				
Ascherman	44	235	46	25
Competency/sanity	20	104	41	22
Dayton				
Ascherman	6	17	40	32
Competency/sanity	26	77	57	46
Toledo*				
Ascherman	5	20	78	74
Competency/sanity	4	16	22	21

*The Toledo center was not contracted to perform these evaluations until very late in the data-collection period.

Source: Compiled by the author.

of each sample that were referred for Ascherman and competency/ sanity evaluations.

With the notable exception of Columbus, whose caseload was 44 percent Ascherman, the centers' Ascherman referrals constituted only 17 percent or less of the total caseloads.* Similarly, competency/sanity referrals comprised no greater than 26 percent of the six centers' caseloads. The remaining referrals to the centers were distributed across the categories mentioned above, though the bulk typically fell under the rubric of "general evaluation."

The project research team gathered data on the types of evaluation procedures employed at the six centers and at LSH. Individual clinical interviews, the compilation of social case histories, and psychological testing (of personality, organicity, and intellectual functioning) were found to be typical of all centers and of LSH. The latter facility, in contrast to the centers, was also found to perform substantial numbers of medical and neurological examinations on its clients. This greater diversity of evaluative techniques at LSH was coupled with the administration on the average of greater numbers of interviews and tests. For example, five of the six LSH samples were tested on an average of over three instruments, while the average number of instruments employed at the six centers nowhere surpassed three and was under two at three of the centers. Furthermore, while at least one psychiatric interview is standard operating procedure at LSH, as few as 58 percent of one center's clients were interviewed by a psychiatrist.

On the other hand, the research team has serious and extensive reservations about these data, most of which revolve around the contention that quantity is neither inherently desirable nor synonymous with quality. The greater numbers and varieties of examinations conducted at LSH may represent an indiscriminate "shotgun" approach reflecting inflexibility or a lack of individualization of evaluation techniques to client needs. Furthermore, the professional qualifications of the evaluators must be considered. Data gathered during the Toledo evaluation clearly demonstrated that personnel of the center surpassed their LSH counterparts in this regard. While data addressing

---

court orders for evaluation typically simply referred to the statute number.

*The Columbus center does not accept cases without court orders. Some of these Ascherman cases. may therefore represent referrals that at other centers are categorized generally as "presentence."

this issue were not gathered in the other evaluations there is reason to believe that the Toledo findings are generalizable to the other centers. Indeed, it is unclear from some of the LSH records if the medical doctors conducting the "psychiatric" interviews are in fact psychiatrists or even licensed physicians.

Across the country, institutions for the criminally insane have, of late, come under attack for their inability to attract high-caliber clinicians. Ohio is not unique in this regard, and this was one of many problems that led to the class-action suit filed against LSH in May 1973. In its September 1974 Interim Order, the court hearing the Davis v. Watkins litigation directly addressed this issue in an effort to define what constitutes qualified clinical personnel, stating that "anyone qualifying as a 'qualified mental health professional' must demonstrate a sufficient degree of proficiency in the English language so that they are able to communicate effectively with patients."[2] Besides the communication problem, the employment of recently immigrated clinicians in the forensic psychiatric system could also be criticized from the perspective that defines mental disorders in terms of their larger cultural framework. To the degree mental disorders are caused by or correlated with cultural variables, a clinician not well versed in that culture is seriously hampered in his efforts to evaluate and treat these disorders. Furthermore, the centers' evaluations are frequently conducted on an outpatient basis. As such, the client seen at the center is not uprooted from home or employment, nor does he face the stigma of institutionalization at LSH and the subsequent problems of reintegration into the community upon return. By the same token, center staff are able to observe the client in his natural setting as opposed to the artificial living situation of LSH. This provides center evaluators not only the opportunity to more thoroughly assess the client's interactions with his normal daily environment but also the possibility of consulting directly with the client's significant others, including family, employers, friends, and so on.

Related to all this is the finding that the respective center staffs have close working relationships, formal and informal, with criminal justice referral agents in the area. The two groups are easily accessible to one another and communications are generally good. The existence of the center at the local level saves both time and money incumbent upon transportation of both clients and expert witnesses back and forth between the community and LSH.

In the final analysis, the advantages of the centers appear to far outweigh the finding that LSH administers greater numbers and varieties of examinations.

The research team gathered data on the evaluation results recorded in the files of all six centers and LSH. Some of these evaluation results were explicitly spelled out in reports to referral agents; others were contained in examination summaries that formed the bases for the formal reports. Besides evaluation results addressing specific statutory questions, the most frequently recurring statements were assessments of clients' dangerousness, probation risk, probability of repeating, and amenability to treatment. The studies of all six centers found a proportionately greater number and variety of evaluation results in center files than in the records of the LSH sample.

One of the most notable findings of the study is that evaluation results on the questions of Ascherman candidacy (as mentally ill, mentally retarded, or psychopathic offenders) and competency/sanity differed little between the centers and LSH. Evaluators from both sectors were more likely than not to find clients as competent/sane or as inappropriately included under the Ascherman rubric. Of those referred to the centers for evaluation under the Ascherman statute, 72 percent were evaluated as not Ascherman candidates; this compares with 63 percent referred to LSH. Only one center, and only one LSH sample, found fewer than 60 percent ineligible for Ascherman.

Evaluation results for competency/sanity were even more definitive and practically identical overall for the centers and LSH. Seventy-two percent of the center clients and 73 percent of the LSH clients were found competent/sane. Four of the centers and their respective LSH samples were within seven percentage points of one another in their conclusions regarding competency/sanity. The two remaining combinations showed divergent results: In one the center found 83 percent competent/sane and its respective LSH sample was 67 percent competent/sane; in the other the center found 64 percent competent/sane and LSH 85 percent. In no instance were fewer than 60 percent evaluated as competent/sane.

The actual decision of the court, of course, may or may not be in agreement with the conclusions reached by the evaluators, whether from the centers or LSH. In fact, compared to the clinical evaluators, the courts found greater percentages of clients ineligible as Ascherman candidates and lesser percentages of clients to be competent/sane. Thus, while the centers found 72 percent ineligible under Ascherman, the courts found 89 percent ineligible, and while LSH found 63 percent not Ascherman, the courts found 73 percent. On the other hand, the centers evaluated 72 percent competent/sane and the courts found only 67 percent competent/sane; LSH found 73 percent competent/sane and the courts found 66 percent.

Overall, agreement rates between the centers and the courts, and between LSH and the courts, are nevertheless quite high. This is especially true with regard to competency/sanity. Two of the LSH samples were in complete 100 percent agreement with the courts on competency/sanity cases, and none fell below 85 percent agreement. While one of the centers had as low as 67 percent agreement on competency/sanity cases, three had agreement rates of 90 percent or above. On Ascherman evaluations, LSH ranged from 76-94 percent agreement and the centers from 75-85 percent agreement with the courts. When competency/sanity and Ascherman agreement rates are combined, LSH had a higher rate than the center in some locales but the center had a higher rate than LSH in other locales with no consistent pattern evident.

The research team also gathered data on the recommendations for disposition that the centers and LSH forwarded to the courts.

TABLE 8.6

Recommendations for the Six Centers and the LSH Samples

	Centers		LSH	
	Percent	Number	Percent	Number
Probation	23	392	10	9
Mental health outpatient	33	572	13	12
Social life intervention	12	209	—	—
Drug/alcohol program	7	117	15	14
Mental health inpatient	15	256	25	23
Due process incarceration	7	125	35	33
Further evaluation	4	63	2	2
Total		1,734		93

Source: Compiled by the author.

Table 8.6 reveals that 33 percent of the combined centers' recommendations were for mental health outpatient care and another 23 percent for probation. In contrast, 35 percent of LSH's recommendations were for due process/incarceration and another 25 percent for mental health inpatient care. Only 7 percent of the centers' recommendations were for due process/incarceration. While not reflected in Table 8.6, the researchers found all six centers made substantially higher numbers of recommendations than did LSH. In the course of conducting the evaluations, the research team learned that there is considerable debate concerning whether or not evaluation results should be accompanied by recommendations. Some courts and clinicians define the purpose of evaluations simply to report on the status of the client regarding the reason for referral; others believe the clinicians should additionally forward their professional opinions regarding appropriate court disposition. It appears that personnel of LSH are enamored of the former viewpoint and personnel of the centers of the latter.

To further enhance the interpretive value of the data, recommendations for mental health outpatient care, probation, drug or alcohol treatment, and social life intervention were combined under the rubric of "return to the community," and recommendations for incarceration and mental health inpatient care were combined under the rubric of "institutionalization." The resultant distribution is presented in Table 8.7, which indicates that, overall, 76 percent of the centers' recommendations were for the clients' return to the community compared to 32 percent of LSH's recommendations and, conversely, 21 percent of the centers' recommendations were for institutionalization compared to 67 percent for LSH.

As with evaluation results and court decisions, the fact remains that actual court dispositions may not go along with clinical recommendations. Of the centers' clients, 49 percent were placed on probation, 32 percent were incarcerated, and 11 percent were remanded to mental health inpatient care. The courts clearly incarcerated persons more frequently than the centers recommended. Of LSH's clients, 40 percent were incarcerated, and 28 percent each were placed on probation and remanded to mental health inpatient care. These dispositions are generally more congruent with LSH's recommendations.

TABLE 8.7

Categorized Recommendations for the Six Centers and LSH Samples
(in percent)

| | Return to Community | | Institutionalize | |
	Center	LSH	Center	LSH
Akron	82	0	18	100
Butler	83	43	17	57
Cincinnati	70	36	30	64
Columbus	76	50	24	50
Dayton	79	43	21	57
Toledo	65	19	17	76
Mean Percent	76	32	21	67

Source: Compiled by the author.

As with recommendations, court dispositions were categorized under "return to the community" and "institutionalization." While the centers overall recommended a 76 percent return to the community, the courts actually returned only 59 percent. Conversely, the centers recommended institutionalization for 21 percent, but the courts institutionalized 41 percent. Overall, the agreement rate between the centers and the courts is 78 percent with regard to returns to the community but only 39 percent with regard to institutionalization.

In contrast, more congruence between LSH and the courts is again evident. LSH recommended return to the community for 32 percent and institutionalization for 67 percent; the courts returned 29 percent to the community and institutionalized 69 percent.

Another way of looking at these data is to note that the bulk of the centers' clients are returned to the community, while the majority of LSH's clients are institutionalized. But this interpretation must again consider the inpatient-outpatient distinctions between the facilities and the possibilities that more serious cases are being screened through the centers to LSH.

TIME INVOLVED IN MOVING THROUGH THE SYSTEM

The research team computed the average number of days between the various stages of the evaluation process for all six centers and for the samples of LSH referrals from the geographical areas served by the respective centers. Three phases of the evaluation procedure were examined: date of referral to date of admission, date of admission to date of final report, and date of final report to date of court disposition. The average number of days between referral and admission for all six centers combined is 8.55, compared to 11.17 for the combined LSH samples. While the difference of 2.62 average days reflects favorably on the centers, there is definite evidence that the 11.17-day figure for LSH is grossly underestimated. Since 1971 when the administration of LSH adopted a very limited admissions policy in the wake of severe overcrowding at the institution, the admission of clients to LSH has routinely involved long waiting periods after the actual signing of the court order. Throughout the conduct of the center evaluations, the research team received numerous reports of one- to three-month delays between the decision to refer clients to LSH and actual acceptance of clients at the institution. Thus, in the final analysis, the research team suspects that referral dates in the LSH files are less a reflection of the court order date than the date actual transportation proceedings were initiated.

Table 8.8 depicts the average number of days between admission and report, and report and disposition, for all six centers and their respective LSH samples.

TABLE 8.8

Processing Times for the Six Centers and the LSH Samples

| | Mean Number of Days Between | | | |
| | Admission and Report | | Report and Disposition | |
	Center	LSH	Center	LSH
Akron	21.90	31.98	30.13	44.29
Butler	21.52	29.79	16.45	43.80
Cincinnati	8.89	37.78	36.90	54.00
Columbus	23.26	29.27	40.08	60.43
Dayton	15.57	30.78	30.02	47.26
Toledo	41.50	41.40	21.70	39.80
Grand mean	22.11	33.50	29.21	48.26

Source: Compiled by the author.

With the very slight exception of Toledo, all centers average fewer days between admission and report than LSH. The greatest differential is between Cincinnati and LSH, the former facility averaging 29 fewer days. All six centers combined average 11.39 fewer days between admission and report than LSH. An examination of the number of days between report and disposition finds all six centers averaging less time than LSH. The Butler center and LSH display the greatest differential (27 days). All six centers combined average 19.05 fewer days between report and disposition than LSH.

In summary, the centers overall consume substantially less time than does LSH at all phases of the evaluation procedure.

COST ANALYSIS

Various types of cost analyses were conducted by the researchers for each of the six centers under consideration in this integrative report. Some of these analyses yield meaningful comparisons across centers and others do not. The simplest and most gross cost analysis is the division of total budget by total client caseload. This analysis was performed for all six centers, and the results are contained in Table 8.9. It must be borne in mind in interpreting these data that the budgetary and caseload figures employed correspond to the respective data-collection periods that vary both in length and calendar

TABLE 8.9

Cost per Client Based on Budget and Caseload Size for All Six Centers

Center	Time Frame	Budget	Case-load	Cost per Client	Adjusted Cost per Client
Akron	March 1974– December 1974	63,325	170	373	—
Butler	February 1974– February 1975	72,000	145	497	—
Cincin- nati	July 1973– December 1974	161,967	218	743	430
Colum- bus	January 1973– December 1974	212,055	536	396	—
Dayton	October 1972– February 1974	149,305	183	816	462
Toledo	July 1971– December 1973	471,900	869	543	459

Source: Compiled by the author.

TABLE 8.10

Costs for Ascherman and Competency/Sanity Evaluations at the Six Centers

Center	Evaluation Type*	
	Ascherman	Competency/Sanity
Akron	468	494
Butler	565	665
Cincinnati	549	586
Columbus	425	398
Dayton	520	638
Toledo	560	389
Grand mean	515	528

*The cost figures for both Ascherman and competency/sanity evaluations were computed for each center. The means of the two are the figures presented in this table.

Source: Compiled by the author.

year(s). Thus, for example, the Akron figures are from March through December 1974 while the Toledo data are from July 1971 through December 1973. Furthermore, the data-collection period at all centers included only those cases that had been completed and not those that were still in progress during the time frame tapped.

An examination of Table 8.9 reveals that costs per client range from $816 at Dayton to $373 at Akron. A number of very important qualifications must be made with regard to some of these cost figures. Most significantly, the Cincinnati, Dayton, and Toledo costs are all inflated as a result of small numbers of referrals in the early days of the centers' operations compared to later months. If adjustments are made in the cost data to reflect this fact, the Cincinnati cost drops to $430, the Dayton cost to $462, and the Toledo cost to $459. Thus, in the final analysis, costs per client are very similar among the six centers. The range from the most expensive to the least expensive is only $124, and all centers have an average cost per client of under $500.

Of particular interest is the cost accruing to evaluations under the Ascherman and competency/sanity statutes at the centers compared to LSH. Table 8.10 summarizes these cost figures. Ascherman evaluation costs range only $140, from $565 at Butler to $425 at Columbus. Competency/sanity evaluations range $276, from $665 at Butler to $389 at Toledo. Since Ascherman evaluations at LSH cost $2,011, the center with the lowest cost is $1,586 more economical than LSH and the center with the highest cost is still $1,446 more economical than LSH. Competency/sanity evaluations at LSH cost $1,095, so the center with the lowest cost saves an average of $706 and the center with the highest cost saves an average of $430. All centers combined evaluate Ascherman referrals at an average cost of $515, or $1,496 less than LSH, and competency/sanity referrals at $528, or $567 less than LSH.

SUMMARY

The findings presented clearly indicate that the anticipated benefits of forensic psychiatric centers listed in Chapter 7 are in large measure being realized by the centers in Akron, Butler County, Cincinnati, Columbus, Dayton, and Toledo. The caseload sizes of significantly greater proportions than served by LSH prior to the centers' openings are clear testimony that the centers are supplementing the evaluation and treatment services of LSH, lightening LSH's caseload from the counties served by the centers, and preventing the institutionalization of some individuals and thus the disruptive influence on the client, his family, and the community of such institutionalization, not to mention the easing of the reintegration problem. Cost analyses demonstrated that the centers negate a sizable proportion of costs incumbent upon institutionalization at LSH. Generally speaking, the centers are providing not only evaluations, recommendations, treatment, and emergency intervention services but also consultation and education services for local criminal justice system agents. The centers are performing Ascherman and competency/sanity evaluations in significantly shorter spans of time than typical of LSH, and the periods between referral and admission and release and court disposition are also much shorter for the centers. Given all this, it is not too surprising that most criminal justice system referral agents strongly endorse the centers and describe them as quite superior to LSH.

NOTES

1. Ohio Revised Code, 2947.25.
2. Davis v. Watkins, 384 F. Supp. 1196 (1974) at 1198.

9

FINDINGS:
THE STATEWIDE SERVICE DELIVERY SYSTEM

Eric W. Carlson

INTRODUCTION AND SYSTEM OVERVIEW

It is a frequently cited truism that no study should proceed without a clear conceptualization of the phenomenon that is being studied. A holistic approach, in the tradition of general systems analysis, assures that the entire scope of the phenomenon will, at least initially, be considered. In addition a somewhat functionalist approach is taken as a method for organizing existing knowledge of the Ohio forensic psychiatric service delivery system (FPSDS). In line with these aims, the first question that must be addressed is: How shall the FPSDS be defined? The answer to this question is determined, to a large extent, by the focus of the study, and the answer, in turn, influences the findings that emerge. In general, we accept the popular notion that a system is a set of elements and the relationships that exist among those elements.[1] We propose to begin with this concept of a system, although as we proceed the concept will become less element-centered to allow greater flexibility in disregarding and modifying element definitions. In addition we consider human organizations as falling within the category of open systems, that is, those that exchange energy and information with their environment and seek to maintain some stable internal equilibrium.[2]

There are a large number of entities in the selected jurisdictional area (Ohio) that could be considered elements in the FPSDS. In a very gross sense one might define the major elements as the agencies reporting to the Division of Forensic Psychiatry and/or purporting to offer forensic services; the clinicians in the state who are willing to work with forensic clients; and the aggregate of Ohio's mentally disordered offender population. One can increase the discrimination of these categories by further subdividing them, which in turn enriches any model derived from them by providing more detail. For example, the agencies might be broken down by type of funding, specific services offered, or size of caseload. The degree of discrimination chosen is dictated by the aim of the study being conducted. In this case we are interested in the effect of service delivery policy on the system, its clients, and those who support it; thus, we have chosen to operate from the lowest applicable level, that of the individual forensic facility.

A second factor that must be considered when defining a system is the issue of focus, or the problem to be addressed. The focus of this study is an exploration of alternative modes for the delivery of forensic services to criminal justice clients. With this in mind, there are still a number of elements that can be chosen to be included in the system and that have some detectable or theoretical effect on the FPSDS. In this study the major alternatives considered are the community-based forensic center and the large inpatient institution. The question is: Are they in fact alternatives?

A large portion of the effort expended in this study and prior studies was directed toward gaining familiarity with the FPSDS.[3] The techniques utilized were direct observation of participants in the system, the questioning and interviewing of persons working within the system and those in contact with it, and the gathering of descriptive data relative to the system. The following section describes the elements and processes within the system.

SYSTEM ELEMENTS

Overall, the Ohio FPSDS consists of five elements: the community forensic psychiatric centers, Lima State Hospital, the courts that refer forensic clients, local and state corrections agencies, and civil mental health institutions. The relationships among these elements will be discussed at length in this study. In addition to these five elements there are also two immediate environments that exercise considerable influence over the FPSDS: the legal and the administrative environments at both state and local levels. The effect of these environments is to set limits on the capability of the PFSDS to perform, and thus they can be viewed as constraints on the system.

The Community Forensic Centers

The community forensic centers are an element of growing importance in the FPSDS. Although three such centers have for some

time borne a portion of the forensic examination caseload for specific courts in Cincinnati, Cleveland, and Painesville, it was not until the early 1970s, when the state of Ohio began to encourage the establishment of forensic centers, that a statewide pattern of growth developed. *
In 1976 there were 11 organizations in the state operating as forensic psychiatric centers. Nine centers, which are funded wholly or in part by state or federal funds, are located in Akron, Columbus, Cincinnati, Dayton, Hamilton (Butler County), Portsmouth, Springfield, Toledo, and Zanesville. In addition, there are centers in Cleveland and Painesville that operate independently of the state and are primarily locally funded.

The establishment of forensic centers was intended to achieve a number of objectives that can be reduced to two categories: treatment objectives and evaluation objectives. Research into the operation of the individual forensic centers indicates that, in general, only the evaluation objectives are being pursued.[4] Lack of resources for treatment, increasing evaluative caseloads, and a narrow conception of mission are all factors that appear to contribute to this situation. Without judging the merits of this narrowing of objectives, it can be said that the primary goal of the community forensic centers appears to be the production of information for decision makers in the criminal justice system.

The following evaluation process from a "typical" forensic center illustrates the process of information generation. First, the center director receives either an offender or notification that an offender has been referred to the center for examination; at the same time the referral agent, usually a court, notifies the center of the question concerning the defendant that must be answered. Often the question is asked by simply referring to the statute number authorizing the examination and assuming that the examiners will know the question. At other times the specific question will be posed; for example, "Is he sane?" "Is he competent?" "Is he dangerous?" and so on. Once it is determined by the center that the offender will be accepted for examination, and that the question can be legitimately addressed, the process that follows is geared almost entirely to answering the question. The centers use a variety of methods to generate information. Most begin the process with a social history that is developed by an in-house staff member. In a large number of cases, particularly those involving misdemeanors or referrals from municipal courts, the process ends here. In other cases, however, the process continues to the stage of psychological testing. Testing is frequently though not always

---

*The Cleveland clinic began operation in 1925.

handled by outside consultants. In some additional cases there is a psychiatric examination. It most often is conducted by consulting psychiatrists because few centers are large enough to justify a staff psychiatrist. Finally, and only rarely, consultants are utilized to address special neurological or psychiatric problems.

The final step in the process is the consolidation of the reports written by the separate individuals in the process into a statement of evaluation results. This statement usually addresses the original question asked, though there are cases in which it does not. The extent to which individual staff members and consultants participate in a particular evaluation varies, but the overall process and the order of intervention seem to hold generally within and between centers.

Once the information has been generated by the center, the use that is made of it is at the discretion of the original referral agent. The agent is free to accept or reject any of the information provided by the center. In practice, we have found a high degree of agreement between the recommended dispositions of defendants by the centers and the referral agents' dispositions. This agreement may reflect two factors. First, the results of the examinations may be highly accurate or at least highly acceptable to the referral agents. Second, some referral agents may "rubber stamp" the recommendations of the centers out of deference to the expertise of center personnel. It should be borne in mind, however, that the decision to pass dispositional responsibility to the center lies with the referral agent and not with the center. The referral agent has, in effect, acted by abdicating his responsibility.

While referral agents ask a number of questions of the centers, the most frequently raised are:

Is the defendant competent/incompetent to stand trial?
Was the defendant sane/insane at the time of the alleged offense?
Is the defendant covered under Ohio's psychopath statute (Ascherman Law)?
Is the defendant dangerous?
What is the "best" sentence for the defendant, taking into account the likelihood that he will respond positively and also his degree of dangerousness?
How can this probationer/parolee best be treated while in the community?
Does this person who is being held in a local detention facility have a mental problem?

The quality of the centers' responses to these questions from the point of view of the referral source appears to have a large effect on the impact that the centers have on the other elements of the FPSDS.

If referral agents regard the information provided by the centers as inaccurate or incomplete, they will tend to use less of the centers' services and the relative importance of the centers will decline. This could lead to an increase in the importance of LSH as an information generator or, if LSH continued to be only a limited resource, it could lead to a general denigration of the value of forensic psychiatric information to the Ohio criminal justice system. Thus the influence of the centers on the system may well be directly related to the perceived value of the information that they generate for referral agents.

Lima State Hospital

Lima State Hospital is a critical element in the FPSDS. The institution is a maximum-security inpatient psychiatric facility that has for a number of years served as the only major facility for the evaluation, treatment, care, and custody of forensic clients. Setting treatment aside for the moment, LSH has performed two basic functions. First, it has conducted examinations of offenders for the courts in a manner quite similar to that described above regarding the forensic centers. Second, it has served as an institution of custody for offenders committed as "criminally insane," a group consisting primarily of persons found incompetent to stand trial, persons found committable under the psychopath statute, and persons committed after being found not guilty by reason of insanity. LSH has also served as a place of custody for offenders who have been committed to Ohio correctional institutions but have developed mental difficulties while incarcerated that preclude their remaining in that institution, and for inmates of civil institutions who prove dangerous and difficult to handle.

The function most extensively reviewed in this study is the examination function. It cannot be totally separated from the custody function, however, because a considerable portion of the facilities and resources at LSH are utilized by examination cases. This has become particularly critical since the Interim Order in Davis v. Watkins[5] that demands a reduction in population. Clearly, examination capability can be traded for custody capability or vice versa.

The Courts

The courts are another critical element in the FPSDS, particularly from a decision-making point of view. The vast majority of the input into the FPSDS, in the form of offenders, is generated by the courts. The courts are responsible for referring persons for both examination and custody. In addition to this influence over the input to the system, the courts also exercise considerable influence over the general operation of the system through judicial review and the quasi-executive powers of the higher courts.

All municipal, county, and common pleas courts in Ohio are potential sources of referrals to the FPSDS. Each has the legal authority, if not functional capability, of ordering defendants into the FPSDS under the auspices of a variety of statutes. This ability to make what are largely discretionary referrals to the FPSDS, on the basis of often vague and poorly articulated legal criteria, places considerable influence over the FPSDS in the hands of the referring courts.

Our evaluations of the individual centers provide some evidence that the standards for referral held by the courts can change markedly in a relatively short period of time, a situation that can lead to a rapidly fluctuating referral rate. For example, the average referral rate from the courts of Montgomery County increased by over seven times during the period between 1971 and 1974.[6] If this rapid change were to occur in just a small percentage of Ohio's most populous counties, the result for the FPSDS would be a literal explosion of the forensic caseload, which would necessitate rapid administrative and perhaps legislative reaction.

At a more general level the state and federal courts are exerting a considerable effect over the operating parameters of the FPSDS. There can be little doubt that the interim decision in Davis v. Watkins has had a profound effect on the population level at LSH and a direct result also on the offender population in other Ohio institutions, both mental health and criminal.

This dual function served by the courts complicates the analysis of the system because we can no longer simply speak of the influence of the courts; instead we must recognize qualitatively different forms of influence. These can be labeled as "referral influence," which describes the relationship of the courts to individual defendants (that is, referral to the system, commitment to the system, and so on), and "control influence," which describes the ability of the courts to set standards for the FPSDS that affect all or large groups of defendants. Control influence ranges from relatively gentle hints by the courts that something should be done, which might be apparent through judicial commentary, to direct intervention in the operation of an organization in the FPSDS, such as the court actions in the Davis v. Watkins case.

Local and State Correctional Facilities

Correctional facilities serve as important sources of referrals in the FPSDS. In most areas with community forensic centers it has been accepted that emergency psychiatric problems that occur in the local detention facility will be handled by the center. Depending on the stage in the criminal justice process that the offender has reached, he may be referred to other appropriate agencies if he is diagnosed as in "need" of further custody or treatment. In addition, state correctional facilities have traditionally used LSH as a holding and treatment facility for persons who develop psychiatric problems while incarcerated. A large number of these interinstitutional transfers occurred during the research period.

Corrections also serves a radically different role from that of the referral agent, which tends to influence strongly the character of the FPSDS in Ohio. The FPSDS is often viewed as spanning the boundary between the mental health and criminal justice systems. This notion suggests that the trappings of both systems should be apparent, and indeed they are. It is suggested, however, that the trappings of corrections are often more in evidence and more influential in the FPSDS than are the trappings of mental health. The traditional heavy emphasis on security for virtually all forensic offenders, regardless of their behavior patterns, is an excellent example of this phenomenon as is a more central concern with the legal status of offenders in the FPSDS than with their mental health status.

Civil Mental Health

The importance of the civil mental health organizations and institutions to the FPSDS has only recently begun to be discussed in Ohio.[7] Historically, the systems have been kept largely independent of each other, based primarily on the perceived differences of forensic and civil mental health clients. This independence was preserved and enhanced by the past administrative association of forensic psychiatry with corrections in the state Department of Mental Hygiene and Correction.

In the past, civil mental health institutions have served two functions in relation to the delivery of forensic services. First, they have served as a referral source for LSH. Patients who are assaultive or escape-prone are often transferred to LSH.[8] This practice is interesting because it is an explicit recognition of the high level of security consciousness at LSH. Second, the civil institutions have served as a custody facility for forensic clients who, for any number of reasons, have fallen out of the criminal justice system. In many areas of the state it is the practice of the courts to allow the dropping of criminal charges against defendants in return for the defendants' voluntarily signing themselves into mental institutions.

Recently, civil mental health has been assuming new functions in relation to the FPSDS. The civil mental institutions in Ohio are now performing court-ordered forensic evaluations of criminal justice clients at almost one-third the rate of LSH. Courts complain either that they are unable to gain admission to LSH for their clients or that the process at LSH is too slow for their needs. The result has been that civil institutions have begun to assume a portion of the examination role.

Civil mental health is also becoming a receiving area ("dumping ground") for offenders previously held at LSH. The court-mandated population reduction at LSH is in part being accomplished by the transfer of forensic clients who are not in need of maximum security to the civil institutions.

SYSTEM ENVIRONMENTS

In addition to these five basic elements in the FPSDS, there are a number of other influences on the system that are too important to be dismissed, in particular the legal and the administrative environments.

The Legal Environment

First, the legal environment includes the statutes under which the FPSDS performs its functions. These include the Ascherman Act, the competency/sanity statutes, and the large number of other statutes that allow a defendant in the criminal justice system to be either examined or treated by mental health professionals. These statutes are, in essence, the constraints on the system; they are intended to define the population to be handled by the FPSDS and the outer boundaries of the permissible processes to be utilized within the system.

Second, the legal environment, which includes the basic values and processes that set the character of American jurisprudence (such as the presumption of innocence until guilt is proved, competency on the part of the defendant at the time of the trial, and due process) serves as an important influence shaping the behavior of the FPSDS.

The Administrative Environment

The administrative environment of the FPSDS in Ohio has a number of facets. The state Division of Forensic Psychiatry is a separate, but not necessarily equal, branch of the Department of Mental Health and Mental Retardation. The Division of Forensic Psychiatry is charged with the administration of LSH, the maintenance of psychiatric facilities for the state correctional institutions, and the support and coordination of community-based forensic services. Since the agency has only recently assumed a role in community-based services, it is primarily institutionally oriented, an orientation that may be a source of difficulty when the division attempts to coordinate community-based services.

Traditionally, the most important role of Forensic Psychiatry, from the division's point of view, has been the operation of LSH. The major portions of its budget and staff resources have been and still are expended there. This focus on LSH has caused the division to ignore its other functions, particularly when problems arise at LSH. The problems at LSH that caused the Davis v. Watkins suit have yielded a steady stream of court orders and threats of orders regarding conditions at LSH, which have virtually paralyzed the division. The functions of the division regarding community-based services have, until recently, received only minimal attention.

This situation has resulted in a crisis of leadership within the community-based forensic centers. Fortunately, the appointment in June 1974 of a full-time employee of the division as coordinator of forensic centers has improved the situation. Concurrently with the appointment of the new coordinator, the directors of the individual forensic centers have formed an association to begin to address a number of the needs they felt were not being adequately addressed by the Division of Forensic Psychiatry.

This general lack of leadership for the forensic centers was probably largely the result of the problems at LSH, but the method of establishing and funding the centers cannot be ignored as a contributing factor. The centers are funded through a variety of local, state, and federal sources. Individually, they are often funded from a number of sources, in one case as many as six. [9] This leads to serious questions about who shall influence the operation of the center. In addition to these multiple funding problems, several of the centers were established through local rather than state action; consequently, their staff feel little loyalty toward state administrators.

ACTIVITIES AND FUNCTIONS

One way to analyze the activities of the FPSDS in Ohio is to examine the basic functions it performs. It is reasonable to hypothesize that the system performs four functions, and the activities of all its elements can be placed in one or more of these categories. This functional typology of activities allows the commonalities between organizations to be emphasized rather than the divergences. These functions include information generation, treatment, custody, and decision making.

Information generation is a function that is performed for persons outside of the FPSDS. When evaluations of defendants for competency to stand trial, Ascherman committability, or drug dependency are performed by an organization in the FPSDS, that organization "acts as if" it were solely in the business of providing information.

Forensic psychiatric service decisions can be categorized in two ways. First, there is decision making that is concerned with the operation of the forensic services system. Decisions to transfer clients within or between institutions and those regarding treatment modalities and security are all examples of decisions that concern either the operation of the institutions within the system or persons who have been committed to the custody of the system by some referral agent. A second form of decision making is evident when the recommendation of agents of the forensic psychiatric system are accepted by referral agents as the final decision determining the fate of the offender. This is a case where the decision maker, as defined by law, has ratified a decision made within the forensic psychiatric system.

The custody function requires little explication. A number of clients find themselves indefinitely committed to the care of the FPSDS. These are persons who are committed under the Ascherman Act, the competency/sanity statute, or any of a number of alternative statutes.

The treatment function, although difficult to define, must at least be noted. Even clinicians have difficulty agreeing on precisely which activities constitute treatment. The entry of the courts into this area as standard-setters under the concept of "right to treatment" has also failed to provide a clear concept of treatment. For purposes here, treatment is regarded as activity undertaken by FPSDS personnel to improve the offender's ability to cope with his life situation, or to bring his behavior within socially acceptable limits. It is not necessary to discuss treatment at the individual level; thus, this definition is offered only to signify what is meant when the word "treatment" is used. This function is included in our typology because treatment activities are being carried out in the FPSDS. The controversy surrounding the definition of treatment and the questioning of the benefits of the function are not material to the purpose of the study.

Table 9.1 is an attempt to illustrate the functions performed by each of the elements in the forensic system. The table includes both the legally mandated and traditional functions, as well as functions that have been assumed during the past few years. For example, LSH regularly performs the information-generation function when it evaluates offenders referred by the criminal justice system. It also routinely

TABLE 9.1

Functions Performed by Elements of Forensic Psychiatric Service
Delivery System

Functions of FPSDS	LSH	Forensic Psychiatry Centers	Correc- tions	Civil Mental Health	Courts
Information generation	X	X	—	O	—
Decision making (major decisions)	O	O	—	O	X
Custody	X	—	X	O	—
Treatment	X	X	X	O	—

X = mandated or traditional.
O = assumed.

Source: Compiled by the author.

performs the custody function when it holds persons indefinitely committed. As an adjunct to the custody function, treatment is also provided. Finally, there is some reason to believe that LSH may perform
a decision-making function with regard to the labeling of offenders.
This occurs when referral agents, such as courts, abdicate their responsibility to make decisions by deferring to the expertise of examining mental health professionals and accepting without question their
decisions regarding client mental status. This is clearly an assumed
function, because the courts are charged with the responsibility of
making the decision, and their choice not to make the decision may
well be a conscious one.

The Information-Generation Function—
Forensic Examinations

There are six basic processes carried out in the FPSDS that fall
under the information-generation or examination function. These are:
the Ascherman examination, the examination to determine competency
to stand trial or sanity at the time of the offense, the psychiatric presentence examination for mitigation of sentence or recommendation
for probation, examinations of probationers and parolees to determine
current mental condition and most successful supervision methods,

examination to determine drug dependency, and emergency interventions for persons incarcerated in either state or local facilities. The nature of each process is in large part determined by the statute governing its use, although in practice statutory provisions are often ignored or misapplied. The processes are also strongly influenced by applicable executive orders and by the formal and informal policies of the courts, corrections, and mental health agencies.

In practice, the procedures followed for several of these examinations may appear very similar. However, they should be discussed separately in light of the very different statutory authorities involved. Table 9.2 illustrates the seven types of examinations conducted at LSH and the forensic psychiatric centers.* Examinations are broken down into the number of each type conducted at LSH and at the centers, with accompanying percentages of total examinations for each.

The Ascherman Examination

This is a postconviction examination required of all persons convicted of selected crimes such as rape, sexual battery, corruption of a minor, endangering children, and so on. This examination, which can also be ordered when the courts feel it is advisable, is intended to determine whether an offender can be regarded mentally ill, mentally retarded, or "psychopathic." Appropriate dispositions are provided for each category by the Ascherman statute.

Table 9.2 indicates that a large percentage of the forensic examinations conducted in Ohio fall into this category. In this sample of admissions to LSH, 56 percent of all examinations were conducted under the Ascherman Act. For a combined sample of cases seen at four community forensic centers (reflecting operations at the Cincinnati, Columbus, Butler County, and Akron centers) the proportion of Ascherman examinations to total examinations was 31 percent.

At LSH the process for conducting an Ascherman examination is rather formally prescribed. It involves an initial intake interview by a social worker, followed by requests for information regarding the criminal justice, mental health, and other pertinent records of the defendant. The defendant receives a thorough medical examination by a physician or assistant at intake. There is also an intake psychiatric interview conducted by a psychiatrist and a psychological interview and testing conducted by a psychologist or an assistant. Later, a staffing session is held and a final report prepared for the court that

---

*The table includes examinations for the civil mental health system, which are not one of the prescribed major functions of LSH.

TABLE 9.2

Examinations by Type, Lima State Hospital and Community
Forensic Centers, 1968-74

Examination	LSH	Percent of Total	Centers	Percent of Total
Ascherman	1,839	55.9	315	30.7
Competency/sanity	1,321	40.1	171	16.7
General presentence examination	—	—	393	38.2
Drug dependency	11	0.3	96	9.3
Probation and parole	1	0.1	34	3.3
Civil	119	3.6	—	—
Emergency	—	—	18	1.8
Total	3,291	100.0	1,027	100.0

Source: Compiled by the author.

addresses the specific question: Is the defendant mentally ill, mentally retarded, or psychopathic? There is no information that indicates that the appropriateness of these referrals is ever questioned
by LSH personnel.

The process at the centers is more eclectic and less well defined. The center directors are often faced with referrals that, although made under provision of the Ascherman statute, are clearly
not intended to be Ascherman examinations. The process at the centers is more flexible in order to accommodate these inappropriate
referrals by addressing the concerns of the referral agent, even when
the agent does not fully understand the implications of the statute used
for referral. An attempt is made to answer not only the Ascherman
questions but also questions pertaining to dangerousness, probability
of repeating, and possible disposition.

These attempts to meet the needs of the court result in a less-
structured examination. It usually begins with the intake interview
conducted by a social worker and proceeds to an examination conducted
by a psychologist, which may include psychological testing. Frequently, if there are no outstanding problems, or the crime involved
is not particularly serious, the examination process will end with the
psychological examination. The psychologist will serve as the court
witness, if required. If the case is difficult, or the crime particularly serious, a psychiatrist may examine the defendant. The center's

decision to utilize psychiatric evaluation is very situational and often determined by the center's perception of the proclivities of the presiding judge. It is clear from previous research, however, that psychiatric time is used much more sparingly by the community forensic centers than by LSH.[10]

The Competency/Sanity Examination

The trial courts of Ohio are authorized to order the examination of any defendant whose competency to stand trial is questioned, whose current sanity is questioned, or whose sanity at the time of the offense is questioned.[11]

Data in Table 9.2 indicate that this is the second most common examination conducted at LSH, accounting for 40 percent of the examinations conducted during the sample period. For the combined sample of four forensic centers, competency/sanity examinations accounted for 17 percent of the total, which placed them third in examination type.

At LSH the process for conducting the competency/sanity examination is quite similar to the Ascherman procedure. The major difference is in the questions that must be answered. There are three distinct questions that can legitimately be addressed within the limits of this statute: Is the defendant competent to stand trial? Was the defendant sane at the time of the offense? Is the defendant currently sane?

Like LSH, the process at the community forensic centers for conducting competence/sanity examinations is similar to that used for Ascherman referrals. There is some evidence, in terms of the number of contacts with mental health professionals, that these examinations are somewhat more thorough at the centers than are Ascherman examinations, although the trend seems to be to expend fewer resources, particularly psychiatric time, on this category.[12] This has occurred because the center directors feel that they are receiving a significant number of competency/sanity referrals that are considered inappropriate and that could better be handled as general presentence examinations. An additional point should be noted: The community centers are very reluctant to conduct examinations for which the expressed purpose is to determine sanity at the time of the offense. At least one center refuses even to accept these referrals because of the difficulty of addressing that question. *

---

*The Cincinnati Court Psychiatric Center has a policy of refusing to address the question of sanity at the time of the offense because they feel that it is impossible to determine.

The Presentence Examination

While the general presentence examination is not routinely conducted at LSH, it is one of the most frequently employed at the community forensic centers. A number of provisions in Ohio law appear to allow this type of examination for felony offenders, although no statutory authority for the use of this type of examination could be found for misdemeanor offenders. In spite of some question about the authority to conduct them, these examinations account for 38 percent of the caseload at the forensic centers. The persons who receive these examinations appear to be persons who would not have been examined prior to the opening of the forensic centers and thus represent additional examinations that have not been drawn away from LSH. The rather large number of misdemeanor offenders in this group is particularly supportive of this conclusion.

Probation/Parole Examinations

Probation/parole referrals constitute a second category of examination type that is relatively rare at LSH. The aim of the examination is to assist the probation or parole officer in supervising his client. In effect, this examination is often a psychiatric adjunct to the normal presentence report, although it usually takes place after the judge has agreed to place the offender on probation. Frequently, one of the conditions of probation is that the defendant participate in this examination. Occasionally, however, behavior problems that occur while the offender is on probation or parole precipitate the examination, and the results are utilized to assist in the decision to revoke or continue probation or parole.

Only about 3 percent of the examinations appear to fall into this category, although this may be an understatement in terms of the use of the examination for probationers because a large number of these referrals appear in forensic center records as treatment, rather than examination referrals. There is little indication, however, that the number of parolees is understated.

The Drug Dependency Examination

The drug dependency examination is conducted under an Ohio law that authorizes the utilization of probation for a person convicted of any misdemeanor or probationable felony for the purpose of receiving treatment for drug problems.[13] To ascertain whether probation is warranted, the defendant receives a medical and psychiatric examination to determine if he is drug dependent, if he is in danger of becoming dependent on drugs, or if he may be rehabilitated through treatment for drug problems.

These examinations are conducted at both LSH and the community forensic centers, although at neither have they become a major referral source. They account for less than 1 percent of the LSH examinations and only 9 percent of the referrals to the forensic centers.

The actual process of the examination, both at LSH and the centers, is unclear. This seems to be due to the small number of these examinations and to some uncertainty among clinical personnel over what their content should be.

The Emergency Examination

The emergency examination occurs only at the forensic centers. When a person incarcerated in a local lockup exhibits perceived signs of some severe mental disorder, it is common practice in areas with forensic centers for a detaining authority to contact the center and request assistance. All the centers appear willing to handle these problems. The frequency of these examinations is probably understated in the records of the centers. Data indicate that only about 2 percent of the examinations are in this category, although it is suggested that they frequently are listed as competency/sanity examinations with the court order being written after the initial interview with the defendant. *

The process used in conducting these examinations is, to a large extent, determined by the exigencies of the situation, although it usually involves an interview with the defendant at the jail or lockup rather than his transportation to the forensic center. The circumstances surrounding the referral and the availability of forensic center staff determine which type of professional personnel will visit the local lockup and interview the offender.

Treatment and Custody

As stated earlier, it is recognized that treatment and custody are quite different functions. They are, however, discussed in the same section because significant portions of the treatment for offenders in Ohio occur in a custody situation. In addition, as also stated earlier, it is not germane to include a detailed discussion of treatment

---

*Because most centers prefer not to conduct examinations without the authority of a court order, emergency jail examinations are conducted very informally. The records of such examinations are begun upon the later receipt of a court order that (because the offender often exhibits symptoms of psychosis) generally relies on the authority of section 2945.40.

processes. Thus, this section will consist largely of a discussion of the custodial function of forensic psychiatry in Ohio.

Indefinite Commitments to Lima State Hospital

There are at least ten sections of Ohio law that allow persons to be indefinitely committed to LSH. Persons covered include those found to be mentally ill, mentally retarded, or psychopathic under the Ascherman statute; persons found incompetent to stand trial; mentally ill prisoners transferred from Ohio's prisons; dangerous or homicidal civil mental health patients; mentally ill persons who have served the maximum sentence in a correctional institution; and persons covered by Ohio's drug dependency statutes. For the period 1968 through 1974, 2,469 persons were indefinitely committed to LSH.

TABLE 9.3

Total Annual Commitments to LSH by Examination or Indefinite Commitment, 1968–74

Year	Examination		Indefinite		Total
1968	664	60.0[a]	442	40.0	1,106
		20.9[b]		18.7	
1969	724	66.6	363	33.4	1,087
		22.8		15.3	
1970	668	62.8	395	32.7	1,063
		21.0		16.7	
1971	500	60.1	332	39.9	832
		15.7		14.0	
1972	186	42.9	248	57.1	434
		5.9		10.5	
1973	219	42.6	295	57.4	514
		6.9		12.5	
1974	217	42.7	291	57.2	508
		6.8		12.3	
Total	3,178[c]		2,366[d]		5,544

[a]N = row percent.
[b]D = column percent.
[c]This number excludes 119 mentally ill and probate cases.
[d]This number excludes 105 cases held beyond maximum sentence.
Source: Compiled by the author.

Table 9.3 presents all commitments to LSH for the seven-year period, categorized by examination commitments and indefinite commitments. It clearly indicates that LSH is becoming increasingly custody and treatment oriented. Indefinite commitments as a percentage of all commitments to LSH rose fairly steadily from 40 percent in 1968 to over 57 percent of the admissions in 1974. This reflects either an increasing concentration of LSH resources on custody and treatment or a decreasing emphasis on examination, or possibly a combination of both.

Although LSH has been the primary inmate institution for forensic psychiatry in Ohio, the custody and treatment functions have also been carried out at the Junction City Treatment Center and the Chillicothe Treatment and Research Center.

Custody and Treatment Alternatives to LSH

The Chillicothe Treatment and Research Center has served primarily as an evaluation unit for inmates of the Department of Rehabilitation and Corrections facilities who are being considered for placement in the Junction City program. Recently, however, it has served as a holding facility for persons transferred back to correctional institutions from LSH, after having been classified as "not dangerous to self or others and not in need of maximum security."

The Junction City facility, with a capacity of about 100, has functioned as a small, special-services facility administering an experimental treatment program designed to reduce recidivism. The small capacity of this unit has precluded its ever being a major custody facility for forensic psychiatry, and current serious budgetary and small population problems raise doubts about its continued operation.

Although LSH, Chillicothe, and Junction City are the primary centers of the custody and treatment function in the Ohio FPSDS, there is some evidence that it may occur in other locations. The Division of Forensic Psychiatry provides funds for some staff who supply forensic services in Ohio's correctional institutions. To the extent that these services allow offenders to remain in their current institutions even though they could conceivably be mentally ill, the provision of these services allows the institutions to serve a custody function that would otherwise fall to LSH. An example of this is the provision of psychotropic drugs to offenders who would not otherwise be able to remain in the institutions without them because of behavior deterioration.

The civil mental health institutions also support the custody function of LSH in at least two ways. First, there have been small but substantial numbers of persons indefinitely committed to civil institutions under the authority of the competency/sanity and Ascherman laws. This is a clear assumption of the custody function by civil mental health units. Second, there is a significant body of evidence, largely anecdotal, that it is the practice of many courts, prosecutors, and police agencies to practice informal diversion of defendants to the civil mental institutions. This practice, although often questioned on the grounds that it may violate a defendant's constitutional rights, serves to shift a significant number of persons who would become custody cases for the FPSDS to the civil sector. The extent of this practice is difficult to ascertain because it often falls within the legitimate areas of discretion available to courts, prosecutors, and police— areas that are often discussed only with great reluctance.

Decision Making in the FPSDS

As previously stated, decision making can be conceptualized in at least two ways. First, there are a large number of decisions that must be made regarding the operation of the system. In this section one is concerned primarily with decisions that would be made, or at least ratified, by persons in the position of institutional superintendent or above. Examples would be the decision to intake, transfer, or discharge clients, decisions regarding the level of security required for classes of clients, and decisions regarding the conditions under which clients in custody exist.

The most salient observation that can be made regarding this concept of decision making in the FPSDS is that it is so fractionalized and uncoordinated that the elements of the FPSDS waste a great deal of time working at cross-purposes. For example, the interim Davis v. Watkins order mandated, in effect, that clients be transferred to the least restrictive setting if custody were indeed required. This led to the reevaluation of the entire population of LSH and the subsequent transfer of a number of persons back to the correctional system from which they had originally been referred. The problem with this decision, however, was that correctional facilities were already operating at capacity. The correctional system was not prepared to handle the influx of transfers from LSH. The result has been that a chain reaction of transfers, retransfers, and retransferred-transfers has been set off.

This situation was not cited to label the personnel in any particular segment of the system as villain; as with many complicated situations, this is one in which no one can be singled out. When the court required that clients be transferred to the least restrictive setting, it limited the range of decision making for the rest of the FPSDS. The decision option at LSH to continue holding particular groups of clients was taken away. The only option available was to return the clients to their point of origin, that is, corrections of mental health. Unfortunately, these systems were already full. At each point in the process, from the court through corrections, the options were simply not available; they were constrained by budgetary limitation, by law, or by public opinion.

A second concept of decision making concentrates on the individual client and his official entry into the FPSDS. This is a direct outgrowth of the information-generation function. In theory, agents of the FPSDS who examine clients under the various statutes are acting only as expert witnesses of the courts. The authority to make the decision to label a client as a psychopath, mentally ill, drug dependent, or any other status is in the hands of the court. In practice, this may not always be the case. If the courts merely ratify the recommendations of the agents of the FPSDS regarding client disposition, a significant change in the locus of the decision making has taken place.

As previously mentioned, research indicates that there is a high degree of agreement between evaluation recommendations and eventual court disposition, which is not, however, evidence that the courts have abdicated their role. It may simply be indicative of the accuracy of examinations. In the course of the research, however, other information emerged that may cast further light on this issue. Evaluators who are unknown to the court (that is, those who are not local) tend to be called more infrequently into court to testify concerning the condition of the defendant. This suggests at least the possibility that courts have more confidence in local agents of the FPSDS and would tend to ratify their judgments on client disposition more frequently than the judgments of more remote evaluators. One implication of this is that the development of local forensic centers is conducive to the shifting of disposition decision making from the courts to mental health professionals.

This framework is offered as both a description of, and a tool for, understanding and interpreting the activities of Ohio's FPSDS. It establishes a context within which policy issues relating to the FPSDS can be addressed. The following material contains more focused discussions of these issues, although it is hoped that a broader perspective can always be quickly reestablished by referring to this framework.

FINDINGS

Two basic samples were used to generate the findings that follow: a sample of 5,792 consecutive admissions to LSH, and a sample of 1,065 admissions to the Akron, Cincinnati, Columbus, and Butler County community forensic centers.

The LSH data were gathered to establish existing referral patterns to the hospital. The data elements gathered included county of commitment, referral source, referral reason, criminal charge, and number of prior admissions to LSH. Comparable data elements were selected for the center sample.

In addition a survey of criminal justice and mental health agencies was conducted to determine attitudes regarding the provision of forensic services. Agencies and individuals surveyed included court judges, probation and parole officers, sheriffs, jail superintendents, and superintendents of correctional and mental health facilities.

Forensic Services—Issues of Supply and Demand

The first issue to be addressed is the demand for forensic services. Since LSH is important in this process, the first step is to gain a notion of the role it plays. Table 9.3, which listed commitments to LSH by year, graphically illustrated the sharp drop-off that occurred during late 1971 and 1972 as a result of charges of patient abuse and generally poor conditions at LSH. The number of examination commitments in 1972 dropped to 28 percent of what they had been in 1968. This decrease is particularly significant because it occurred in spite of a steady increase in criminal prosecutions during that period and because the forensic centers had not yet begun to pick up a major portion of the examination load from LSH.

If the level of examination commitments seen from 1968 through 1972 is indicative of the demand for examination services by the courts of Ohio, it is important to discover what happened to the cases not sent to LSH from late 1971 on. Clearly, a considerable number of cases were involved. If the average for 1968 through 1970 of 6,853 is taken as a base, then 1972 was 499 cases below base, 1973 was 466 below, and 1974 was 468 below for a total of 1,433 under what would have been expected, given a straight-line projection of the prior three years.

Beginning with the establishment of the Toledo center in 1971, the six centers evaluated in this study began serving ever-increasing local client populations (see Table 8.1, which illustrates the numbers of clients referred to forensic centers supported by state effort). During 1972, given the low caseload, it is unlikely that the centers absorbed a significant portion of the excess cases from LSH, with the possible exceptions of the Toledo and Lucas County area. During 1973 and 1974 the volume of referrals to forensic centers grew to the point where the latter were probably absorbing a considerable portion of referrals that would have gone to LSH had the difficulties of 1971 not occurred. The number of referrals is so large, in fact, that either the centers were encouraging a significant number of referrals on their own, or the referral agents were referring persons who would previously not have been examined. The 914 referrals that occurred in 1973 were considerably more than one would have expected to find at LSH based on 1968 through 1970 performance.

Table 9.4 lists the forensic referrals to civil mental health institutions for examination and indefinite commitments by year. The trend here is toward a significant increase in referrals, though the trend does not seem to be radically altered by the changes at LSH during 1971. Indeed, it appears that this trend was well established beknown about the referrals that are appearing at the civil mental health institutions. Discussion with the superintendent of one institution suggests that these referrals are largely misdemeanor offenders from local county and municipal courts. The most common referral reason suggested was alcoholism. These cases appear to represent a significant increase in forensic referrals and not referrals that would previously have gone to LSH.

This discussion suggests that two phenomena are occurring. The examination function of the FPSDS is being shifted radically among the elements of the system. There are indications that the forensic centers and possibly the civil mental health system are picking up the load from LSH. At the same time, however, the total examination load or demand is increasing. Table 9.5 is an attempt to demonstrate this increasing demand. In an absolute sense, the table is far from accurate since it contains estimated figures, mixed calendar- and fiscal-year data, and does not include some examinations at Springfield and Cincinnati for which data were unavailable. Nevertheless, it represents our best estimate of the total number of forensic examinations conducted in the state from 1971 through 1974 by examining institutions. The important feature of the table is the steady rise in examinations after 1972, which is reflected in the column totals. It is interesting to note that this rate of rise is significantly greater than any increase in the total population of the state.

Predictions of the demand for forensic examinations are currently very risky business because the total number that occur can be heavily influenced by administrative decisions, such as the one in 1971 to restrict the availability at LSH. Our data indicate, however, that given time, referral agents can overcome restrictions by locating alternative suppliers of services. It is unclear what would have happened to demand had the division chosen not to support the development of community-based forensic centers. One possibility is that private psychiatrists would have received an increase in the demand for these services, a second alternative would have been a more rapid growth in referrals to civil institutions, and a third alternative would have been the performance of fewer examinations in total with the

TABLE 9.4

Commitments to Civil Institutions by Type, Year, and Presence or Absence of Local Forensic Centers

	1968	1969	1970	1971	1972	1973	1974
Center Counties*							
Examinations	27	61	109	161	232	353	236
Indefinites	0	6	21	17	8	107	20
Noncenter Counties							
Examinations	10	19	11	25	57	254	97
Indefinites	5	1	3	5	6	122	14
Total							
Examinations	37	80	120	186	209	607	333
Indefinites	5	7	24	22	14	229	34

*Butler, Franklin, Hamilton, Lucas, Montgomery, Summit.

Source: Compiled by the author.

TABLE 9.5

Estimated Total Forensic Examinations, 1971-75

	1971	1972	1973	1974	1975
Forensic centers	171	271	914	1,500	1,864*
LSH	500	186	219	217	218*
Civil institutions	186	289	607	333	333*
Cuyohoga County (Cleveland)	575	508	530	530*	530*
Lake County (Painesville)	12	30	48	48*	48*
Total	1,344	1,284	2,318	2,628	2,975*

*Projected figure.
Source: Compiled by the author.

courts becoming increasingly selective in terms of the offenders examined. The consequences of each of these alternatives should be explored because resource shortages could precipitate the adoption of one of them. Finally, policy makers should not neglect the possibility that provision of these services has in effect created a demand that would otherwise not have been manifested.

The responses to several of the questions in the survey of criminal justice and mental health personnel are relevant to this discussion and provide an alternative method of assessing supply and demand issues for forensic services. All common pleas, municipal, and county court judges were asked to indicate the resources they use for evaluation of the mental status of defendants. One of the most interesting aspects of the responses to this question is that more judges listed the state civil mental hospitals as a source of evaluations than LSH. Some explanation of this can be found by dichotomizing judges into "common pleas" and "other"; 63 percent of the common pleas judges listed LSH as a resource with only 33 percent listing civil mental health hospitals, while only 15 percent of the other (county and municipal) listed LSH as a resource and 36 percent civil mental health. This probably results from the fact that LSH has not regularly been available to municipal and county judges. It should also be noted, though, that even within the counties that have local forensic centers, only 67 percent of the judges list them as a resource. This seems to indicate that the service coverage of the centers is less than complete. In a similar vein, judges were also asked if they "approved of the use of civil mental health facilities for the evaluation of criminal offenders." Of those replying, 80 percent indicated the affirmative, which suggests there is very little opposition to the use of civil mental health facilities for this purpose.

When the judges were asked if their needs for psychiatric evaluation were being met, 61 percent replied that they were not. The result was somewhat better within center counties, where only 24 percent replied that their needs were not being met. This response clearly indicates a significant unmet need for evaluation services.

The judges were also asked to estimate the percentage of defendants who passed through their courts in the last 12 months who were found in need of psychiatric evaluation or treatment. The mean of the responses fell between 6 and 7 percent. Of the respondents, 59 percent felt that the percentage was "increasing over time," 40 percent felt it was "remaining about the same," and less than 1 percent felt it was decreasing.

Probation and parole officers responded to comparable questions in a very similar manner. The only significant difference was that they see a greater number of defendants as being in need of psychiatric services, with the mean lying near 10 percent.

Admittedly, these responses are only subjective, but they indicate that there is a strong opinion among the criminal justice system personnel in Ohio that adequate psychiatric services are not yet available to the courts.

These results taken in conjunction with the trend of increasing referrals strongly suggest that any reduction of the examination function for the FPSDS will have to come from the forensic system. There is no indication that the referral agents in the criminal justice system are willing to reduce their demands for the services either in terms of their actions or their opinions.

An important issue in the supply of all forensic services is the population served by the forensic facility. Basically there are three approaches to defining the service areas of forensic centers: by geographic area served, by proportions of the state population served, and by the courts served and their caseloads. Each of these methods will be discussed here.

The first, and probably least informative, is to define service areas in geographic terms. Of Ohio's 88 counties, 11 contain a forensic center. In addition, these centers serve courts in 17 additional counties for a total of 26. These 26 counties contain 12,888 square miles or 31 percent of Ohio's land area. Though this type of analysis ignores the location of the population of the state, it clearly illustrates the geographic remoteness of forensic services to a large portion of the state.

A second approach to defining service areas is in terms of the population of the areas served. When this strategy is used, the coverage of the centers appears much more favorable. The total estimated population within the counties where the centers are located numbers 4,321,810, or 40 percent of the 1972 Ohio population estimate. This is an impressive figure for only 11 centers, and it is indicative of the concentration of Ohio's population in those nine counties. Whether by plan or accident, Ohio's forensic centers are well placed in terms of population. The above figure is, however, only a portion of the population actually served, because as previously noted, several centers serve more than their home counties. When these additional counties are included in the total population served, the number increases to 5,181,410, or 48 percent of the 1972 Ohio population estimate.

When Ohio's counties are ranked by population and then compared with center coverage, it is interesting to note that the counties that rank seventh through tenth are not covered. These counties (Stark, Mahoning, Lorain, and Trumbull) have a total population of 1,175,400. If these counties, which are located in the northeastern quadrant of the state, were to be included in the service areas of existing centers, or additional centers were established, the total population covered would climb to 6,356,810, or 73 percent of the state population. This reasonably high percentage can be obtained while still serving only approximately one-third of the counties in the state. *

Though it does not appear particularly difficult to serve a relatively large portion of Ohio's population with community-based forensic services, a considerable problem will still exist for a number of the smaller counties. There were 37 counties that made 14 or fewer referrals for examinations to LSH during the period 1968 through 1974. Because of their low populations it is highly unlikely that these counties will even generate enough referrals to support a center designed for strictly forensic services. This is complicated by the fact that there are pockets of these rural counties that do not generate sufficient referrals to support a central facility within a reasonable distance; for the foreseeable future their caseload probably will have to continue to be sent to LSH. Herein lies a problem, for as other more populous counties develop their local forensic services, the quality

---

*These coverages exist in theory only since other replies to the survey indicated that the presence of a center did not guarantee its availability to all potential clients within an area.

variation across the state can potentially become wider and wider. If community-based forensic services continue to provide the quality of services of which they appear capable, this issue will have to be addressed, if from no other point of view than "equal justice."

The third approach to defining service areas is in terms of the courts served and the proportion of the criminal justice clientele served by those courts. At the present time this is an extremely difficult task because the centers are undecided as to whom they will serve. Basically, the centers serve the common pleas courts of their areas, though frequently they will handle municipal or county court referrals on a space-available basis. There are also centers with fee-for-service contracts with courts in counties outside their own. There is also some question about the legal authority of the lower courts to order examinations and services under existing statutes. These questions confront both the personnel at the centers and the courts. They are particularly sharp when relatively minor misdemeanants or juveniles are involved. Given these complications, it should not be assumed that all the courts in the area served by a forensic center receive all or even a portion of the services the center has available.

Although this discussion has focused primarily on the examination function of the FPSDS, the custody and treatment functions cannot be ignored. The research team recognizes that the custody function, in particular, is undergoing dramatic change in terms of the institutions handling the function. Information relating to this function is more difficult to obtain, however, because it is a much less visible process.

It appears that the level of indefinite commitments to LSH has varied much less than the examination level. Table 9.3 indicated that although indefinite forensic commitments decreased significantly in 1972, the decreasing trend seems to have been established prior to 1971. Indefinites in 1972 had decreased to 56 percent of their level in 1968, which is a marked reduction but not nearly as significant a decrease as that evident in examination commitment. Exams in 1972 were only 28 percent of their 1968 level.

When the rather small, but increasing, numbers of indefinite commitments to civil institutions are added, the total commitment level is somewhat erratic, but there remains the suggestion of a slight downward trend. This is contrary to what one would expect, given generally increasing trends in population, in crime, and in persons receiving mental health services. There are several possible explanations for the decrease. First, courts are becoming much more discriminating in their decisions to commit offenders indefinitely. The difficulty courts experience in having persons admitted to LSH may serve as informal pressure to avoid these commitments. The increased concern over the moral and legal ramifications of the indefinite commitments may also operate as a check. Second, the clinicians may be reassessing their position concerning the efficacy of institutional treatment and recommending less of it. This is in line with the creation of community-based facilities and the highly treatment-oriented alternatives to institutions being developed.

The nature of indefinite commitments has altered during the sample period. Prison transfers and civil commitments have remained relatively constant as a proportion of annual indefinites. Drug and parole commitments have never really been significant. Ascherman and competency/sanity commitments are particularly interesting because they have almost reversed as a proportion of annual referrals. In 1968, 50 percent of the indefinite commitments to LSH were Ascherman, while only 18 percent were competency/sanity. In 1974, 45 percent were competency/sanity and only 25 percent Ascherman. This reversal somewhat complicates the custody function of the FPSDS because a relatively larger proportion of its clients are persons who have not been found guilty of any crime, that is, not guilty by reason of insanity or incompetent to stand trial. This situation may also have implications for the type of treatment and security required to deal with the forensic custody population, though they are far from clear.

The issue of facilities available for the custody function was raised in the questionnaire sample by asking all judges surveyed if they "felt there was a need for a local inpatient unit." Seventy-nine percent expressed the need for the services. Probation and parole officers responded with a 76 percent yes.

The availability of treatment in the FPSDS is an issue that has generated more questions than answers. The difficulty of defining the term is probably a significant contributor to the problem, though even when there is agreement over what treatment is, there is disagreement over where it should be conducted. The directors of the local forensic centers have grappled with the issue and each seems to pursue a different policy. Several directors believe that the provision of treatment services is as important as conducting evaluations. At one center the evaluation/treatment split in the caseload is about 50/50. Other directors assigned a low priority to treatment, some reasoning that they are not mandated to do it, others that evaluators and treators cannot in good conscience be the same person.

Judges were asked if they felt "that the court's need for psychiatric treatment services is currently being adequately met." Seventy-six percent replied that it was not; when, however, just the judges presiding in counties with forensic centers were polled the percentage was reversed with 75 percent stating that their needs were being met. The judges who felt most strongly that their needs were unmet were the municipal court judges.

There appear to be several options available for the provision of treatment locally. There are the options of the local forensic center, local civil mental health institutions, and community mental health centers, along with other local public and private facilities. Local civil mental health institutions are somewhat limited in the services they can offer, however, because they are geared to providing inpatient services and because they are located only in a limited number of areas. Community mental health seems like the best potential source of treatment services for forensic clients. The problem seems to revolve around persuading community mental health personnel to accept forensic clients. Again and again the researchers encountered the situation where community mental health either flatly refused to accept persons with criminal-legal problems or accepted them reluctantly and provided very few services. There are strong arguments on both sides of this issue, but in the end there does not seem to be any solid justification for community mental health centers refusing these clients. This subject was raised on the survey questionnaire and the responses are rather interesting. When asked if they "approved of the use of civil mental health facilities for the treatment of criminal offenders," 64 percent of the superintendents of mental health and mental retardation institutions replied yes. Judges approved of using civil facilities by 72 percent. The question that begs for an answer is why with all this support there is so little visible treatment of criminal offenders by the civil mental health system at both the community and institutional levels. It is recognized that a great deal of the contact of the civil institutions with offenders may not be apparent because clients are informally diverted out of the criminal justice system to them. At the local level with regard to community mental health, however, the research team does not believe this qualification applies and suggests that the local mental health centers consider more willingly accepting responsibility for these clients.

Another issue to be addressed is the availability of clinical personnel and their distribution relative to the offender population. At the outset it must be stated that information in this area is very sparse. Despite considerable effort, the researchers were unable to obtain any information regarding the distribution of social workers in the state. Information is available on psychiatrists and psychologists who are licensed, but its usefulness for planning is very questionable because there are a large number of professionals who refuse to handle forensic cases and it is not clear who they are. In any event, in 1974 there were 538 licensed psychiatrists in Ohio; they were licensed in the 40 most populous counties and the number per county ranged from 1 to 163. During this same period there were 1,570 licensed psychologists in 70 counties ranging from 1 to 321 per county. Basing any statements about the distribution of these professionals on these incomplete figures is tenuous. Probably the most informative statement that can be made is that when the number of psychiatrists per county is correlated with county population, the Pearson r is .95; with psychologists the r is .97. Thus, to the extent that forensic clients are distributed in accordance with population, the professional staff is potentially available.

Quality of Forensic Services

There appears to be no satisfactory objective way to address quality issues in the FPSDS, given the current state of research in the mental health and criminal justice fields. As an alternative, some subjective measures of quality were attempted.

Referral agent and mental health staff respondents were asked to rate the overall quality of LSH examinations and also the quality of LSH examinations versus a known alternative (the forensic centers). The quality of LSH examinations seems to be ranked lowest by mental health professionals and highest by the judges who do not have access to a center and therefore use LSH for exams. It is perhaps interesting to note that judges from center counties who are familiar with the forensic center as an alternative to LSH rate the quality of LSH's evaluations lower than judges who have no access to forensic centers. The difference in responses of judges who use forensic centers versus those who do not is dramatic. The center-county judges who obtain what they rate as faster, better-quality evaluations from centers are more critical of LSH. There can be little doubt that judges' standards of quality change radically when alternatives to LSH are regularly provided.

The only conclusions that can be drawn from these subjective ratings are that evaluation service users or referral agents seem to be relatively satisfied with the services of LSH until they are provided a regular alternative. Nonusers of LSH's services seem to rate them more negatively than users. In total there appears to be some unhappiness with LSH, but whether it is caused by something that can be altered is another question. The unhappiness may be just an expression of discontent with the FPSDS in general that has become focused on LSH.

Multiple Admissions to LSH

This final issue is one that was not apparent during the early phases of the forensic study. In the field of corrections the concern is frequently expressed that as alternatives to incarceration are developed, the persons who remain in the institutions will become increasingly more difficult to deal with. They will be the "hard core" who cannot qualify for alternatives to incarceration. We wondered if this situation might also be occurring in institutions such as LSH that are in the process of reducing their populations.

To explore this issue, we examined multiple admissions to LSH. The results were startling. In 1968, 62 percent of the admissions were first admissions; in 1974 only 33 percent were there for the first time. In 1968, 23 percent were second admissions and in 1974, 28 percent were second admissions. Third-time admissions increased from 10 percent in 1968 to 17 percent in 1974. The proportion of fourth-time admissions increased threefold between 1968 and 1974 from 3 to 10 percent, and fifth-time admissions increased fivefold from 1 to 5 percent. In 1968, 15 percent of the admissions were persons who had been there at least twice before. In 1974, 39 percent of the admissions had been there at least twice before. Clearly, if the number of admissions can be taken as at least one dimension in defining whether or not a hard-core custody population is being created, then these data strongly suggest that it is.

SUMMARY AND CONCLUSIONS

The major elements of the FPSDS are the community forensic psychiatric centers, Lima State Hospital, the courts that refer forensic clients, local and state corrections agencies, and the civil mental health institutions. The activities of these elements and the relationships among them are heavily influenced by the legal and administrative environments at both the state and local levels. The activities and processes that occur within the FPSDS can be interpreted in terms of the functions the system performs. These functions include information generation, decision making, custody, and treatment.

The information-generation function, which is most visible in the form of forensic examinations for the courts, is currently shifting from an institutional base at LSH to facilities less remote from the home communities of the clients it serves. Community forensic centers are of growing importance in conducting examinations, but the dramatic increase in examinations being performed by civil mental health institutions should not be overlooked. Professionals within the criminal justice and mental health field are divided on their opinions regarding this function. Our data indicate that there are significant unmet needs for psychosocial services to courts even in areas that are served by community-based forensic facilities, but at the same time our analysis indicates that the provision of the services may be the stimulus to even more demand. There are currently no criteria that unambiguously define a person as being in need of these services. Even the laws that govern these examinations are of little help because they are largely discretionary.

More specifically, our data tend to indicate that referral sources that regularly use the facilities of LSH are reasonably satisfied with the quality of its examination services. LSH is rated favorably on the dimensions of timeliness, usefulness of results, and overall quality of reports. Referral sources that do not regularly use LSH tend to rate it lower on these same three dimensions, while at the same time giving high rating to local forensic centers.

The decision-making function, though not explicitly investigated in this study, appears to be shifting from the courts to the mental health professionals, particularly in those geographic areas served by community forensic centers. Future research should address this issue.

The custody function is also in the process of shifting its base within the system. There can be no doubt that persons now housed in correctional and civil mental health facilities would have remained at LSH had the Davis v. Watkins suit not occurred. The impact of this shift is most directly evident in terms of increasing populations in corrections and civil mental health institutions, though there are a number of less-evident indirect effects that deserve further study.

The treatment function, which is performed in conjunction with the custody function, is currently only poorly defined. This definitional problem (that is, what constitutes treatment activity), appears to be a significant block to meaningful studies of this function and it must be addressed. Furthermore, which agency is responsible for treatment is unclear. When the community forensic centers were established, there was widespread claim that they would begin to assume this function. There is little evidence to suggest that they either have or intend to assume this responsibility. Our data suggest that there is a significant desire, on the part of Ohio courts, for more treatment services. This need, which does not necessarily manifest itself in a demand for inpatient services, seems to result from a general dissatisfaction with the quality of treatment services offered at LSH.

We believe that this description of the FPSDS in terms of the above functions demonstrates the pervasiveness of each function and suggests that all functions must be provided for a coherent system. The value of this analysis lies in the fact that it demonstrates that functions to not disappear just because they have shifted to another part of the system. They change form, and they impact on different groups, but the functions themselves and the demands for them remain.

Overall, there are at least four highly significant conclusions that can be drawn from this report:

The decrease in examination commitments to LSH after 1971 has more than been made up by the increasing commitments to community forensic centers and civil mental health institutions. However, the question of whether LSH and the alternative examining institutions are serving the same client population is still in doubt. The possibility exists that a number of the cases that are now being examined would not have been examined several years ago because they would not have been considered serious enough. The proportion of persons examined who have been convicted or accused of misdemeanors appears to be rising over time, while those accused of felonies appears to be decreasing. Without regard to the makeup of the client population being served, however, the trend toward ever-increasing referrals for forensic services shows no sign of abating and the users of the services report significant unmet needs for services.

There is a serious lack of coordination among the elements of the FPSDS. The Division of Forensic Psychiatry has been unable to serve as a coordinating body for a variety of reasons. Clearly, its personnel are occupied with problems at LSH that at times threaten to consume all the energies of the division. The control that the division is able to exercise over referrals to its facilities is minimal. The division can only play a gatekeeper role that can easily be thwarted by persistent and insistent courts. The forensic centers are funded in a manner that limits the control that can be exercised over them. Finally, even coordination with Corrections is difficult because Corrections views the Department of Mental Health and Mental Retardation as an equal but it does not regard the Division of Forensic Psychiatry as such.

The nature of LSH's population is changing. In one sense it is becoming more hard core while at the same time it consists more and more of persons on incompetency commitments who have not been convicted. An increasing percentage of its commitments is indefinites.

As community forensic centers become more widespread, the dependence of the courts upon them can be expected to increase. The role of the centers appears to be in the provision of information, but there is some evidence that they may become the decision makers by default. Thus the quality of the information they provide must be as high as possible.

NOTES

1. Van Court Hare, Jr., Systems Analysis: A Diagnostical Approach (New York: Harcourt, Brace, and World, 1967), p. 13.

2. D. Katz and R. L. Kahn, "Common Characteristics of Open Systems," in Systems Thinking, ed. F. E. Eioery (Baltimore: Penquin Books, 1969), pp. 86-105.

3. See Nancy J. Beran, Erick W. Carlson, and Harry E. Allen, The Forensic Psychiatric Centers of Ohio: An Integrative Report (Columbus: Ohio State University, Program for the Study of Crime and Delinquency, October 1975); Beverly G. Toomey, Nancy J. Beran, and Eric W. Carlson, An Evaluation of the Akron Criminal Courts Psycho-Diagnostic Clinic: An Experiment in Community-Based Forensic Services (Columbus: Ohio State University, Program for the Study of Crime and Delinquency, October 1975); Beverly G. Toomey, Nancy J. Beran, and Eric W. Carlson, An Evaluation of the Columbus Forensic Psychiatric Services (Columbus: Ohio State University, Program for the Study of Crime and Delinquency, October 1975); Josephine Ann Colli, Nancy J. Beran, and Eric W. Carlson, An Evaluation of the Butler County Forensic Psychiatric Services (Columbus: Ohio State University, Program for the Study of Crime and Delinquency, October 1975); Franklin H. Marshall, Nancy J. Beran, and Eric W. Carlson, An Evaluation of Community-Based Forensic Psychiatric Services in Cincinnati Area (Columbus: Ohio State University, Program for the Study of Crime and Delinquency, October 1975); Nancy J. Beran, Erice W. Carlson, and Harry E. Allen, An Evaluation of the Dayton Center for Forensic Psychiatry: An Experiment in Community-Based Services (Columbus: Ohio State University, September 1974); Nancy J. Beran and Harry E. Allen, An Evaluation of the Toledo Court Diagnostic and Treatment Center: An Experiment in Community-Based Forensic Psychiatric Services (Columbus: Ohio State University, Program for the Study of Crime and Delinquency, April 1974).

4. Ibid.

5. 384 F. Supp. 1196.

6. Beran, Carlson, and Allen, An Evaluation of the Dayton Center for Forensic Psychiatry.

7. See Minutes of the Ohio Forensic Psychiatric Center Director's Association Meeting, Toledo, April 28, 1976.

8. Ohio Revised Code, sec. 5125.03.

9. Beran and Allen, op. cit., p. 55.

10. See studies listed in note 3.

11. Ohio Revised Code, sec. 2945.37-40.

12. See studies listed in note 3.

13. Ohio Revised Code, sec. 3719.51.

10

REMAINING ISSUES AND
RECOMMENDATIONS

REMAINING ISSUES

The findings presented in Chapters 8 and 9 are strongly supportive of the program for community-based forensic services in the
state of Ohio. Numerous unresolved issues nevertheless remain, and
most of them are intimately related to the basic systemic question of
who should be providing what kinds of services to whom. For example, all six community-based centers that were studied in detail have
experienced dramatic increases in caseload size over time. To some,
this state of affairs suggests an excessive definition of criminal justice cases in mental health terms; to others, it suggests a genuine
need being progressively better met. Thus some center directors
express desires for program expansion to accommodate greater numbers and varieties of clients. Others, however, are attempting to
more selectively define the type of client appropriately referred to a
center. Some are working on expanding the scope of their service
capability, while others are trying to reduce it.

The source of burgeoning caseloads, of course, is the criminal
justice system. Agents of this system, however, perceive a contin-
uing unmet need for clinical evaluation and treatment services (especially the latter) even after the opening of the centers. Indeed,
while stating that the centers have become their primary resources
for forensic services, referral agents informed the research team
(and hard data substantiated) that scores of clients are still being referred to civil mental health facilities. Some of these referral agents
would like to see the centers service all forensic clients; others selectively define the type of client they believe to be an appropriate referral to a center and refer all others to other sectors of the mental
health system.

The other sectors of the mental health system, of course, include the state institution for mentally disordered offenders and the civil branches. The former, Lima State Hospital, has not been a readily available resource for the last several years, and civil mental health facilities have therefore been solicited to accommodate some forensic clients, especially those adjudged in need of inpatient care. Some of these facilities have adopted open-door policies in relation to the criminal justice system; others selectively define the type of client they will accept.

Over and again the research team witnessed controversies that ultimately boiled down to this issue of who should be providing what kinds of services to whom. On the face of it, the issues would appear to be conceptually separate and narrow in scope: Should the centers provide all forensic services to all criminal justice agencies in their locales? Should the centers provide treatment services? Should the centers have access to or control over an inpatient unit? Are the centers receiving inappropriate referrals? Invariably, however, efforts to answer these questions led into a morass of confusion over basic systemic issues. Clearly, substantial differences exist among center personnel, criminal justice referral agents, and civil mental health officials regarding the most preferable course of action. Some would like to see the centers providing the totality of forensic services, others would not. Some think the centers should have active treatment programs, others do not. Some believe the centers need inpatient units, others do not. And so on.

Despite all the confusion and disagreement, some conclusions are clear from the data presented in Chapters 8 and 9. In Ohio there is a need for forensic evaluation and treatment services of both inpatient and outpatient varieties. This need is perceived by criminal justice system agents as both growing and not wholly met, and hard data support these perceptions. The forensic centers are impacting substantially upon the need for outpatient evaluation services but, with a few notable exceptions, only minimally upon the need for treatment and not at all upon the need for inpatient services. The civil mental health system, which is equipped to provide treatment and inpatient services, assumes a generally hostile posture toward the criminal justice system. Some question, however, the appropriateness of forensic referrals to civil mental health, claiming that the proper management of certain forensic cases necessitates knowledge of legal parameters not typically a part of clinical training, and that special expertise is required to deal with the highly manipulative style of many criminal justice clients.

RECOMMENDATIONS

After attempting to weigh all of the diverse strands of data from a holistic and integrative perspective, the research team recommended the following:

Continued support should be given to the development and maintenance of forensic psychiatric centers in the state of Ohio by the Department of Mental Health and Mental Retardation and the Division of Forensic Psychiatry. The centers studied in depth in this project are proving to be cost-effective community-based supplements, if not alternatives, to the evaluation services of Lima State Hospital.

Standards and guidelines for the certification of forensic centers and for the conduct of forensic examiners should be developed by the Department of Mental Health and Mental Retardation and the Division of Forensic Psychiatry. In areas without forensic centers, uniform policies for the acceptance of forensic evaluation referrals at civil facilities should be developed.

The centers and the Division of Forensic Psychiatry should evaluate the respective merits of the part-time consultant approach and the full-time employee approach to the staffing of the centers. A wide variety of considerations impinge upon this issue and range from budgetary and caseload variables to the differential refinement of skills in dealing with forensic statutory questions and forensic clients. Correlatively, the research team recommends adherence to the interdisciplinary team approach typical of community mental health. Recent legislation in Ohio qualifying licensed psychologists to testify as expert witnesses under the competency/sanity statutes reflects and supports this increasingly popular orientation.

The role of treatment services at the forensic centers should be reassessed. On the one hand, the provision of treatment might function to minimize staff turnover since most clinicians prefer positions offering them opportunities to do more than conduct mental-status evaluations. Furthermore, in light of the reluctance of civil mental health programs to accept criminal justice clients, the centers may be the only treatment source available to them. On the other hand, the charter of community mental health can easily be interpreted to mandate the provision of treatment services to forensic clients. Another variable that may effectively curtail the role of treatment at the centers is their steadily rising caseloads.

The need for inpatient services for some forensic clients should be addressed. The use of special units, if not the regular wards of civil facilities, should be considered as one possible alternative.

The rights of forensic clients should be recognized and scrupulously protected. An initial step would be to require that all reports that pass from forensic center personnel to the courts be in writing and that clients' rights of access to these reports be recognized. It should also be noted that Lima State Hospital may be becoming a holding institution for difficult cases that would pose special problems in the areas of treatment and review. In all, a broad range of legal problems incumbent upon shifting clients from corrections to mental health and vice versa must be acknowledged and addressed.

Legislation should be proposed by the Department of Mental Health and Mental Retardation to correct vague and confusing statutes in the forensic area. Outstanding examples include the statutes governing incompetency, insanity, and psychopathy.

Substantive communications should be improved among all relevant sectors of the criminal justice, mental health, and forensic systems. While communication breakdowns and gaps are all too frequently blamed for problems that are in fact of much greater complexity, the impression of the research team is that communications among various sectors of the system under study are simultaneously so grossly inadequate and so central to the meaningful provision of forensic services as to constitute a major problem in and of itself. The problem is manifest at a number of levels: between the centers and criminal justice referral agents, between the centers and the Division of Forensic Psychiatry, and between all three sectors and the civil mental health appartus, including the balance of the Department of Mental Health and Mental Retardation. There is a clear need for the Division of Forensic Psychiatry and the administrators of centers to clarify understandings of precisely what services centers are expected to provide for the funding they receive. The Center Directors Association appears to be making significant strides toward developing communications among centers, and the association should be encouraged by state administrators as an organization for policy recommendation and implementation.

DISCUSSION

The question that stands behind many of these recommendations is the same question that has been apparent at various junctures in this book: Why aren't forensic services provided under the aegis of community mental health? The mandate of community mental health is broad and all-encompassing. Comprehensive, continuous, coordinated care is to be provided in both inpatient and outpatient settings and on a partial hospitalization and 24-hour emergency basis. Consultation and education are to be conducted with all manner of community agencies and institutions. With such a mission, community mental health would appear open if not actually obligated to provide a wide range of services for clients in the criminal justice system.

There are other more compelling arguments that can be made for including forensic services within the scope of community mental health. Probably the most important is that professionals in the civil mental health system are by definition in a more neutral position than are professionals in the forensic centers or forensic institutions. Specialized forensic units are arms of the criminal justice system, and their staffs can scarcely be expected to function as independent outside experts. Indeed, one of the problems raised by forensic center staff members during the course of the evaluation project was the difficulty in identifying for whom one was working or, more directly, whose side one was on, the client's or the court's.

Conflicts of interest between the patient and society are not unknown, of course, in the civil mental health system, as involuntary commitment procedures clearly indicate. But the whole point is that these already sensitive issues (including confidentiality between client and clinician) are only aggravated by making the clinician in essence an extension of the court or prosecutor's office. Perhaps some of the manipulative style reportedly characteristic of forensic clients reflects their recognition of this conflict of interest. The clients know full well whose side the clinicians are on.

Inclusion of forensic services under the purview of civil mental health would also discourage the conceptualization of forensic clients as a special category or type of mentally disordered people. The development of specialized units for the evaluation and treatment of mentally disordered offenders perpetuates the myth that criminal justice clients suffer from some unique varieties of mental illness, varieties unknown among other mental patients. There is no empirical support for the contention that the "criminally insane" possess their own private set of mental peculiarities, but the specialized status supports the view that they do. It is a short step from there to the equally erroneous conclusion that these exclusive peculiarities are especially conducive to bizarre and violent behavior.

In a similar vein, the specialized designation of mentally disordered offenders results in a double-barreled stigma. Civil mental patients suffer stigmatization, as do criminal offenders whose mental status has not been questioned. Each of the two major deviance definition and management systems places a burden of stigma upon its clients, as the labels "ex-con" and "ex-mental patient" testify. The "criminally insane" bear both labels, and the combination is likely more than additive when it comes to the resultant stigma.

The counterargument claims that specialized forensic services are advisable because of both the client tendency toward excessive manipulation and the absence of exposure to relevant legal parameters in standard clinical training. But these problems seem neither insurmountable nor sufficient to justify the obverse problems just enumerated. Manipulative behavior is a part of many syndromes and is not unlike other mechanisms and dynamics that mental health practitioners are regularly trained to diagnose and treat, that they frequently encounter among patients, and that they commonly handle quite well. More importantly, it is not as though forensic practitioners have themselves (as yet, anyway) devised procedures especially fruitful in the management of excessively manipulative clients. Should this ever be accomplished, the resultant new knowledge could be integrated into existent clinical training programs.

A similar line of reasoning applies to the lack of knowledge regarding legal issues. Clinicians who currently function as forensic specialists had to learn about these issues during on-the-job training. Community mental health workers could learn them the same way. No formal education prepares a person for all the contingencies to be encountered in the field. Conversely, cursory study of major issues in the evaluation and treatment of criminal justice clients could be easily included in standard clinical training programs.

From this perspective, separate and distinct labels, facilities, programs, and personnel for forensic clients seem neither necessary nor desirable. If forensic clients possess no special sorts of mental problems, then civil mental health should prove adequate to the clinical task. Community mental health in particular provides a service base more all-inclusive and diversified than heretofore known in the mental health field. Specialized forensic services represent a costly and unnecessary duplication of resources. That such specialized services are undesirable is evidenced by the compromise in professional clinical neutrality, the implication of unique client pathology, and the double stigma on the client that they promote.

We are not reneging on our earlier recommendation that continued support be given to the development and maintenance of forensic psychiatric centers in the state of Ohio. What we're suggesting is that attention be directed toward ultimately bringing the administration and operation of these programs under the umbrella of community mental health. In the final analysis, a certain degree of specialization of forensic services would likely occur even under the aegis of community mental health, and this is no more undesirable than any other routinely accepted specialization in adolescent services, geriatric services, acute suicidal services, or whatever. A similar service for forensic clients could address any problems with unusually manipulative clients and enhance staff acquaintance with legal issues.

What seems prudent to avoid, from both practical and philosophical bases, is the degree of specialization that casts mentally disordered offenders as unique types of beings especially prone to vicious and violent acts. That kind of mythology is a disservice to both the mental health and criminal justice systems and to any studied efforts to coordinate the two. More important, it is a disservice to the clients.

11

OHIO'S FORENSIC SYSTEM:
FUTURE PLANS

Timothy B. Moritz

As Seymour Halleck points out, Thomas Szasz always shakes up your belief systems and starts you thinking along new lines. Although you may not agree with him, he certainly challenges you to reexamine the full range of your own beliefs and to test their validity. He challenges you to identify which beliefs have scientific underpinnings and which are more reflective of a philosophical position, a system of morals, or a political philosophy.

A few years ago, when Ohio's civil commitment laws were in the process of being changed, I noted that by a change in administrative policy and philosophy we had substantially reduced involuntary commitments to state mental hospitals—from 85 to 55 percent—in a relatively short period of time. This difference represented something in the neighborhood of 4,000 people.

Since then, we have gone on to enact House Bill 244 to clarify Ohio's laws concerning the civil rights of the mentally ill and to provide much more rigorous due process protections. The trend has continued so that now I am able to report that approximately 75 percent of the people in our state mental hospitals are now there on a voluntary basis. That change from involuntary to voluntary plus the reduction in patient population produced by the discharge of many involuntary commitments means that we have 6,000 fewer people involuntarily committed to our state mental hospitals today then we had two years ago. That's three and a half times less.

As Halleck said, we are changing the trends and, in Ohio, very rapidly and at a very accelerating pace. I know that Szasz's position would be that the 1,750 remaining patients are 1,750 too many. Maybe so, but at least we are changing and moving in the dfrections that he has been advocating, and we certainly have much closer professional and court scrutiny over the process governing the relatively few who remain behind. I think this has also had a positive impact on the internal milieu of our hospitals. Clearly, when patients are there on a voluntary basis, it begins to change the nature of staff-patient relationships, as well as the patient's own self-image.

There is an interesting development under way in a federal class-action suit facing Ohio. The U.S. Department of Justice is trying to get the federal court to issue an order that would make it impossible for patients in one of our mental hospitals in the future to have the free choice of whether they want to stay there or go to some alternative facility. They would like the court to order that we reduce the 700-bed facility to 50 beds, which would force many patients out into the community, whether they want to go or not. I'm a strong advocate of having community alternatives available and of giving the patient a free choice between facilities and types of treatment, but I don't think the federal court has any business telling both the sovereign state of Ohio and all those patients that "Thou shall not live in such and such state hospital whether you want to or not" in that kind of a radical fashion. I think that is government tyranny, and I trust the court will not permit the will of the Department of Justice to prevail upon us.

ADMINISTRATION OF FORENSIC SERVICES

The subject of this chapter is the state of Ohio's future plans for forensic services. The research that led to the conference dealt with the community forensic centers. These centers represent one of the elements of the criminal justice system with which the Division of Forensic Psychiatry is involved. The other elements are the outpatient clinics, the institutions of the Department of Rehabilitation and Correction, and the major inpatient facility, Lima State Hospital. Actually, the division is involved only with the criminal aspects of forensic psychiatry, not the full range. This is partly by design, partly by necessity. It was reflected in the original designation of the division, the Division of Psychiatric Criminology, when it was established in 1966. The subsequent name change occurred partly because doctors resented being referred to as "criminal psychiatrists."

The purpose of the division at the time was to form a bridge between the Divisions of Mental Health and Corrections and to make more of the resources of Mental Health available to Corrections. Although some cooperative efforts were achieved in this bridging function, they could not prevent the ultimate separation of the department into two independent departments: Mental Health and Rehabilitation and Correction. We certainly endorse the split that did occur. The professional staff of the division overwhelmingly preferred to stay with Mental Health and did so.

THE COMMUNITY FORENSIC CENTERS

From the onset the division's major function was to administer Lima State Hospital, Ohio's institution for the "criminally insane." It was in many respects a thankless task. The institution was overpopulated and understaffed. The hospital had no control over admissions. Patients came from all parts of the state and from corrections. To remedy this situation, the decision was made to establish local outpatient evaluation centers. The Massachusetts system was used as a model. The pilot was established in Dayton in 1971 with funding through the Law Enforcement Assistance Administration (LEAA). This center is still the only one that is directly administered through the central office.

The pilot was successful. It was well received by the courts and other criminal justice agencies. It soon became clear that evaluations could be performed locally without sacrificing quality, and that local centers were more responsive to the needs of the local courts. However, pressures for resolution of the population problem at Lima mounted rapidly and forced the division to improvise. Centers in Columbus and Cincinnati were opened through direct contracts with local mental health centers. In Toledo we contracted with an existing incorporated court clinic. Although we prefer not to have centers directly associated with courts or probation departments (in order to keep more flexibility and independence), we contracted with the center in Akron, which was part of the probation department. Independent centers in Springfield and Hamilton were developed with funding through Cincinnati and Dayton, and Cleveland was left to operate its independent court clinic since this was successful in keeping patients out of Lima and no requests for additional funding were received from Cleveland at the time.

Later, centers were established with LEAA funding and contracts with the local 648 boards. The result was a collection of many different types and models, with various levels of staffing (most contracting for professional services), different levels of expertise, and different administrative and liaison skills. Significant differences also developed in the types of services provided, from purely evaluative to treatment, emergency intervention, and consultation and education. And finally, differences developed regarding to whom services were provided, from common pleas and county courts, to municipal courts, jails, and parole and probation departments. Two centers are associated with medical schools.

One of the interesting results to come out of the centers is the Association of Forensic Center Directors. This group formed spontaneously and has been meeting monthly, exchanging viewpoints, sharing information, and gradually becoming a body of expertise that has been invaluable in assisting the division in the difficult task of coordinating the various centers. They have been concerned with training needs, have set aside during their meetings a separate portion of their time for training, and are developing certification standards for forensic centers. This group as a body has accumulated a vast knowledge of the forensic court system and has assisted the department in developing new forensic legislation. One advantage of the group as an independent body is that it has been less sensitive to budgetary concerns and has been able to continue its meetings even in times of austerity.

THE STATE INPATIENT FACILITY

Lima State Hospital, in the meantime, had a number of successive crisis situations. Investigations in 1972 into criminal abuse of patients involving a substantial number of employees resulted in few convictions and left morale lower than ever and the institution's reputation at an all-time low. A federal class-action suit against the hospital and the department began in 1973. In 1974 the Interim Order in Davis v. Watkins was issued, mandating the hospital to provide humane care and adequate treatment in specifying civil rights for the patients. A crucial item was the designation of Lima as a maximum security facility and the establishment of criteria for patients in need of maximum security, thus enforcing the right to treatment in the least restrictive environment. By applying these criteria, the population of the hospital decreased in a few months from 600 to 450. The court order also allowed the hospital to exert some control over new admissions and was an important factor in future planning for security needs in the department. Other federal court decisions also played a role in decreasing the hospital population. Jackson v. Indiana limits the involuntary commitment of a person incompetent to stand trial to a reasonable period of time and resulted in the transfer to civil mental hospitals of a substantial number of patients, some of whom had been held in Lima for over 20 years, and some for relatively minor offenses.

Progress toward compliance with the interim court order was slow at first. This was partly due to the inertia of the system, partly to budgetary problems, to some degree to lack of understanding of the order and its urgency, and to a "waiting for Godot" attitude, in this case, for a final court order that has as yet not been issued.

The urgency became clear when the court on January 21, 1977, issued a contempt citation based on the status as of March 1976. At that point the department moved rapidly, establishing a compliance monitoring system and making additional funds available to hire staff and to make the necessary physical improvements. Some of this, of course, had been under way all along, but it was accelerated at that point.

The staff-to-resident ratio has improved 90 percent in the last 28 months. The current ratio of 214 staff to 100 patients is more than double the national average for public mental hospitals and five times better than Lima was in 1971. Highly qualified professional and management staff have been recruited to provide new leadership. The hospital has now reached a high compliance level that we feel will be acceptable to the court. In the meantime we decided not to wait for the anticipated three-judge panel decision on the constitutionality of the Ohio forensic statutes but to proceed with the development of legislation that would, it is hoped, moot the issues. Legislation was developed in line with recent federal court decisions and introduced in April 1977 as House Bill 565.* This bill represents a major philosophical shift from the present manner in which the criminal offender enters the mental health system.

LEGISLATIVE REFORM

Current statutes dealing with disposition of those found not guilty by reason of insanity, incompetent to stand trial, and penal transfers have concentrated on direct judicial commitment powers with plenary review authority vested in the same committing judges. While recent revisions in the Ascherman Act and incompetency sections allow for more due process, they still place the major decision making for release or transfer in the hands of the court. House Bill 565 is premised on the concept that individuals should not enter into the mental health system unless they meet the stringent requirements of civil commitment criteria. Evaluations by certified forensic centers or by private psychologists or psychiatrists will provide data to the court to make determinations as to insanity at the time of the offense or incompetency to stand trial. Strict time limits for evaluation are required as well as an opportunity for outpatient evaluation by private professionals.

An important aspect of the bill repeals the Ascherman Act, which deals with presentence evaluations and indefinite commitments

---

*This bill was passed in amended form in August 1978.

with suspended sentence for sexual psychopaths or persons found to be mentally ill or mentally retarded. The Ascherman Act, aside from its questionable constitutionality, has been found to be very unworkable in practice for a number of reasons. The individuals previously referred to under this statute can be dealt with under existing statutes that provide for presentence and probation evaluation.

The impact of this legislation is difficult to predict. Fewer patients found not guilty by reason of insanity and incompetent to stand trial will be treated at maximum security facilities. Evaluation and treatment will take place at the least restrictive level. The bill will require a more acute awareness of the security needs of patients and a smoother transition between various levels of security in the system. The treatment system in which the security function is carried out far from the other facilities cannot be seen as responsive to the patient's needs.

FACILITIES AND SERVICES FOR THE FUTURE

In order to facilitate the coordination and integration of security needs throughout the system, and because of the high cost of renovating Lima to meet various standards, and because of traditional difficulties in attracting qualified staff to Lima, we have decided to build three alternate facilities. These regional inpatient units will be located in the Cleveland area, Columbus, and Dayton. They will be built on the grounds of existing hospitals and will operate under the administrative responsibility of those hospitals. We have projected a total capacity of some 300 beds for these facilities. We hope to have all three facilities university-affiliated with active training and research programs in addition to high-quality therapeutic programs, They will be closely integrated into the community forensic and human service systems.

In addition to these three units, we are planning for a facility for the sentenced prisoners transferred from correctional facilities. We are constantly rethinking our future function in corrections. So far, we have provided consultants to the prison system who work primarily on an outpatient basis in a strict psychiatric medical type of practice. The division has a statutory obligation to provide psychiatric services to the Department of Corrections. Whether this situation is in the best interests of the inmates is uncertain. Ultimately, the total mental health needs in the correctional institutions have to be addressed in a much broader sense than has been done in the past. This system of mental health care has to be functionally and administratively closely integrated into the total prison environment and we have to question whether an outside agency is a proper provider of care in such a system.

Much is left to be done in the area of the forensic outpatient
centers. We consider the first phase to be completed. We have established a forensic center at Lima that makes it possible to bring
patients in for evaluation on a one-day in-and-out basis. The courts
have reacted favorably to the concept. We also recently opened centers in the Canton, Youngstown, and Mansfield areas. This means
that all major population centers now have access to forensic centers,
and the need for admission to Lima State Hospital is reduced to a
minimum. As I pointed out earlier, there is a great deal of difference between services provided by the centers and the staffing of the
centers. There is a need to coordinate these services. We will continue to work with and through the Association of Forensic Center
Directors toward that goal.

More coordination is also needed at the central office level.
Two factors will facilitate this process. One is the strengthening and
greater degree of independence of the Division of Forensic Psychiatry,
and the other is increased understanding in the other divisions (Mental Health and Mental Retardation) of forensic psychiatry in general,
through increased involvement in the area. We also need an understanding of our functions and purpose from the other elements of the
criminal justice system. The local centers, through close and con-
stand contacts with the courts, have contributed considerably toward
this goal. The division is planning a series of seminars in which various elements of the criminal justice and mental health systems are
brought together. Opportunities for discussion and for becoming better acquainted with each other will be emphasized.

We realize that many needs for mental health services in the
criminal justice system have not been met. Although the department
has made a commitment to fund services to the county courts, many
municipal courts are in need of similar services. In fact, we see
services to municipal courts as a prevention function since many adult
offenders come to us with a history of a multitude of contacts with the
municipal courts. We are looking at these needs and working toward
a solution through better coordination with local mental health centers.
We are also surveying the mental health needs in county and city jails,
and we find that many of their inmates are in need of various levels of
mental health care. It is hoped that recent federal court decisions
will improve facilities at the jails so that these needs can be met as
much as needed within the facility.

Contacts with medical schools have been facilitated by the forensic centers. We hope to establish fellowships in forensic psychiatry at the medical schools in Cincinnati and Cleveland, and perhaps
in Dayton. Wright State University Medical School has recently been
able to attract a highly qualified and experienced psychiatrist and has
given him a faculty appointment with special responsibilities in forensic
psychiatry and as a liaison to our department's facilities.

In summary, we feel encouraged and excited with the recent trends in forensic psychiatry. Improvements in the care at Lima State Hospital have been considerable. Staffing has increased to the extent that all professional departments are at least adequately staffed with qualified mental health professionals. The population has decreased to 320, compared to a population of 1,300 just six years ago. The new inpatient units will be modern and attractive facilities, meeting all relevant national standards, and will get high priority in providing excellent and intensive care. The community forensic centers are expanding and becoming an integral part of the mental health delivery system. The new legislation will assure that patients will move through the system in accordance with the most recent concepts of care and civil rights. Expansion will continue in the future. So far, legislators have been reacting favorably to our efforts and have responded by providing us with a more adequate budget.

Let me say in closing that regardless of our beliefs on any single issue, we who are clinicians and administrators within the public system must work within the existing legal structure. From our studies of the law and our consultation with many, many attorneys, I don't think the state of Ohio could even pass the laws that Szasz advocates because of federal court decisions. So many of the things that are being advocated at this point would be considered unconstitutional. Until there is a change at that federal level, we have to work the best we can to provide for due process and adequate treatment within the provisions of Ohio law within the framework of the federal court decisions. We are trying to do the best we can within that frame of reference.

DISCUSSION

Question: I have two questions. I believe Dr. Halleck commented earlier that, nationwide, about 40 percent of psychiatric graduate students are foreign born and foreign speaking. Does that hold true for Ohio and do you see that as a problem in terms of communicating with patients? My second question is, Do you feel that taking all of the forensic services in the state and putting them under the state Department of Mental Health and Mental Retardation would be a more effective plan than the existing structure of 648 boards in conjunction with the state?

Moritz: On the first question, I'm not sure of the composition of the psychiatric residency classes operated by the universities in the state of Ohio. I don't think the figure is quite as high as that which you quoted. If we took the psychiatric residency programs that are currently operated by our department, the figure is far higher than that. In fact, last year the department's own residency training program consisted 100 percent of foreign medical graduates. In terms of the actual composition of the staff of state mental hospitals, the foreign graduates are running 70-75 percent of our total medical and psychiatric staff.

This is a matter of supply and demand in the marketplace, and we could speculate for a long time on the reasons concerning that. It's certainly not that we're discriminating against American graduates. It's everything from market economics to stigma and professional job satisfaction that have to be overcome in the process. We have slightly improved this situation in the last two years, but not very much. Yes, for some foreign graduates and for some patients the language barriers can be quite significant. On the other hand, some of our finest psychiatrists and clinicians are foreign born and graduates of foreign medical colleges. It boils down to whether the practitioner and the individual patient can relate to each other. Statistically, nevertheless, I think it's a problem.

With regard to your second question, I don't think I'm in favor of the state of Ohio, or any state, or the federal government operating all services in one network. It's a little scary, especially along the lines of Szasz's statements about social control. In general I think it's better to have things decentralized and with the heavy involvement of the private sector as well as local government. While we're maintaining a flexible position, I would not personally advocate a totally state-controlled and -operated system now.

Question: If I may, I'd like to go back to the first question for a minute. Do you have any plans to alleviate the problems regarding foreign graduate students, and what are they?

Moritz: Yes, we have plans. One thing we've already done is to go to the legislature to get significant increases in salaries with the ability to pay supplemental compensation. Using that, we have recruited some very good people. Second, we have been emphasizing affiliating our facilities, and especially our psychiatric resident training programs, with the universities. To assist in the recruitment and retention of staff, we would like to have the ability to offer university appointments in some cases. At the very least we want the stimulation of the university involvement, and we are moving ahead with that. It's not a fully developed program, but we have quite a few affiliations enacted and several more are under negotiation right now. I'd like eventually to have all of our facilities university affiliated.

We are also, of course, trying to overcome some of the stigma and some of the poor working conditions that have scared both professionals and voluntary patients away in the past. Our emphasis is on physical environment, staffing patterns, and the quality of care to make our facilities more attractive places for good professionals to work as well as for patients to seek voluntary treatment. It's a multi-faceted program and we're making a lot of progress overall, but our recruitment of psychiatrists hasn't quite caught up with some of the other progress we're making.

Szasz: I was really very impressed by what Moritz said, and certainly with the reduction by 6,000 patients in two years. That's a lot more than I have done. And I loved your last point—that you have to operate within the system and within the law. As you know, I am a great believer in operating within the system and the law and not taking the law into one's own hands just because one doesn't like it.

But it seems to me that your presentation really pointed to another major question that just has to be articulated, and that is: Why do we need so many medical doctors? You have managed to reclassify the category of people who belong in Lima State Hospital; if you could next reclassify the running of hospitals so that there would be a minimum number of M.D.s, I think it would be a major step, nationwide, worldwide. We need M.D.s only to take care of people who have diabetes, epilepsy, and possibly to have some control over drugs, and all of this takes very little time. I think we should have the human services—talking, so-called psychotherapy, milieu therapy (more talking), and, of course, job training; everything else that is not strictly medical—in lay hands, or social workers, or psychologists. Frankly, I don't even think you need a Ph.D. in clinical psychology for it; I think a B.A. degree is plenty. I don't mean this in terms of belittling the nature of the job, because what you need for this is not so much technical information but experience and common decency.

I also want to add that these foreign graduates are really hired only for one reason: because they have the M.D. degree. I have nothing against foreigners, obviously, but in my opinion, not speaking good English and not understanding idiomatic English should disqualify one from the job. It's ludicrous to have an M.D. who knows about anatomy but doesn't know about butterflies in the stomach and who doesn't know colloquial English. For that matter, it's even ludicrous to have a WASP psychiatrist from New England taking care of poor blacks in Louisiana or vice versa.

Moritz: The question is certainly a provocative one and certainly something we have all thought about; among the reasons are those you cited. In every single civil rights legal action suit that we're involved in, one of the major issues is to increase the number of qualified professionals as defined by the legal aid societies and the courts.

They cite the exact numbers and ratios of every professional discipline you have to have on your staff. So that's one of the reasons.

Another reason is that outside the forensic system, in the civil system, the federal government won't pay Medicaid or Medicare and the health insurance industry won't pay Blue Cross or other health insurance benefits if you don't meet those standards that are set by either the Department of Health, Education and Welfare or the Joint Commission on the Accreditation of Hospitals. Not only may the state or private-agency provider not get the revenue they need to staff their facilities properly, but also the patient may be ruined financially because his insurance won't pay the bills. He may have to spend his life savings on his treatment, and the whole family could be jeopardized. As always, Szasz's comments are provocative ones that should be considered, but there is a lot of resistance in the system to those kinds of change.

Question: Halleck indicated that he had visited Florida and learned that they are building a 2,000-bed hospital for forensic inpatient care. You commented that the Ohio plan includes 300 beds. Is that because you feel that's all we need, because we're not going to have a lot of inpatients, or do you have other plans for additional inpatient facilities?

Moritz: I think it's probably a combination of many things. I can't comment on Florida's plans, but we don't think we have 2,000 people who need that kind of facility today. I think we probably treat a higher percentage of our people in the civil system in both state hospitals and in the community. We must use probation and parole a lot more than they do. Since we have a higher total population than Florida we're obviously treating our people in a less restrictive way.

Question: Do you feel that 300 is probably all we're going to need for the near future?

Moritz: Yes, although it's a little hard to project this population because while our mental health population is decreasing, the general prison population has been increasing. This may be an indication that people are beginning to do what Szasz is advocating. In the state of Ohio and nationally, we are having fewer people involuntarily committed to mental hospitals and more people being locked up in jails, for better or for worse.

ABOUT THE EDITORS AND
CONTRIBUTORS

NANCY J. BERAN is an associate professor of sociology and the Lavelle Professor of Criminal Justice at Ohio Dominican College. She received a doctorate in sociology from Ohio State University. Her teaching interests include deviance, criminology, and corrections courses as well as sociological theory and methods courses and interdisciplinary studies.

BEVERLY G. TOOMEY, who has studied both psychology and the sociology of deviance, earned her Ph. D. in social work at Ohio State University. She currently teaches human behavior theory, deviance and law, and research methodology courses in the College of Social Work at Ohio State University.

ERIC W. CARLSON received his Ph. D. in public administration from Ohio State University. Formerly associate director of the Ohio State University Program for the Study of Crime and Delinquency, he is currently an assistant professor of public administration at the University of Arizona.

SEYMOUR L. HALLECK, author of countless books and articles and a well-known forensic psychiatrist, received the Sutherland Award of the American Society of Criminology in 1978. Dr. Halleck received an M. D. and a Ph. B. from the University of Chicago and he now teaches both psychiatry and law at the University of North Carolina.

NICHOLAS N. KITTRIE is professor of criminal and comparative law at the American University Law School. He is past president of the American Society of Criminology and is currently Dean of the Law School. Dr. Kittrie has degrees in law and international studies from Georgetown University.

TIMOTHY B. MORITZ is the director of the Department of Mental Health and Mental Retardation in the state of Ohio. A board-certified psychiatrist, he received his medical degree from Cornell. Dr. Moritz has extensive experience in community mental health and has coauthored articles on drug abuse, alcoholism, and mental health.

DEE ROTH is chief of the Office of Program Evaluation and Research of the Ohio Department of Mental Health and Mental Retardation. Ms. Roth completed her M. A. and some doctoral studies in sociology at Ohio State University. She is a founding member and secretary-treasurer of the Executive Committee of the National Association of State Mental Health Research Directors and also is a member of the Region V National Institute of Mental Health Steering Committee on Evaluation.

THOMAS S. SZASZ is a professor of psychiatry at the State University of New York at Syracuse. His nontraditional approach to mental illness is reflected in more than a dozen books and the fact that he is a cofounder of the American Association for the Abolition of Involuntary Mental Hospitalization. Dr. Szasz received both his undergraduate and medical degrees from the University of Cincinnati.

ALIENATION IN CONTEMPORARY SOCIETY: A
Multidisciplinary Examination
edited by
Roy S. Bryce-Laporte
Claudewell S. Thomas

LEGALITY, MORALITY, AND ETHICS IN CRIMINAL
JUSTICE
edited by
Nicholas N. Kittrie
Jackwell Susman

OFFENDERS AND CORRECTIONS
edited by
Denis Szabo
Susan Katzenelson

REFORM IN CORRECTIONS: Problems and Issues
edited by
Harry E. Allen
Nancy J. Beran

TREATING THE OFFENDER: Problems and Issues
edited by
Marc Riedel
Pedro A. Vales

VICTIMS, CRIME, AND SOCIAL CONTROL
Eduard A. Ziegenhagen